Oneness Pentecostals and the Trinity

Gregory A. Boyd

BAKER BOOK HOUSE
Grand Rapids, Michigan 49516

Copyright © 1992 by Baker Books
a division of Baker Book House Company
P.O. Box 6287, Grand Rapids, MI 49516-6287

Printed in the United States of America

Library of Congress Cataloging-in-Publication Data

Boyd, Gregory A., 1955–
Oneness Pentecostals and the Trinity / Grégory A. Boyd.
    p.   cm.
Includes bibliographical references.
ISBN 0–8010–1019–5
    1. Oneness doctrine (Pentecostalism)—Controversial literature.
2. Trinity—History of doctrines—20th century. 3. Oneness Pentecostal
churches. I. Title.
    BX8763.B68   1992
    232'.8—dc20   91–48111

To my loving wife Shelly.
A better companion
for this spiritual journey we call life
could never be found.

Contents

Preface

The Oneness heresy begins with the conviction that the orthodox Christian doctrine of the Trinity is fundamentally incompatible with a faith that there is only one God. Therefore, the Father, Son, and Holy Spirit cannot in this view be real, distinct, coequal persons in the eternal Godhead, but are only different roles that one divine person temporarily assumes. Though this heresy can initially appear relatively harmless, in rejecting the Trinity this belief actually cuts to the heart of all that is essential to the Christian faith.

Throughout its history, the church has occasionally confronted views similar to the Oneness belief. In the early church these views were known variously as Sabellianism, Modalistic Monarchianism, or Patripassianism. In the past these views were always rejected by the orthodox church as dangerous heresies.

Not since the early third century, however, has the Christian church had to confront the Oneness heresy to anything like the extent that it must do so today. From its informal beginnings seventy-five years ago amidst the fledgling American Pentecostal movement, different sects embracing the Oneness heresy have grown to number over one million in the United States and close to five million worldwide on conservative estimates. (For more detailed statistical information on the Oneness movement, see Appendix D.) This means that Oneness believers—almost all of whom have remained within the Pentecostal movement—constitute one of the three largest antitrinitarian professing Christian movements both in this country and in the world!

Moreover, it has been my experience, confirmed by many others who have since left the Oneness movement, that former trinitarian Christians make up the largest single group of people who become new converts in Oneness churches. In their eyes, trinitarian denominations are mission fields. I have confronted an increasing number of pastors who have lost some of their congregations to Oneness proselytizers. One pastor even reported that during a series of revival meetings where many people were coming forward in response to the evangelistic message, Oneness believers would actually pose as altar counselors in order to then steal the new converts over to their "true" church.

Despite these alarming facts, the majority of trinitarian Christians, and even trinitarian Christian leaders and educators, remain completely uninformed about this movement. While thousands of books and articles have been written on other antitrinitarian sects, such as Jehovah's Witnesses, Mormonism, Armstrongism, or The Way International, next to nothing has been written on Oneness Pentecostalism. In fact, only two books have been published critiquing Oneness Pentecostalism from a theological perspective: Carl Brumback's *God in Three Persons* (Tennessee: Pathway Press, 1959) and F. J. Lindquist's *The Truth About the Trinity and Baptism in Jesus' Name Only* (Minneapolis: Northern Gospel Publishing House, 1961). Neither of these works is exhaustive in its exposition or critique of the movement, and both are very dated.

Not only this, but Christian works on "alternative religions" or "cults" in America hardly ever include any discussion of Oneness Pentecostalism; and in those few instances where they do, the differences between Oneness Pentecostals and orthodox Christianity are watered down, especially concerning baptism and tongues. Hence, for example, in Ruth Tucker's work *Another Gospel* (Grand Rapids, Mich.: Zondervan Publishing House, 1988), the author states that "except for the denial of the doctrine of the Trinity, the United Pentecostal Church is not significantly different from other Pentecostal groups" (p. 385). As we shall see, this view is very mistaken. This perhaps explains why she confines her treatment of the United Pentecostal Church International (UPCI) to one page in an appendix, whereas a cult like "The Way," which is a fraction of its size, is given an entire chapter.

Finally, the doctrine of the Oneness Pentecostals is frequently misunderstood in the secondary literature, as for example in Ronald Enroth's *A Guide to Cults and New Religions* (Downers Grove, Ill.: InterVarsity Press, 1983). In this work Enroth compares the Oneness view of God to that of The Way International (p. 15). The antitrinitarianism of these two groups, however, has only a denial of the Trinity in common.

Given the widespread ignorance concerning Oneness Pentecostalism, it is hardly a mystery as to why this group is as successful as it is in evangelizing mainstream trinitarian Christianity.

There are, I believe, two basic reasons for this ongoing ignorance. First, whereas most other antitrinitarian sects tend to be tightly structured in an authoritarian fashion and are thus easily identifiable as opponents to traditional Christianity, Oneness Pentecostalism has always been a relatively disunited movement. The United Pentecostal Church International (UPCI) is the largest of all the Oneness denominations, having approximately half a million members in the United States and roughly the same number elsewhere. But there are in fact several hundred much smaller Oneness Pentecostal organizations, and even the UPCI is the result of a merger between two smaller Oneness denominations. Its presence on the Christian scene is thus much less conspicuous than that of other heretical Christian groups.

Second, whereas other antitrinitarian groups reject the Trinity by denying that Jesus Christ is equal with the Father, the Oneness Pentecostals reject the Trinity by denying that Jesus Christ is in any sense *distinct* from the Father. But because the doctrine of Christ's divinity hits closer to home than the doctrine of the Trinity for most Christians (and especially for most Pentecostals), the Oneness error on the God-head can seem more innocuous than the subordinationist error. So again, the error of Oneness Pentecostalism has largely escaped the atten-tion of Christian leaders.

As a matter of fact, however, the inconspicuousness and apparent harmlessness of this theological aberration renders it all the more dan-gerous and makes the need for Christians to be informed about it all the more urgent. The rapid growth of the Oneness movement testifies to its profound impact—despite its inconspicuousness. And the dangerous nature of this form of antitrinitarianism is no less real because of its affirmation of the deity of Christ. As the early Fathers who first fought this heresy saw, and as I shall maintain in this book, the denial that the Father, Son, and Holy Spirit are eternally distinct "persons" within the Godhead indirectly undermines the Christian view of God's character, God's revelation, and God's salvation by grace.

It is, I shall therefore argue, no mere coincidence that the present form of this Oneness antitrinitarianism is also accompanied by a num-ber of other radical theological aberrations that run directly counter to some of the most fundamental concepts Christians have always believed about God and about salvation. Hence almost all Oneness Pentecostals today not only deny the Trinity, they also deny that one is saved by grace through faith alone. Almost all Oneness Pentecostals also maintain that one must be baptized by immersion "in Jesus' name" (not the tra-ditional "Father, Son, and Holy Spirit"), and that one's salvation hangs on this mode and formula. Furthermore, one must speak in tongues if one is to claim to have the Holy Spirit and be saved. Finally, it is usu-ally held that one must live a strictly regimented "holy" life "worthy of the Lord," involving various extreme "standards," if one is to be saved. Indeed, I shall maintain that it is not an overstatement to see this par-ticular antitrinitarian heresy as teaching salvation-by-works to an extent almost unparalleled in the history of Christianity.

The Oneness belief, then, is as harmful as it is influential, and I believe it is time that trinitarian Christians begin to take notice of it.

Throughout this work, I shall primarily have the United Pentecostal Church International in mind in my polemic against Oneness Pentecostalism. There are four reasons for this. First, the UPCI is by far the largest and most influential of the Oneness organizations. Second, the UPCI publishing house, Word Aflame Press, publishes and distributes almost all of the Oneness apologetic material circulating in the United States today. Third, the UPCI is very representative of what is standard among almost all Oneness Pentecostal groups (a modalistic view of God, Jesus' Name baptism, and tongues as the initial evidence of the Holy Spirit), while avoiding many of the various eccentricities that sometimes characterize its smaller Oneness counterparts. Finally, because my own four-year involvement in Oneness Pentecostalism was primarily (though not exclusively) in a UPCI church, it is the one I am most familiar with on a firsthand basis.

There are three purposes that have governed the writing of this work.

1. It has been the ongoing task of the church to reaffirm in diverse times and places its trinitarian faith over and against alternatives, which continually assail the church. The church needs to reflect continually on the meaning and validity of its trinitarian faith in each new situation in which it finds itself and against each new challenge it confronts.

This book therefore seeks to be a reflection and reaffirmation of the decision the third-century church made when it opted for its trinitarian faith over and against the very popular, and less metaphysically demanding, modalistic monarchian belief that was then sweeping Western Christianity. As this belief has again arisen to a degree that must give us some concern, we must seek once again to reaffirm the biblical foundation and central theological significance of the trinitarian view of God that has nurtured the church throughout the ages. If successful, we shall have thoroughly refuted the Oneness heresy and reaffirmed the validity and centrality of the doctrine of the Trinity.

It is hoped, then, that this work will prove informative and helpful to any who seek to understand more clearly the church's trinitarian faith.

2. In keeping with the above point, this work seeks to serve as a guide to individuals involved in any way with Oneness Pentecostalism. It is hoped that this work will prove helpful to believers who come in contact with, or are even evangelized by, Oneness adherents, as well as

to questioning individuals who are either still in this movement or who have left the movement but remain confused by it.

3. Finally, I have written this book with a special eye toward Christian leaders who have been or will be confronted with Oneness Pentecostalism. I have each year received an increasing number of calls from pastors or other church leaders who are having any number of members in their congregations negatively influenced by the Oneness teaching and want to know how to combat it. Indeed, recently a sizable trinitarian congregation in my locale completely converted over to the Oneness Pentecostal doctrine. This is tragic and entirely unnecessary. It is simply the result of a lack of understanding of what this teaching is all about and why it is fundamentally unbiblical.

If this work does anything to better inform and equip those in leadership positions who are responsible for others, and if this work thereby reduces the number of such incidences of individuals and churches being swept away by this heresy, it will have accomplished its goal.

There are numerous individuals to whom I am indebted in writing this work. The idea for it arose out of my conversations with a number of close friends who have, with me, struggled in their spiritual journey out of the UPCI. Dave and Terri Churchill as well as my sister Anita Boyd deserve special mention for their insights and feedback. I am also greatly indebted to my good friend Robert Bowman of the Christian Research Institute for his continual input, and especially for his skillful help in editing this book. I am greatly indebted to my wife, Shelley, whose love and support have remained constant throughout the difficulty and confusion of leaving the Oneness Pentecostal movement together, and without whose patience this work would not have been possible. Finally, I am of course eternally grateful to my Lord and Savior Jesus Christ, who revealed his grace and truth to me and who has called me to his ministry. My prayer is that this work will glorify him as one aspect of this ministry.

Abbreviations of Works Cited

Oneness Pentecostal Works

(The following are published by Pentecostal Publishing House or Word Aflame Press, Hazelwood, Missouri, unless indicated otherwise.)

Bernard, Holiness	David Bernard, *In Search of Holiness: Series in Pentecostal Theology,* vol. 3 (1981)
Bernard, New Birth	David Bernard, *The New Birth: Series in Pentecostal Theology,* vol. 2 (1984)
Bernard, Oneness	David Bernard, *The Oneness of God: Series in Pentecostal Theology,* vol. 1 (1983)
Chalfant	William Chalfant, *Ancient Champions of Oneness: A History of the True Church of Jesus Christ* (1982)
Ewart	Frank J. Ewart, *The Name and the Book* (Chicago, Ill., Daniel Ryerson, 1936)
Fauss	Oliver Fauss, *Baptism in God's Plan* (1986)

Fitch   Theodore Fitch, *God the Father Is Omnipresent Spirit* (Council Bluffs, Iowa: Fitch, n.d.)

Graves   Robert Graves, *The God of Two Testaments* (USA: Robert Graves & James Turner, 1977)

Gray   David Gray, *Questions Pentecostals Ask* (1987)

Haywood   G. T. Haywood, *The Victim of the Flaming Sword* (Indianapolis, Ind.: Temple Book Store, n.d.)

Jordan   J. Mark Jordan, *Measures of Our Faith* (1987)

Magee   Gordon Magee, *Is Jesus in the Godhead or Is the Godhead in Jesus?* (1988)

Miller   John Miller, *Is God a Trinity?* (Princeton, N.J.: Miller, 3d ed., 1922)

Morehead, Foundations   Keith Morehead, *Fictional Foundations of Trinitarian Thought* (St. Paul, Minn.: Oneness Ministries, 1988)

Morehead, Mystery   Keith Morehead, *God's Mystery, That Is, Christ Himself* (St. Paul, Minn.: Oneness Ministries, n.d.)

Norris   S. G. Norris, *The Mighty God in Christ* (St. Paul, Minn.: Apostolic Bible Institute, n.d.)

Paterson   John Paterson, *The Real Truth About Baptism in Jesus' Name* (1953)

Pugh   J. T. Pugh, *How to Receive the Holy Ghost* (1989)

Reeves, Dimensions   Kenneth Reeves, *God in 13 Dimensions*, Bk. III (USA: Reeves, 1986)

Reeves, Godhead   Kenneth Reeves, *The Godhead* (USA: Reeves, 7th ed., 1962)

Reeves, Supreme   Kenneth Reeves, *The Supreme Godhead*, Bk. II (USA: Reeves, 1984)

Reeves, Tongues   Kenneth Reeves, *The Holy Ghost With Tongues* (Ill.: Inspiration Books, 1966)

Sabin, I–VI   Robert Sabin, ed., "Oneness News," vols. I–VI (St. Paul, Minn.: Oneness Ministries, Spring 1986–March 1987)

Sabin, Battle	Robert Sabin, *The Battle of Chattanooga: Written Rebuttal of the John Ankerberg Show* (St. Paul, Minn.: Oneness Ministries, n.d.)
Sabin, Gender	Robert Sabin, "The Gender Gap," a Oneness Ministries handout (St. Paul, Minn., n.d.)
Sabin, Irrefutable	Robert Sabin, "Irrefutable Reasons Why the Theory of the Trinity Cannot Stand," a Oneness Ministries handout (St. Paul, Minn., n.d.)
Sabin, Jesus	Robert Sabin, "Who Is Jesus Christ?" a videotaped debate with Robert Bowman, Jr., held at Apostolic Bible Church (St. Paul, Minn.: Oneness Ministries, January 1990)
Sabin, Let Us	Robert Sabin, "Let Us Make Man," a Oneness Ministries tape (St. Paul, Minn., n.d.)
Sabin, Seminar	Robert Sabin, handout material from a "Oneness Seminar" held at Apostolic Bible Church, St. Paul, Minn., 1986
Sabin, The Man	Robert Sabin, "The Man Jesus Christ," a Oneness Ministries handout (St. Paul, Minn., n.d.)
Sabin, Transfer	Robert Sabin, "Transfer Theology/Transfiguration Theology," a Oneness Ministries handout (St. Paul, Minn., n.d.)
Sabin, Truant	Robert Sabin, "The Truant Person of the Holy Ghost," a Oneness Ministries handout (St. Paul, Minn., n.d.)
Springfield	Marvin Springfield, *Jesus the Almighty* (Portland, Oreg.: Parry Mail Advertising Service, 1972)
Streitferdt	Thomas Streitferdt, *The Word Became Flesh* (Orange, N.J.: Lutho Press, 1961)
Urshan, Almighty	Andrew Urshan, *The Almighty God in the Lord Jesus Christ* (Portland, Oreg.: Urshan, n.d.)
Urshan, Divinity	Andrew Urshan, "The Divinity of Jesus Christ, or the Absolute Deity of the Son of God According to the Old and New Testament," *Pentecostal Witness* 3 (April 1927)
Urshan, Life	Andrew Urshan, *The Life Story of Andrew Bar David Urshan: An Autobiography*, Oneness Pentecostal Pioneer Series (Stockton, Calif.: W.A.B.C. Press, 1967)

N. Urshan, Consider	Nathaniel Urshan, *Consider Him? David's Son and David's Lord* (St. Louis, Mo.: Pentecostal Publishing House, n.d.)
Weisser, Heresy	Thomas Weisser, *After the Way Called Heresy* (USA: Weisser, 1981)
Weisser, Three	Thomas Weisser, *Three Persons: From the Bible or Babylon?* (USA: Weisser, 1983)
Why?	Kelsey Griffin, Dan Segraves, Ralph Reynolds, Rick Wyser, *Why?: A Study of Christian Standards* (1984)
Yadon	C. Haskell Yadon, *Jehovah-Jesus? The Supreme God: Son of God, Son of Man* (Twin Falls, Idaho: Yadon, 1952)

Oneness Tracts

(All published by Word Aflame Press)

#102   "Why?"

#105   "Water Baptism according to History and Scripture"

#108   "Why Did God Choose Tongues?"

#126   "Why I Do Not Have a Television"

#6109   "Why We Baptize in Jesus' Name"

#6111   "New Testament Salvation"

#6121   "Who Is God?"

#6125   "60 Questions on the Godhead With Bible Answers"

#6132   "The Baptism of the Holy Spirit"

#6141   "Saving Faith"

#6144   "Gift of the Holy Spirit"

#6145   "Speaking With Tongues"

#6146   "Water Baptism"

#6154   "The Promise Is Yours"

#6155   "Grace + 0 = Salvation?"

Other Works Cited

Alexander   Joseph Alexander, *Commentary on the Prophe-cies of Isaiah* (Grand Rapids, Mich.: Zondervan, 3d printing, 1970)

Barnes   Albert Barnes, *Notes on the Old Testament, Explanatory and Practical: Isaiah, Vol. 1* (Grand Rapids, Mich.: Baker Book, rpt. 1950)

Bettenson   Henry Bettenson, ed., *Documents of the Christian Church* (London, Oxford, New York: Oxford University Press, rpt. 1973)

Bowman, Oneness   Robert M. Bowman, Jr., "Oneness Pentecostalism and the Trinity: A Biblical Critique," *Forward* (Fall 1985)

Bowman, Trinity   Robert M. Bowman, Jr., *Why You Should Believe in the Trinity: An Answer to Jehovah's Witnesses* (Grand Rapids, Mich.: Baker Book, 1989)

Brumback   Carl Brumback, *God in Three Persons* (Cleveland, Tenn.: Pathway Press, 1959)

Bruner   Dale Bruner, *A Theology of the Holy Spirit: The Pentecostal Experience and the New Testament,* Shirley Guthrie and Charles Hall, trans. (Philadelphia: Westminster, rev. ed. 1963)

Dunn   James Dunn, *Christology in the Making: A New Testament Inquiry Into the Origins of the Doctrine of the Incarnation* (Philadelphia: Westminster, 1980)

Enroth   Ronald Enroth, et. al. *A Guide to Cults and New Religions* (Downers Grove, Ill.: InterVarsity Press, 1983)

Herbert   A. S. Herbert, *The Book of the Prophet Isaiah: Chapters 1–39* (Cambridge, Mass.: Cambridge University Press, 1973)

Kelly, Creeds   J.N.D. Kelly, *Early Christian Creeds* (New York: Longman, 3d ed., 1972)

Kelly, Doctrines   J.N.D. Kelly, *Early Christian Doctrines* (San Francisco: Harper & Row, rev. ed. 1978)

Leupold   H. R. Leupold, *Exposition on Isaiah* (Grand Rapids, Mich.: Baker Book, 1977)

Lindquist	F. J. Lindquist, *The Truth About the Trinity and Baptism in Jesus' Name Only* (Minneapolis, Minn.: Northern Gospel Publishing House, 1961)
Mauchline	John Mauchline, *Isaiah 1–39* (London: SCM, 1962)
Moule	C.F.D. Moule, *The Origin of Christology* (Cambridge, Mass.: Cambridge University Press, 1977)
Prestige, Fathers	G. L. Prestige, *Fathers and Heretics* (London: S.P.C.K., 1954)
Prestige, God	G. L. Prestige, *God in Patristic Thought* (London: SCM, 1952)
Reed	David Reed, *Origins and Development of Theology of Oneness Pentecostalism in the United States*, Ph.D. dissertation, Boston University, 1978
Wainwright	Arthur Wainwright, *The Trinity in the New Testament* (London: SCM, 1962)
Young	Edward Young, *The Book of Isaiah*, vol. 1 (Grand Rapids, Mich.: William B. Eerdmans, 1965)

Introduction
Confessions of an Ex-Oneness Pentecostal

The present status of the Oneness heresy on the world scene and the present lack of reliable information on this movement are themselves enough reason to render a work such as this necessary and even urgent. But this work also represents a more personal urgency, for it is the result of my own wrestling with the theology of the Oneness movement over the past sixteen years. It may prove helpful to share some of this with the reader.

My involvement with Oneness Pentecostalism began when I was, at the age of sixteen, converted into a United Pentecostal Church. Like many teenagers, I was searching for something to belong to, to believe in, to identify with. Moreover, my involvement with drugs and the "party scene" was already growing old for me, and I wanted something different—radically different.

Well, I certainly found it. In this strict religious community I found a highly structured lifestyle, which on the surface made my initial break with my past life of sin relatively easy. I also found a belief system that initially made pretty good sense to me and supplied clear answers to almost all the questions about life I had been asking for so long.

The UPCI also supplied me with a strong sense of community I could identify with; coming from a broken home, this was something I longed for. Indeed, I soon internalized the certain "elitist" mentality that largely characterizes many Oneness communities, for we all believed we had a "truth" possessed by very few others. In our view, we alone were the people who knew the one true God; we alone knew who Jesus truly was; we alone were baptized correctly; we alone walked "worthy" of the Lord; we alone, in a word, were "saved." Other "so-called Christians"—the trinitarians—were deceived into believing in three gods, but we had the genuine "apostolic faith." Belonging to this group, I was certainly "a somebody," which at this point in my life was extremely important.

My honeymoon with the Oneness faith, however, was quite short-lived. I quickly discovered that "the holiness standard" (the community lifestyle rules), which initially seemed freeing to me, became very burdensome. I discovered that even the threat of hell, spoken of so often from the pulpit, was not enough to motivate me to change permanently certain aspects of the sin-character that I had acquired in my pre-UPCI life. I thus spent a lot of my time feeling like God didn't like me very much and believing that I was in fact going to end up in hell. This is not an uncommon feeling among Oneness Pentecostals (though they rarely admit it until they are out of the movement).

All of this changed, however, about a year and a half after my conversion, and that is what began to initiate my departure from the UPCI. For the first time in my life I experienced God's *grace*. Standing in a church parking lot one October Sunday evening in 1976, feeling hopelessly sinful and lost, having just heard yet another powerful "live-holy-or-go-to-hell" sermon, I "happened" to open up my Bible to Romans, chapter 8.

As I read the first verse, "There is therefore now no condemnation to them which are in Christ Jesus . . ."(KJV) my spiritual eyes were opened in a way they had never been opened before. The words NO CONDEMNATION reverberated in my mind like a thousand church bells chiming at once. The eternal and infinite love, joy, peace, and freedom of God Almighty flooded my heart that moment in a manner impossible to describe adequately. That moment I knew I was saved, for I knew I was—because of Jesus' sacrifice alone—loved just as I was. I was accepted unconditionally.

My motivation for living for God was instantaneously changed from the fear of hell to a gratitude for heaven. And the bondage of sin I had previously been experiencing through legalism was now obliterated by grace. Because this way of thinking and living was diametrically opposed to the theology of Oneness Pentecostalism, however, my experience of grace was the "beginning of the end" of my journey through this movement.

Once the sect's legalism had lost its grip on my mind, other aspects of its teaching slowly began to lose their grip on me. I first began to see that my experience (and Paul's theology) of grace was fundamentally incompatible with the Oneness understanding of the baptism of the Holy Spirit. As we shall see, in the theology of Oneness Pentecostalism one receives the saving presence of the Holy Spirit only *after* one has acquired sufficient faith, has purified oneself, and has fully yielded to God. This reception, moreover, must always be evidenced by speaking in tongues.

For this reason, people who have not spoken in tongues are not regarded as having the Spirit and as being saved, and they are encouraged to "seek" this "gift" continuously. But, it seemed to me, all of this meant that salvation was a reward, not a gift (cf. Rom. 4:4–5). Also, as I grew in my own knowledge of Scripture, the view that tongues was "the initial physical evidence" for the baptism of the Holy Spirit began to appear on ever shakier ground to me.

Shortly after this, I also began to question the Oneness view of Jesus' Name baptism for the remission of sins. The view that God's forgiveness literally hung upon one's baptism—and upon the exact words spoken during baptism—struck me as inconsistent with salvation by grace alone. It seemed to reduce the all-loving God I experienced that October night to a nit-picky Deity interested only in behavioral propriety. Moreover, this doctrine also increasingly struck me as lacking adequate biblical support.

The final belief to crumble for me was the Oneness Pentecostal antitrinitarian view of God. This is frequently the last belief to be abandoned by ex-Oneness believers because the doctrine of the Trinity is usually caricatured so badly within Oneness circles that one tends to associate any talk of "three persons" with crude tritheism for quite some time, even after leaving the group. The Oneness doctrine is also the belief that Oneness groups invest the most energy in defending, and the one that, on the surface, is the most difficult to refute.

My modalistic view of God finally fell during my first year of attending seminary. I was at this time constantly getting into debates with educated trinitarians who didn't fit my tritheistic stereotype and who had much better scriptural support for their positions than I did for mine. I also discovered at this time that the earliest post-apostolic Fathers were clearly far more trinitarian than they were Oneness (see chapter 7), and this could not be explained if the apostles had in fact been teaching something like the Oneness doctrine. My personal affiliation with Oneness Pentecostalism thus came to an end in late 1979.

My departure from the Oneness movement, however, did not spell the end of my involvement in it, for I continued to have a number of friends and relatives in the sect, some of whom I had personally recruited. This involvement gradually grew into something of a ministry to Oneness Pentecostals and to ex–Oneness Pentecostals as I began to work with them through the theological and personal issues that this movement created for them. This book is an outgrowth of that ministry.

1

Understanding Oneness Pentecostalism

Before trying to critically evaluate the Oneness Pentecostals' interpretation of the Godhead, we ought first to try to examine their position sympathetically. In particular, we ought to understand what they feel are the strengths of their position and what are the main biblical arguments in support of their view. In this chapter, then, I shall be summarizing the Oneness Pentecostals' case for their rejection of the Trinity. Since we are interested in the truth and not simply in knocking down a "straw man," the focus here will be on the best and most frequently heard arguments in support of the Oneness position. Furthermore, since the purpose of this chapter is to explicate the Oneness position, not to criticize it, I shall here be presenting those arguments with little by way of critical commentary. They are for the most part the same arguments I used zealously against trinitarianism when I was a Oneness Pentecostal.

For non-Oneness readers, this chapter will enable a fair evaluation of Oneness doctrine. For Oneness readers, this chapter will be an assurance that the critique of Oneness doctrine presented in the succeeding chapters is based on an accurate, firsthand understanding of the Oneness position.

The Basic Argument for the Oneness View

Oneness doctrine is based on a particular understanding of two scriptural truths. These Bible-based beliefs serve as the foundation for the Oneness view of God and of Jesus Christ. The first biblical truth is that *there is only one God,* and the second is that *Jesus Christ is God.* From these two truths, Oneness groups deduce that Jesus Christ is God in his totality, and therefore that Jesus must himself be the Father, Son, and Holy Spirit. This implies, of course, that the orthodox doctrine of the Trinity, which maintains that Jesus Christ is the second "person" of the Trinity, eternally distinct from the Father and Holy Spirit, is an erroneous doctrine.[1]

Premise One: There Is Only One God

There can be no question that the Bible does indeed teach these two foundational premises of Oneness theology. Thus, first of all, Oneness Pentecostals are absolutely correct in emphasizing that the Bible uniformly and unequivocally teaches that there is only one God. Certainly it was the proclamation, "Hear, O Israel, The LORD our God, the LORD is One" (Deut. 6:4), that formed the cornerstone for everything that was distinctive about the faith of God's people in the Old Testament. The message of God's uniqueness and singularity is driven home literally hundreds of times throughout the pages of the Old Testament (e.g., Isa. 42:8; 43:10b–11; 44:6). This strict monotheism is by no means forgotten when we enter the New Testament era. Rather, it forms the presupposition of the Christ-centered faith articulated in the New Testament (e.g., Mark 12:29; 1 Cor. 8:4b–6; Eph. 4:4, 6; 1 Tim. 2:5).

It is therefore an incontestable fact that the Bible is monotheistic through and through, as Oneness believers tirelessly point out. No biblical author would have ever entertained the notion that there could be more than one supreme being. This is the cornerstone to ancient and contemporary Judaism and the first foundational stone to Oneness theology.

Premise Two: Jesus Christ Is God

The second foundational premise of Oneness theology, the deity of Christ, is also certainly biblical. While certain groups have attempted to dispute this truth, we must happily agree with the Oneness Pentecostals that the biblical case for the complete deity of Jesus Christ is actually very solid. Throughout the New Testament, Jesus is honored with the titles *God* (e.g., John 1:1; 20:28; Titus 2:13; 2 Peter 1:1; 1 John 5:20)[2] and *Lord* (e.g., John 20:28; Rom. 10:9–13; Phil. 2:9–11; Heb. 1:10). Moreover, Christ is everywhere portrayed as speaking and acting with the authority of God (e.g., Matt. 5:22, 28; Mark 2:5–12; etc.). And he commands an honor, respect, and commitment that is wholly inappropriate for any ordinary human being (e.g., Matt. 5:11; 8:18–22; 10:39; Luke 12:50–53; John 5:23; 10:30). Christ is worshiped (Matt. 28:17; Heb. 1:6), receives prayer (Acts 7:59; 1 Cor. 1:2; 2 Cor. 12:7–10), and is the one who shall judge all men (Matt. 25:31–46; John 5:21–22; 2 Cor. 5:10). In short, Jesus Christ *is* God; he is the incarnation of the one and only true God.

Conclusion: Jesus Is the Father, Son, and Holy Spirit

It must, then, be taken as solid scriptural truth that there is only one God, and that Jesus Christ is, in every sense of the term, himself this God. Oneness Pentecostals are quite right in drawing attention to these truths. And, with these two fundamental truths of Scripture, every orthodox believer must stand in full agreement.

Yet, it is precisely this agreement that exists between trinitarians and Oneness believers that gives the Oneness arguments against the orthodox doctrine of the Trinity much of their apparent persuasive power. For, these Oneness groups argue, only their position is consistent with these two foundational truths. Only if Jesus is himself Father, Son, and Holy Spirit can the unity of God and the full deity of

Christ be acknowledged with consistency. And, for most Oneness Pentecostals, being consistent on this point is one of the necessary prerequisites for salvation itself (see, for example, Sabin, III, 1).

The prolific Oneness writer David Bernard expresses the logic involved here when he writes concerning the fatherhood of Christ, "If there is only one God and that God is the Father (Mal. 2:10), and if Jesus is God, then it logically follows that Jesus is the Father" (Bernard, Oneness, 66; cf. Graves, 59).

So, too, it is customarily argued by Oneness adherents that if there is only one God and that God is the Holy Spirit, and if Jesus is indeed God, then it must logically follow that Jesus is himself the Holy Spirit (see Bernard, Oneness, 128f.; Graves, 69f.; Magee, 26). And, from the other direction, it is argued that if Jesus is in fact fully God, if indeed "the fullness of the Godhead" dwells in him (Col. 2:9), then it must follow that "all His [God's] attributes, power and character . . . is in Jesus. Father, Son, Holy Ghost, Jehovah, Word . . . are all in Jesus" (Bernard, Oneness, 216; cf. Graves, 136–37).

Hence the UPCI and other Oneness groups argue that only their belief is compatible with the two most central truths of Scripture. By contrast, it is argued that the doctrine of the Trinity "detract[s] from the important biblical themes of the oneness of God and the absolute deity of Jesus Christ" (Bernard, Oneness, 298). This doctrine "violates the Shema" and "denies . . . the sole and supreme Deity of Jesus" (Sabin, IV, 4; and Sabin, Irrefutable).

On the surface, this argument appears to have great force, so much so that many sincere trinitarian Christians have been convinced by it. In chapters 3 and 4, I will be explaining why this argument is actually unsound. However, it is important to feel the force of the argument in order to appreciate why Oneness Pentecostals can be firmly convinced that their position follows logically from the Bible's teachings.

Beyond this simple but sweeping argument, Oneness Pentecostals offer a number of specific points in support of their position. The rest of this chapter will summarize these additional arguments.

Arguing That Jesus Is the Father and the Holy Spirit

Jesus Is the Father

Oneness Pentecostals employ two basic strategies in arguing for the conclusion that Jesus is God the Father. First, they argue that certain prooftexts directly identify Jesus as the Father. Second, they argue that what is said about God the Father—and what could be true of him alone—is said also of Jesus Christ.

Perhaps the text most frequently cited by Oneness Pentecostals to support their view that Jesus is the Father as well as the Son is Isaiah 9:6, where Jesus is called "Mighty God, Everlasting Father." Since "there is only one Father," it follows that "Jesus must be God the Father" (Bernard, Oneness, 66; cf. Graves, 147–48; Reeves, Godhead, 90).

There are several other texts that Oneness Pentecostals also take to be identifying Jesus as the Father. In John 10:30, Jesus says, "I and the Father are one." In other texts in the Gospel of John, Jesus says that to know, believe in, and even to see him is to know, believe in, and see the Father (John 8:19; 12:45; 14:7–11). Jesus is said to relate to Christians as their heavenly Father in certain texts (John 14:18; Rev. 21:6–7). Less frequently, some Oneness writers have claimed that when Paul speaks in his salutations of "God our Father and the Lord Jesus Christ" (e.g., Rom. 1:7; 1 Cor. 1:3), the word "and" (Greek, *kai*) actually means "even" or "who is." This allows them to conclude that these salutations should be translated, "Grace be unto you and peace from God our Father, even the Lord Jesus Christ" (Graves, 51ff.; Bernard, Oneness, 207ff.).

The second strategy used by Oneness Pentecostals to prove that Jesus is the Father is to cross-reference passages in which both Jesus and the Father are said to perform certain divine functions. For example, the Bible says both that the Father raised Jesus from the dead (Gal. 1:1) and that Jesus raised himself from the dead (John 2:19–22). The Father answers prayer (John 15:16), but so does Jesus (John 14:14). The Father gives the Holy Spirit (John 14:16), but so does

Jesus (John 15:26; 16:7). The Father draws all men to Jesus (John 6:44), but Jesus draws all men to himself (John 12:32). The Father will raise the dead (Rom. 4:17; 1 Cor. 6:14), but so will Jesus (John 6:40). By piecing together texts such as these, Oneness exponents conclude that "Jesus is himself the Father as well as the Son" (Haywood, 17). The arguments used to support this conclusion will be examined in chapter 3.

Jesus Is the Holy Spirit

The Oneness arguments for seeing Jesus as identical with the Holy Spirit follow the same pattern as their arguments for seeing Jesus as being identical with the Father. First of all, there are a few texts that Oneness believers interpret to teach explicitly that Jesus is the Holy Spirit. Second, Oneness Pentecostals cross-reference several texts in which Jesus is said to do things that elsewhere are said to be done by the Holy Spirit.

Oneness believers argue that Jesus is explicitly called "the Spirit" in 2 Corinthians 3:17, which in the King James Version reads, "Now the Lord is that Spirit; and where the Spirit of the Lord is, there is liberty." Jesus, it is argued, is "the Lord" here, and he is explicitly identified as the Spirit who opens up the heart of believers (Bernard, Oneness, 132, cf. 196; Graves, 78; Magee, 25). Also frequently cited in support of this position is Romans 8:9–11, where "the Spirit," "the Spirit of God," the "Spirit of Christ," "Christ," and "the Spirit of him who raised Jesus" appear to be used interchangeably. This, it is argued, would not be possible if Jesus and the Spirit (and the Father) were not personally identical (Bernard, Oneness, 130, 132; Graves, 74–75, 148).

The cross-referenced texts that Oneness Pentecostals believe demonstrate the identity of Jesus with the Spirit are similar to those cited to prove that Jesus is the Father. Both Jesus and the Spirit raised Christ from the dead (John 2:19–21; Rom. 8:9–11). Both will raise dead believers on the last day (John 6:40; Rom. 8:9–11). Both dwell in the hearts of believers (John 14:16; 2 Cor. 13:5; Col. 1:27). Both are called the Comforter (Greek, *parakletos* [John 14:26; 1 John 2:1]).

Both are portrayed as intercessors for the believer (Rom. 8:26; Heb. 7:25). Both sanctify the church (Eph. 5:26; 1 Peter 1:2). Both will provide words to the disciples in times of persecution (Mark 13:11; Luke 21:15).

From piecing together texts such as these, Oneness exponents conclude that "Jesus is the Holy Spirit" (Graves, 78), though his role as Spirit differs from his role as the Son. Again, this type of reasoning can be, and has been, initially persuasive to trinitarian believers who have not been previously informed of it. I will be responding to these arguments in chapter 5.

Conclusion: Jesus Is the Father, Son, and Holy Spirit

It is a given that Jesus is the Son. But if the Oneness interpretation of the biblical passages discussed above is correct, Jesus is also the Father and the Holy Spirit. Oneness Pentecostals find this teaching brought together in one place in Matthew 28:19. Here Jesus tells the disciples to baptize all nations "in the name of the Father and of the Son and of the Holy Spirit." Yet, in the Book of Acts, we find them consistently baptizing everybody "in the name of Jesus Christ" (Acts 2:38; etc.). This, it is argued, must imply that "Jesus" is the name of the Father, Son, and Holy Spirit. To reinforce this conclusion, Oneness Pentecostals point out that in Matthew 28:19, baptism is said to be performed in "the name," not in "the names" of the Father, Son, and Holy Spirit. From the singular "name" they deduce that the Father, Son, and Holy Spirit must be one person—and that person, of course, must be Jesus.

One of the implications of this Oneness interpretation of Matthew 28:19 is that trinitarian baptism is unbiblical and invalid. In fact, the Oneness position implies that all non-Oneness believers, including all trinitarian Christians, are unsaved. We shall be examining the Oneness doctrine concerning baptism and salvation in chapter 6.

If Jesus is indeed the Father and the Holy Spirit as well as the Son, what are we to make of all those passages that at least appear to distinguish the Father, Son, and Holy Spirit? No one disputes that throughout the Gospels Jesus continually referred to "the Father" and to "the Spirit" at least as though they were, in some real sense, distinct from himself. Nor can anyone dispute that this distinction at least appears to be found throughout the rest of the New Testament.

We turn, then, to examining how Oneness theology answers this question, focusing first and foremost on the distinction between the Father and the Son.

Jesus and the Father in Oneness Theology

In order to make the Oneness doctrine that Jesus is both the Father and the Son work, Oneness Pentecostals must offer an explanation of two prominent aspects of the biblical teaching about Jesus Christ. They must explain, first, how the Father and the Son can be distinguished in Scripture and yet Jesus be both of them. And second, Oneness theology must explain why the Bible speaks of Jesus Christ as existing before his birth in Bethlehem. We will take these two questions in order.

The "Oneness Key"

The basic answer given by Oneness Pentecostals to the question of the distinction in Scripture between the Father and the Son is this: The distinction between the Father and the Son is the same distinction as between the humanity of Jesus Christ and the deity of Jesus Christ. For Oneness Pentecostals, to say that Jesus is both the Father and the Son is to say that he is both God and man.

Here it needs to be kept in mind that it is the standard understanding of orthodox Christianity that Jesus was both God and man. Trinitarians agree that Jesus was fully God and fully man. But the Oneness position differs in applying this doctrine of Jesus as God and man to the distinction between the Father and the Son. That is, whereas trinitarians hold that it is the Son of God, as distinct from the Father, who is fully God and fully man, Oneness Pentecostals hold that the description of Jesus as being "fully God and fully man" refers to Jesus as being both the Father and the Son. "Both identities, father and son, God and man, were in the same one [person]" (Sabin, The

Man). In other words, as fully God, Jesus is "Father," and as fully man, Jesus is "Son."

Hence, whereas the Sonship of Jesus is for trinitarian Christians an aspect of his *divinity*, for most Oneness writers it is only an aspect of his *humanity*. "Jesus is God in spite of the sonship and not because of the sonship" (Reeves, Dimensions, 64). As the very influential Oneness author Gordon Magee expresses it, "The Son is the flesh or humanity" (Magee, 21). In short, the Son is, not God, but the man in whom God was incarnated, the man in whom God dwelled. The Son is "the permanent body" of the Father (Norris, 6). So, too, Robert Sabin writes, "God became a man, and He will be a man forevermore" (Sabin, VI, 3). And frequently Christ is called "the last," "permanent," and "complete" theophany of the Father, in contrast to the temporary theophanies of the Old Testament (see Reed, 282ff., for a discussion).

It should be parenthetically noted, however, that some Oneness authors in the past have denied the future eternality of the Incarnation. In these views, the humanity (the Son) of Jesus was assumed only for the purpose of redemption, and once this work is completed the humanity will be discarded (see, for example, Jensen, 8; Fitch, 41).

It should also be noted that not all Oneness authors absolutely restrict the title "Son" to the humanity of Jesus. Hence Reeves, for example, says that "Sonship . . . is a term used to identify a result of two natures fused through the virgin birth" (Reeves, Godhead, 104; Dimensions, 63, 69). So also Bernard writes that "'Son' does not always refer to the humanity alone but to the deity and humanity together as they exist in the one person of Christ" (Bernard, Oneness, 100). What unites these variant views on the sonship of Christ is that all Oneness Pentecostals agree that the Son does not exist as such apart from the incarnation of the Father.

Being both the Father and the Son while on earth, Jesus could, according to Oneness theology, alternate between the two natures. Oneness authors sometimes refer to this "insight" as the "Oneness key" to interpreting correctly the Scriptures and understanding correctly who Jesus was, and how he could be both God and man, both

Father and Son (e.g., Magee, 28, 45; Bernard, Oneness, 213; Reeves, Godhead, 32–33). Thus, in Oneness belief, Jesus can be understood to act and speak sometimes as God (Father) while at other times as a human (Son). This means that when reading the Bible we must always ask whether Jesus is acting in the role or capacity of God or in the role or capacity of a man (McGee, 7, 14; Bernard, Oneness, 87–88, 172).

Bernard confesses that sometimes this "key" is not as easy to discern as one might wish: "Sometimes it is easy to get confused when the Bible describes Jesus in these two different roles, especially when it describes Him acting in both roles in the same story. For example, He could sleep one minute and calm the storm the next minute. He could speak as man one moment and then as God the next moment" (Bernard, Oneness, 88). But, in any case, whenever Jesus is portrayed as learning, praying, being tempted, dying, and the like, Scripture is portraying him as the Son of God—which is to say, as a real human being. However, whenever Christ is portrayed as knowing all things, as being eternal, as making divine claims or receiving divine respect, and the like, Scripture is portraying him as God the Father.

The paradoxes sometimes drawn from this Christology are most striking. Reeves, for example, contends that ". . . God in the assumed nature of man . . . was baptized as man, but not as God. Therefore, God as God was not baptized by John the Baptist, but Jesus as man was immersed by John the Baptist" (Reeves, Dimensions, 35). Similarly, he argues that "God could not die in His deity, but his humanity could be put to death" (ibid., 71). Likewise, Stanley Herron writes that Jesus "combined in His person the part and role of two without being two for He and the Father are One. He did as Man what He could not do as God and He did as God what He could not do as Man" (Sabin, IV, 5–6).

To summarize, then, according to Oneness theology, whenever Jesus is distinguished from the Father—when he is said to love and be loved by the Father, to honor the Father, to be sent from the Father, and so forth—Scripture is referring to Jesus as Son. But when Jesus is portrayed in divine terms and when he is not distinguished from the Father, Scripture is portraying him as being himself the Father.

Therefore, as paradoxical as it sounds, for Oneness theology Jesus was and is both the *Father* who loved and sent his Son, and the *Son* who loved and obeyed the Father. He was both the *Son* who prayed to the Father, and the *Father* who answered the Son (Magee, 7–8, 18; Jordan, 62–63). He was both the *man* who experienced God-forsakenness, and the *God* who at least appeared to forsake his Son on the cross (Ewart, 13; Sabin, IV, 5; VI, 3–4).

And yet, Oneness Pentecostals insist, Jesus was only *one* person. If he appears to be more than that, if the Father and Son appear to be more than distinct "natures" and rather appear in the Gospels as actual distinct "persons," this can only be *an illusion* assumed for the sake of revelation. As the reputable Oneness author and preacher Robert Sabin argues, God had to produce an "apparent separation" between himself (as Father) and the man Jesus (the Son), for otherwise Christ would not have been a genuine man and thus "a fit mediator." Hence, Christ and the Gospel writers employ a "language of separation" or a "language of plurality" when they speak of the Father *as though* the Father were distinct from himself. But "in truth," Sabin continues, "the Father and Son can never be separated" (Sabin, Gender). The problems that this understanding of Christ raises will be addressed in chapter 8.

It must again be remembered that trinitarians fully agree that Jesus was both God and man, and therefore agree in principle that some things said of him in Scripture emphasize his humanity, while other things said of him emphasize his deity. While the way this is worded and worked out may vary, up to this point trinitarians may basically agree with the Oneness distinction between Jesus as God and man. However, what distinguishes the Oneness understanding of this "duality" between the deity and humanity of Christ is that this dual nature of Christ is, for Oneness Pentecostals, also "the key" to understanding the relationship between the Father and the Son in Scripture. For trinitarians, by contrast, the relationship between the Father and Son is not a relationship between two "natures" of one person (how can two "natures" relate?); rather, it is a relationship between two divine, real (not "illusory") "persons."

Moreover, because the Father and Son relationship in the New Testament at least *appears* to be a relationship between two "persons," two "whos" (each "loves," "yields," "talks," etc., to the other), the Christ of Oneness theology can come across as having two very distinct personalities within himself, which operate within him at different times and can even talk to each other. Here, too, the Oneness understanding of Jesus as God and man, Father and Son, differs from orthodox trinitarianism, for trinitarians have always affirmed that the Word *became* flesh, and the *one* person of this union was the God-man, Jesus Christ. Hence, they never see Jesus as talking *to himself* when the Son is speaking to the Father or the Father is speaking to the Son.

The Preexistent Christ

One very important implication of the Oneness equation of "the Son of God" with the humanity of Jesus is that it means that Jesus as the Son of God cannot be eternal, as the orthodox church has always believed. The distinctness of the Son from the Father is the distinctness of a finite human being from the eternal God. It is, therefore, not an eternal distinction. Hence, while Jesus Christ existed from eternity as the Father, according to Oneness theology, Jesus Christ the Son had a definite beginning in time—a beginning that dates from his conception in the womb of Mary (Graves, 43–48; Reeves, Godhead, 53–54; Sabin, Seminar; Bernard, Oneness, 104; Reeves, Dimensions, 59–60). In support of this position, Oneness Pentecostals cite a number of biblical texts (Luke 1:35; Gal. 4:4; Heb. 1:5–6).

There are, of course, places where Scripture at least appears to teach that Jesus Christ, as the Son of God, preexisted with the Father. For example, various passages in the Gospel of John seem to teach the Son's preexistence (e.g., John 1:1, 15, 30; 6:62; 8:58; 17:5). Jesus even speaks repeatedly about coming down out of heaven from the Father (John 6:33, 38, 41, 50–51, 58; 13:3; 16:28). Paul also seems to speak of Christ as preexistent (especially in Col. 1:15–17 and Phil. 2:6–7). Similarly, Paul, John, and the author of Hebrews refer to the world being created through Jesus Christ the Son (John 1:3; 1 Cor. 8:6; Eph. 3:9; Col. 1:15–17; Heb. 1:2). How does Oneness theology handle these texts?

Preexistent as the Father

There are four different sorts of answers that informed Oneness exponents customarily give to explain verses such as these. First, wherever Jesus is referring to himself as eternal (e.g., John 8:58), the previously mentioned "key" concept of Christ being both the Father and the Son is utilized, for this, in Oneness exegesis, means that Christ is both eternal and temporal. It is, then, the voice of the eternal Father in Christ that is for the moment speaking when he refers to himself as existing eternally.

Preexistent in God's Foreknowledge

This explanation will not work, however, for passages that speak of Jesus Christ or the Son *as distinct from God or the Father* as preexisting Christ's human existence. For example, those passages that speak of God's creating the world "through Christ" are impossible to explain through any reference to Christ's supposed personal identity as the eternal Father. For here, clearly, it is Christ as *distinct* from God the Father who is said to be present at creation (though Bernard, remarkably, seems to miss this implication in even these verses, see Bernard, Oneness, 115–16).

To explain passages such as these, most Oneness authors appeal to the concept of God's foreknowledge. This is the second way in which Oneness authors get around the actual preexistence of the Son in Scripture. According to this exegesis, to say that the Father created the world through Jesus Christ means only that God created the world "with a view towards" or "for the sake of" Jesus Christ, the future man (Son) in whom he planned to dwell. In other words, God's plan of redemption through this man was at the forefront of the Father's foreseeing mind when he created the world. "The divine purpose for Christ existed from the beginning, not the one in whom it should be fulfilled" (Sabin, Seminar). And again, "When God did the creating, he did it totally alone, but toward God, facing him in time, was the ideal figure, the envisaged image of one in God's mind whom God was to be" (Sabin, I, 1).

According to standard Oneness theology, then, the Son of God can be said to preexist ideally—in God's forevision and purposes—but not in actuality. "The Son pre-existed in the mind of God only" (Springfield, 19; cf. Magee, 29). He was, one might say, the Father's "super-idea" (Hermann, 88). Even the glory that Christ said he had "with the Father before the world began" (John 17:5) was, in this view, really only an ideal glory: it was the foreseen glory of the crucified, resurrected, and ascended Christ (Sabin, Seminar; Haywood, 34; Bernard, Oneness, 183–84). Parallels are frequently drawn with verses that speak of individuals being foreknown before they are born (Jer. 1:5), of Christ being (ideally) "slain from the foundation of the world" (Rev. 13:8), and of the church being (ideally) "chosen from the foundation of the world" (Eph. 1:4; 2 Tim. 1:9) (Sabin, Seminar).

For the vast majority of Oneness authors, it is this ideal forevision and not a "substantial entity" or "person" that is referred to by John's concept of "the Word," which was in the beginning with God and was God (John 1:1). "The Word," quite simply, was God's plan and purpose in creation and redemption. In standard Oneness theology, then, it was simply the purpose and plan of God, not Jesus as the preexistent Son of God, that was "enfleshed" in the Incarnation (Sabin, V, 1–2; Bernard, Oneness, 60–61, 102–3). Yet it was God himself, they concede, who was "enfleshed," for John tells us that God's purposes are not only "with" him, they are identical to him: "and the Word was God."

Preexistent as a Finite Dimension

While the majority of Oneness authors hold to this interpretation of the preexistent Logos as an ideal in God's mind, there exist a minority who do not, and some of these are the most learned and articulate from among the Oneness camp. The writings of this small branch of

Oneness Pentecostalism generally tend to reflect much more appreciation for biblical scholarship, the early church fathers, and the scriptural difficulty of maintaining the standard modalistic Oneness doctrine. Specifically, they recognize the difficulties (to be discussed in chapter 4) of consistently maintaining that "the Word" is simply an idea in God's foreseeing mind prior to the Incarnation. They recognize the extreme difficulties involved in reducing all of those passages that speak of Christ's preexistence distinct from the Father to a merely ideal existence. And yet, this view desires to remain "Oneness" by rejecting any notion of there being any eternal personal distinctions in the Godhead.

What this faction of the UPCI maintains is that the preexistent Word is an actual distinct "dimension" or "aspect" of God prior to the Incarnation. God is essentially omnipresent Spirit (Father), yet there is, in this view, a "finitized" dimension of God that can be called God's "image," "shape," "form," "face," or "expression." Within this faction there are two subgroups. The majority maintain that this "aspect" or "dimension" of God is essential to God and hence eternal (Paterson, Reeves, Springfield). This view comes very close to trinitarianism in many ways. The smaller group holds that this aspect of God was assumed in time, prior to creation (Yadon, Fitch). This view is somewhat similar to that of the Jehovah's Witnesses, and even more like that of the Arians in the fourth century.

Kenneth Reeves, who holds that God's "Image" is eternal, is the most prolific published UPCI spokesperson for this version of Oneness theology. He writes: "There is One God and God is One, but God is a being of unlimited quantity, of innumerable qualities, infinite intelligence, almighty power, with many facets to His nature and manifestations. One aspect to His Being is His Image or Shape or Form, identified as the Word in John 1:1–3" (Reeves, Supreme, 21–22).

In this camp, then, "the Word" exists "from the beginning" (and for most, "from eternity"), and the Word is, in some sense (e.g., as an "aspect" or "dimension"), genuinely distinct from God the Father. This Word, it is maintained, was manifested in angelic form as "the angel of the Lord" in the Old Testament (Reeves, Dimensions, 95ff.; Yadon, 50), and was then manifested as "the only begotten Son" in the New. But, as Reeves tirelessly argues, the Word does not in any sense constitute a distinct "person" in the Godhead (see Reeves, Godhead, 74–75; Dimensions, *passim*), and hence members of this group remain (at least in their own view) distinctly Oneness in their theology. "The Father and the Word are the same Being, but the Word-Image is a specific aspect of that substance in a form or image" (Reeves, Dimensions, 55).

The Commissioned Son

We have thus far seen that Oneness exponents get around the traditional concept of "the eternal Son" by interpreting Scriptures that have traditionally been taken to imply Christ's preexistence as Son as referring either to Christ's preexistence as God the Father, to Christ's ideal preexistence in the mind of the Father, or (for a minority) to Christ's preexistence as a finitized aspect of the Father ("the Word").

But what, we might finally ask, is to be made of the many passages that speak of Christ as being "sent into the world" by the Father? Do these not presuppose that the Son preexists with the Father prior to his sending?

The small faction of Oneness people following something like the teaching of Reeves have no difficulty with these passages, for in their view this simply means that the Father sent his Word or "image" into the world. "God has an image, shape or form . . . that can come down or go up . . ." (Reeves, Dimensions, 94–95). So, for example, concerning a passage like Philippians 2:7–8, Reeves can say, "The form or image of God took the form of a servant" (Reeves, Supreme, 66; cf. Dimensions, 27).

The majority of Oneness people, however, do not follow this teaching, because they do not acknowledge that Christ, as distinct from the Father, preexisted in any substantial manner. The explanation they offer for the "sending" passages is that Christ is said to be "sent by God into the world" in the same manner in which ordinary prophets are said to be "sent by God." This phrase, in their view, is thus equivalent to saying that the sent one was "commissioned" by God (Sabin, V, 3–4; Sabin, Seminar; Bernard, Oneness, 184; Magee, 36). Hence, for example, John the Baptist is said to be "sent from God," yet clearly he didn't preexist with God prior to his sending (John 1:6). And Jesus even draws a parallel between his being sent and the sending of the disciples when he prays, "As you [God] sent me into the world, I have sent them into the world" (John 17:18).

Hence, it is argued, the only difference between the sending of the man Jesus and the sending of the disciples is that Jesus received his sending directly from the Father who dwelt within him and was united to him, whereas the disciples' sending was commissioned by Jesus himself. And, it is concluded, there is therefore no reason to assume that the language of Jesus being "sent by God" implies any concept of preexistence.

Oneness Pentecostals, then, employ a number of different strategies to show that the Bible does not teach that Jesus preexisted his birth as a person distinct from the Father. We will be critically examining these strategies in detail in chapter 4.

The Son and the Spirit in Oneness Theology

In addition to explaining the apparent distinction between Jesus and the Father in the New Testament, Oneness theology must account for the apparent distinction between Jesus and the Spirit. If Jesus is personally identical with the Spirit, how is it that he can refer to the Holy Spirit as "another Counselor," as a distinct "he" whom he (Jesus) would send, and who would have distinct activities to perform?

The standard Oneness response to this question is to say that the Holy Spirit is simply another name for the Father. Hence Jesus' distinctness from the Spirit is to be understood along the same lines as Jesus' distinctness from the Father explained above. "The one God is Father of all, is holy, and is a Spirit. Therefore, the titles Father and Holy Spirit describe the same being" (Bernard, Oneness, 129, cf. 131).

But, one must ask, why then did Jesus refer to the Holy Spirit as "another" counselor and as another "he"? According to Oneness theology, Jesus did this in order to distinguish the revelation and activity of God in the Son from the revelation and activity of God outside the Son, and especially in the believer. The different roles of God, it is thus argued, require that Scripture speak of God *as though* each activity were a distinct "person," in just the fashion as Jesus spoke of the Father, his divine nature, *as though* "it" were a distinct person.

> . . . when Jesus spoke of the Holy Ghost as one might speak of a third individual, it was to differentiate as to the kind of self revelation or manifestation indicated. . . . The variety and diversity of God's self revelation forces Him [God] to use language that may seem to imply plurality of individuals, but if such is accepted literally the effect would be a belief in a plurality of Gods. [Reeves, Godhead, 51–52; cf. Bernard, Oneness, 195f.]

The logic here is pretty straightforward. Once it is assumed—as Oneness Pentecostals do—that any talk about "three persons" in the Godhead is equivalent to tritheism, then of course when Scripture clearly speaks in just such terms (as Reeves admits), Scripture must be talking *figuratively.* The (apparently) distinct personhood of the Holy Spirit, therefore, can only be a literary device, a "poetic personification," no different from (say) the notion that "wisdom," an attribute of God, can poetically be described as a woman "crying" and "pleading" with individuals, as well as a being "created" by God in the beginning (see Prov. 8; cf. Sabin, Truant, Notes). Again, as with the Son so with the Spirit: God uses "the illusion of separation" for the purpose of revealing his fullness.

If this explanation seems strained, it is actually necessary, given the Oneness assumption that the Trinity is unacceptable for other reasons. Once one concludes that there *cannot* be three "persons" in the Godhead, one must conclude that every appearance that there are in fact three "persons" is only illusory. We shall end this chapter by turning our attention to the remaining arguments from which Oneness Pentecostals conclude that the Trinity is unacceptable in the first place.

The "Errors" of the Trinity

Oneness Pentecostals make a number of serious accusations against trinitarian theology. They argue that (1) the Trinity contradicts the biblical teaching that there is only one God and that Jesus is that God; (2) the Holy Spirit as a "third person" is often "absent" in Scripture; (3) the Bible often speaks of the Father alone as "God" as distinct from Jesus Christ; (4) the doctrine of the Trinity employs extrabiblical language; (5) the Trinity is of pagan origin; (6) some arguments for the Trinity are clearly unsound; and (7) the Trinity is self-contradictory and therefore illogical. I will conclude this chapter with a careful explanation of these seven arguments, which will then be answered in chapter 2.

1. The Trinity, Monotheism, and the Deity of Christ

We have already examined the two foundational pillars of Oneness theology—monotheism and the deity of Christ. Both Oneness and trinitarian believers profess to adhere to these foundational truths. It is the unanimous position of Oneness adherents, however, that the doctrine of the Trinity is grossly incompatible with both of these facts.

First of all, Oneness Pentecostals argue that trinitarian doctrine is inevitably tritheistic and thus is inherently incompatible with biblical monotheism. For example, Bernard writes, "Despite the protests of trinitarians, their doctrine inevitably leads to a practical form of tritheism . . . trinitarianism emphasizes threeness in God while the Bible emphasizes the oneness of God" (Oneness, 288). Reeves repeatedly calls trinitarians "modified tritheists" (Godhead, 30) or even "tri-Godists" (Dimensions, ch. 2), maintaining that a "three-headed God is implied or expressed" by this doctrine (Godhead, 53).

Second, Oneness exponents maintain that trinitarianism is impossible to square with the biblical portrayal that in Christ all the fullness of God dwelt in bodily form (Col. 2:9). "Trinitarianism," writes Bernard, ". . . denies that the fulness of the Godhead is in Jesus because it denies that Jesus is the Father and the Holy Spirit" (Oneness, 289). Sabin concurs, adding that trinitarianism "denies the sole and supreme Deity of Jesus," for "if you separate Christ from the

Father you automatically separate Him from Deity" (Sabin, IV, 4, 5; cf. Norris, 13; Small, 90). So, too, he argues that trinitarianism maintains that God "sent somebody else" while God himself remained "a bystander, a spectator" (what he calls "deputationalism"), whereas Oneness believers know that "He did not send somebody else, but He came Himself" (what he calls "theocarnationalism," ibid., 1–5).

2. The Absent Holy Spirit

Another commonly employed argument used against the doctrine of the Trinity is that "there are abundant Scriptures which relate Father/Son and omit mention of a third person" (Sabin, Irrefutable; cf. Truant; Bernard, Oneness, 195, 207–8). Hence, for example, John says that "our fellowship is with the Father and with his Son" (1 John 1:3), but omits mentioning the Holy Spirit. Jesus speaks of the Father as knowing the Son, and the Son as knowing the Father, but omits mention of the Spirit (Matt. 11:27). Similarly, while God and the Lamb are envisioned on the throne in the Book of Revelation, nowhere is the Holy Spirit "cited" (e.g., Rev. 21:22–23). And in none of Paul's opening salutations does he mention the Holy Spirit, though he always mentions "God our Father and the Lord Jesus Christ" (e.g., 1 Cor 1:3; 2 Cor. 1:2; Gal. 1:3). This, it is argued, is not what one would expect if in fact the biblical authors thought that there was any inherent "threeness" about the nature of God (cf. Yadon, 70), and if the Holy Spirit was considered to be a coequal "person" of the Trinity.

3. The Only True God—The Father

Yet another frequently raised argument is that Scripture frequently calls the Father "God" alongside of Jesus or the Holy Spirit (Sabin, Seminar; Reeves, Godhead, 15, 22–23). Paul's salutations, cited above, are a case in point. So, too, Scripture speaks of God's sending Jesus, exalting Jesus, and creating the world through Jesus (John 3:16; Phil. 2:9–10; 1 Cor. 8:6). It contrasts God, whom "no one has ever seen," with the unique Son ("the One and Only") who manifests him (John 1:18). Jesus expressly addressed the Father as "the only true God"

(John 17:3). And both Jesus and the Holy Spirit are mentioned along-side of "God" in 2 Corinthians 13:14.

The argument here is this: If Jesus (and the Spirit) are in fact God in some sense "alongside" God the Father, it would be improper to limit the title "God" to the Father in these contexts. In other words, the exclusivity of its use in referring to the Father seems to presuppose a contrast with Jesus. This, it is maintained, is incompatible with the trinitarian view, but not with the Oneness view. For, as we have seen, Oneness believers argue that when such contrasts are made, they are made with a view of Jesus as a man, as the Son, not divine.

4. Unbiblical Terminology

Yet another frequently raised objection to the Trinity is that "the language of the trinitarian theory is not in Scripture" (Sabin, Irrefutable; cf. Morehead, Mystery; Reeves, Godhead, 49; Bernard, Oneness, 262). The Bible never uses such words as *Trinity, eternal Son, coequal, consubstantial,* and *three persons.* If the apostles had believed such a doctrine, it is argued, why didn't they say so? Would it be necessary to use terminology that is foreign to Scripture if in fact our beliefs are in harmony with Scripture?

5. Pagan Origins

Related to this last argument is the frequently raised (though never substantiated) contention that the concept of the Trinity did not originate from the Bible at all, but from pagan philosophy and religion. It is claimed that a type of trinity can be found in Plato, in Babylonian religion, in Mithraism, and in Hinduism, and that it crept in and perverted Christianity from these outside sources (see, for example, Reeves, Dimensions, 121ff.; Bernard, Oneness, 264ff.; Sabin, Seminar; Sabin, III, 7–8; Weisser, Three, *passim*; Chalfant, 115ff.).

6. The Logic of the Trinity

The orthodox trinitarian church has always admitted, freely and joyfully, that the doctrine of the Trinity is a mystery that is beyond reason. The creeds, in a nutshell, confess that there is one God and that this one God exists fully, and eternally, in three distinct "persons."

This confession is certainly mysterious, for it clearly implies that God is not quantifiable—he can exist completely in three distinct ways at the same time throughout eternity. This is the mystery of the Trinity.

For Oneness exponents, this mystery is, at best, illegitimate: "It is wrong to state that the Godhead is a mystery when the Bible clearly states that God has revealed the mystery to us" (Bernard, Oneness, 289). At worst, however, this mystery is really a self-contradiction. After all, it is difficult to see "how there can be three persons of God in any meaningful sense and yet there be only one God" (Bernard, Oneness, 290; cf. Reeves, Dimensions, 15).

According to these authors, to say "three persons in one God" is, then, a self-contradictory and therefore meaningless statement. Oneness exponents are also fond of arguing that the doctrine of the Trinity, beyond being contradictory itself, leads to a number of other contradictions. Some of these supposed contradictions are the following (cf. Reeves, Godhead, 54ff.; Hermann, *passim*; Bernard, Oneness, 286ff.; Sabin, Irrefutable):

If the Father and the Spirit are distinct "persons," then Jesus must have had two spiritual Fathers. For the Father, of course, is the Father of the Son (1 John 1:3), yet Scripture also says that Jesus was conceived by the Holy Spirit (Luke 1:35).

If the Father, Son, and Holy Spirit are really distinct "persons," then Jesus had to have the entire Trinity dwelling within him, for he was full of the Holy Spirit (Luke 4:1), and yet he repeatedly said the Father did the work in him (John 14:10). Indeed, each believer must be indwelt by the entire Trinity, for Scripture at different times says that we have dwelling within us the Father (Eph. 4:6), Jesus (Gal. 1:16; 2 Cor. 13:5), and the Holy Spirit (John 14:16). And, as Kenneth Reeves asks, "How can the Three be in heaven, and the Three be in each believer at the same time?" (Reeves, Godhead, 55).

The Bible says that there is only one Spirit (Eph. 4:4), and yet the doctrine of the Trinity requires that there be three Spirits, for the Father and Jesus Christ, as well as the Holy Spirit, are called "Spirits" (John 4:24; 2 Cor. 3:17).

If the Son is the second person of the Trinity and truly divine in his own right (as opposed to just being the humanity of God incarnate), how is it that he had to pray to the Father (Matt. 11:25), obey the Father (John 8:29), and receive everything he had from the Father (John 3:34–35; 5:19, 30)? If Christ is indeed "God the Son," Oneness Pentecostals ask, how is it that he did not know some things (Mark 13:32), and that he admitted that he was less than the Father (John 14:28)? How is it that he could genuinely die (Matt. 27:50)? Can God die? And how is it that his kingdom will eventually come to an end (1 Cor. 15:24–25)?

7. Weak Arguments for the Trinity

A final frequently used tactic in attempting to refute the doctrine of the Trinity is to attack certain weak arguments that, on a popular level, are sometimes used to substantiate the doctrine of the Trinity. In exposing the vulnerability of such arguments, Oneness proponents believe they have successfully undermined the biblical foundation of the Trinity.

Thus, for example, it is not uncommon to find trinitarians arguing for the doctrine of the Trinity on the basis of the fact that the word for God in the Old Testament is *Elohim*, which is the plural of the word *El.* Hence it is thought to imply a plurality in the Godhead.

Unfortunately, this is indeed, as most Hebrew scholars recognize, a very weak argument on which to base the doctrine of the Trinity. When a numerical plurality is intended, the corresponding verb(s) in the context will be plural. When the one true God is referred to as *Elohim,* however, the corresponding verbs are always singular. Moreover, as Bernard notes, the term is applied to the one angelic being who wrestled with Jacob (Gen. 32:30) and to the one golden calf the Israelites worshiped (Exod. 32:1, 4, 8) (Bernard, Oneness, 147). Hence it is easiest and best to understand the plural of *Elohim* when referenced to Yahweh as denoting a plural of majesty (see also Morehead, Foundations, 9ff.).[3]

Even weaker is the argument that the Hebrew word for "one" (*echad*) used in the Shema ("Hear O Israel, the Lord our God is one

Lord") refers to a unified one, not an absolute one. Hence, some trinitarians have argued, the Old Testament has a view of a united Godhead. It is, of course, true that the meaning of the word may in some contexts denote a unified plurality (e.g., Gen. 2:4, "they shall become one flesh"). But this really proves nothing. An examination of Old Testament usage reveals that the word *echad* is as capable of various meanings as is our English word *one*. The context must determine whether a numerical or unified singularity is intended. And, while the use of *echad* in the Shema leaves open the possibility of a unified view of the Godhead, one cannot at all base such a view of the Godhead on the word itself (Morehead, Mystery, 9; Morehead, Foundations, 24–28; Bernard, Oneness, 152ff.; Sabin, IV, 6).

Don't Conclude Too Quickly!

I have presented above some of the most frequently raised objections to the doctrine of the Trinity stated by Oneness adherents. To uninformed trinitarians who have not been prepared for them, they can initially be devastating.

In this chapter I have attempted to present the best arguments of the Oneness exponents in favor of their position. I have tried to do so in as much detail as necessary, with as much force as the arguments warrant, and without critical comment.

These arguments have successfully converted significant numbers of professed trinitarians from "the faith which was once delivered" (Jude 3 KJV) to Oneness Pentecostalism. To those who find these arguments persuasive, may I urge you not to accept them uncritically. Don't conclude in favor of Oneness Pentecostalism too quickly or too easily. Although these arguments must be taken seriously, they can be soundly refuted. It is to this task, then, that we shall address ourselves throughout the rest of this book.

The Trinity
Truth or Error?

n the first chapter I presented the Oneness adherents' arguments for their modalistic understanding of the Godhead as well as their arguments against the orthodox understanding of the Trinity. The remainder of this work will be devoted to responding to these arguments and presenting the biblical basis for a belief in the doctrine of the Trinity.

I begin my reply in this chapter by answering the seven general accusations against trinitarian theology that are most frequently raised by Oneness believers.

Monotheism and the Deity of Christ

As pointed out in chapter 1, Oneness believers unanimously maintain that the doctrine of the Trinity contradicts the biblical teaching that there is only one God and that Jesus is the Incarnation of this

God. Rather, they maintain that only their position that Jesus is himself the Father, Son, and Holy Spirit squares with these two foundational biblical truths. Though this argument has an initial appeal, it is actually misguided. Three things may be said to demonstrate this.

First, trinitarians have always maintained that there is only one God and that God is indivisible. God cannot be "divided up into thirds" so to speak. To say that there are "three Persons in the Godhead" has never been taken to mean that there are "three separate people who are God" or that "God is a committee," as Oneness believers mistakenly accuse trinitarians of believing. Any belief in three gods has always been understood to be heresy from a Christian perspective. This fact of church history would be impossible to understand, however, if in fact the doctrine of the Trinity was itself inherently tritheistic. Therefore, that Oneness Pentecostals *think* it is tritheistic is more the result of their misunderstanding of what this doctrine is all about than it is the result of the orthodox doctrine itself.

The doctrine of the Trinity simply states that God fully exists in three personally distinct ways. This is, as already stated in the first chapter, admittedly paradoxical, since it means that God is nonmaterial and nonquantifiable. As Scripture says, "God is Spirit" (John 4:24), and thus he cannot be quantified into "thirds." God is therefore *fully* present in each of the three ways he eternally exists. But who would limit God by claiming that this is impossible? And what is so illogical or tritheistic about this? As I shall show in chapter 8, even the Oneness Pentecostals admit that God can and does fully exist in more than one way at the same time. Yet no one would accuse them of polytheism for doing so.

This brings us to a second point: Because God is indivisible, the doctrine of the Trinity has always affirmed the complete deity of Jesus Christ. Indeed, this has always been the central point of this doctrine! Throughout the ages the church has, by means of the Trinity, emphatically defended the complete deity of Christ against all subordinationistic heresies.

"For in Christ all the fullness of the Deity lives . . ." (Col. 2:9). This isn't a truth discovered by Oneness people in the second decade of this century. Trinitarians have from the beginning been emphatic on just this central truth! Jesus Christ is "our great God and Savior" (Titus 2:13), our "Lord and God" (John 20:28), the "God [who is] over all" (Rom. 9:5), and the one who is "the beginning and the ending," beside whom there is no other (Rev. 1:8, 17–18 KJV; cf. Isa. 44:6). He is therefore to be the object of our faith and worship. None of this is a "Oneness truth" (as they claim). It is, and has always been, a *trinitarian* truth! It is a truth that has been emphatically preached and preserved down through the ages (as the Lord promised, Matt. 16:18) by the orthodox trinitarian church against any who would assail it. It is, therefore, presumptuous at best, if not positively absurd, for Oneness believers to think that *they* are the sole champions of this truth—against the trinitarians. Indeed, I have yet to find one valid Oneness argument for the deity of Christ that has not already been used by a trinitarian for the same purpose. Oneness exponents make their case on borrowed trinitarian capital.

This leads us to a third and final response. We have seen that trinitarians have always held to the singularity and indivisibility of God as well as to the complete deity of Christ. They have done this because these are clear biblical teachings. But they have never rationalistically concluded from this, as the Oneness movement has done, that Jesus must therefore himself be the Father, Son, and Holy Spirit—because this simply is not a biblical teaching (see chs. 3–7). In Scripture, Jesus is portrayed as being truly God, but he is *not* portrayed as being all there is to be said about God, for God is also portrayed as Father and as the Holy Spirit, distinct from Christ.

It is only a nonscriptural and rationalistic assumption about what the singularity and indivisibility of God must mean and about what the deity of Christ must imply that leads Oneness believers to such an unscriptural position. Because they do not see how God can fully exist as Son as well as Father and Spirit, they fly in the face of Scripture and collapse the three together! A far wiser methodology has been followed by the church throughout the ages, however. Rather than tell Scripture what the singularity and indivisibility of God *must* mean, the church has allowed Scripture to tell us what these truths *in fact* mean. And rather than tell Scripture what the deity of Christ *must* imply, the Church has allowed Scripture to tell us what this truth *in fact* implies. When we, following the church, do this, we discover that God can be truly one while also embodying a triunity, and Jesus can be truly God without thereby exhausting all there is to be truly said about God.

Indeed, as will be shown in chapter 8, it is the Oneness Pentecostals who end up being unable to consistently affirm the Incarnation, precisely because they think it requires a denial of the Trinity. As I shall show, the Incarnation actually presupposes the Trinity!

The "Absent" Holy Spirit

The second general Oneness argument against the Trinity discussed in the previous chapter was that the Holy Spirit is frequently "absent" when the Father and Son are mentioned together, and this, they claim, is not what one would expect if God is in fact triune. There are four responses that can be made to this argument.

First, this Oneness contention is a classic case of an "argument from silence," which is universally recognized to be an invalid form of argumentation. To state this succinctly, *an omission does not constitute a denial.* If I am with my two daughters at a public speaking engagement and I introduce them as "my children, Denay and Alisha," this does not mean that I do not have a son. To conclude that I don't have a son because I didn't mention him would be an argument from silence. In truth my omission only means that I, for whatever reasons, didn't deem it expedient to mention him. Nor does the fact that I didn't mention my wife, my father, or my grandfather imply that I don't have a wife, a father, or a grandfather. Since an omission does not constitute a denial, arguments from silence are never valid.

So also, the fact that the Holy Spirit is not always mentioned alongside the Father and the Son does not in the least entail that the Holy Spirit is not "on a par" with the Father and the Son. Indeed, this same distorted logic would lead us to conclude that the Father doesn't have a Son because, after all, the Son is frequently not mentioned when the Father is referred to. The lameness of this reasoning is obvious.

Second, it seems that this argument, if valid, would actually go against the Oneness position. For, if being consistently mentioned alongside of the Father and the Son is necessary for the Holy Spirit to be regarded as a divine "person," it seems that the Oneness debators are conceding that the Father and the Son *are* distinct divine "persons"—but this is something they would not want to do. If they are not conceding this, what is the point of their argument?

Third, the weakness of this argument can be easily demonstrated by pointing out that the Holy Spirit *is* frequently mentioned alongside of the Father and/or the Son as a distinct "person." Consider, for example, the status given to the Holy Spirit in passages such as these:

> ". . . go and make disciples of all nations, baptizing them in the name of the Father and of the Son *and of the Holy Spirit*" (Matt. 28:19, emphasis added).
>
> May the grace of the Lord Jesus Christ, and the love of God, and the *fellowship of the Holy Spirit* be with you all (2 Cor. 13:14, emphasis added).
>
> For through him [Jesus] we both have access to the Father *by one Spirit* (Eph. 2:18, emphasis added).

Such passages could be easily multiplied (see ch. 5), but the point is already clear. The real question is not "Why isn't the Holy Spirit *always* mentioned alongside the Father and the Son?" but "Why is the Holy Spirit *so frequently* mentioned alongside the Father and the Son?" If the Holy Spirit is simply another name for the presence or power of God, as Oneness theology maintains, such triadically structured verses would seem quite inappropriate.

Fourth, there are two very good reasons as to why the distinct personhood of the Holy Spirit is a bit more obscure than that of the

Father and of the Son (though Oneness theology denies that even these two are distinct "persons"). First, it was not necessary, or even expedient, for the third "person" of the Trinity to be revealed as such until just prior to the beginning of the church age. Before this, and even occasionally after this, the Holy Spirit is sometimes (though not always) portrayed in relatively impersonal terms. With the teachings of Jesus, however, it becomes very clear that the Holy Spirit is God existing in a distinct personal way. Thus, for example, he is consistently referred to as a "he" and has personal activities and qualities ascribed to him (e.g., he counsels, convicts, speaks, leads [John 14:15–16; 15:26; 16:12–15]). And so it continues throughout the New Testament.

Even more significant, however, is the relatively obscure (though no less important) role the Holy Spirit has within God's plan of redemption. It is the business of the Holy Spirit to work within believers, pointing them away from himself to the person of Jesus Christ who reveals the Father. The Father, revealed in the Son, is "out there" as it were, and hence this is where God gives himself to us as an object of faith. But it is the miraculous work of the Holy Spirit to work behind the scenes and create in us the ability and desire to see God revealed in his glorified Son.

Jesus succinctly summarizes this theme, found throughout the New Testament, when he says concerning the Holy Spirit: "But when he, the Spirit of truth, comes, he will guide you into all truth. He will not speak on his own; he will speak only what he hears. . . . He will bring glory to me by taking from what is mine and making it known to you" (John 16:13–14).

The work of the Holy Spirit, then, is to bring glory to Jesus Christ. He is not unlike a photographer who is constantly present with two companions and taking their pictures, but who is himself usually not in the picture. So, too, the Holy Spirit is sometimes behind the scenes when Scripture is referring to the Father and the Son. His occasional omission, however, certainly does not entail his nonexistence.

God Distinguished from Jesus?

The third general argument that Oneness Pentecostals employ in their attempt to refute the doctrine of the Trinity is the contention that God and Jesus are frequently distinguished in the New Testament (e.g., Rom 15:30; 2 Cor. 13:14; Gal. 4:6; etc.). This, it is argued, would not have been done if Jesus were the second "person" of the Trinity and fully God in his own right. Rather, they maintain that only the Father is God, and when he is distinguished from Jesus in Scripture it is because Jesus is being portrayed in his humanity, namely, as the Son. In truth, they maintain, Jesus is both the Father and the Son, the Father being his "divine side," the Son being his "human side." There are three arguments that clearly show this reasoning to be in error.

First, the Oneness Pentecostals need to explain why it is that whenever God and Jesus are being distinguished, it is never Jesus and the Son who are distinguished. That is, if Jesus is both the Father and the Son, why does Scripture always limit Jesus' explicit identity to the Son? Why does Scripture never refer to "Jesus and the Son" when it refers to God (the Father) and the man in whom God dwelt—if in fact Jesus is, as Oneness believers claim, both the Father and the Son?

Related to this point is the incredibly awkward reading that the Oneness Pentecostal understanding of Jesus creates for those passages that distinguish God from Jesus. So, for example, Oneness Pentecostals would have us understand Paul in 2 Corinthians 13:14 to be saying: "May the grace of the Lord Jesus Christ, and the love of God (who is also Jesus Christ), and the fellowship of the Holy Spirit (who is also Jesus Christ) be with you all."

The question is, why does Paul distinguish Jesus Christ from God the Father and the Holy Spirit in this and every similar passage if in fact he believes Jesus is really all three?

Similarly, the Oneness Pentecostals would have us understand all of Paul's salutations as saying, "Grace and peace to you from God our Father (who is Jesus Christ) and the Lord Jesus Christ" (Gal. 1:3).

Even more remarkably, in Paul's many praises, Oneness Pentecostals hear him say, "Praise be to the God and Father of our Lord Jesus Christ (who is himself the Lord Jesus Christ) . . ." (Eph. 1:3). Can anyone really believe that Paul would have penned such convoluted sentences? Can one really accept that his readers would have understood him in this fashion when he *never once* modifies this formula by saying something like "Praise be to our Lord Jesus Christ who is the Father of the Son"? If Paul really thought that the Father was simply the "divine side" of Jesus, would he not at least occasionally have spoken like this?

Second, if it is true that Jesus cannot be God when he is mentioned alongside the Father who is called God, the same must hold true for the Holy Spirit. Often the Holy Spirit is spoken of in distinction from "God," just as the Son is, and often in the very same passage (e.g., 2 Cor. 13:14; Gal. 4:6). Now Oneness Pentecostals (unlike Jehovah's Witnesses, who are more consistent on this point) do not want to deny that the Holy Spirit is God. But then there is no longer any reason to deny that Jesus is being spoken of as God when he is referred to alongside "God the Father." The locution "God and Jesus" no more implies that Jesus is subordinate to God than the locution "God and the Holy Spirit" implies that the Holy Spirit is a subordinate being.

Third, if Jesus cannot be God when the Father is called God beside him, it would follow that God the Father cannot be Lord when Jesus is called Lord beside him (see Bowman, Trinity, 72–73). But this is how Paul always speaks. He opens all his letters, as we have seen, with a blessing "from God our Father and the Lord Jesus Christ." He elsewhere says that for believers "there is but one God, the Father . . . and there is but one Lord, Jesus Christ . . ." (1 Cor. 8:6). Indeed, he even frequently distinguishes between the "one Spirit," "one Lord," and "one God and Father" in whom Christians believe (Eph. 4:4–6; cf. 1 Cor. 12:4–6; 2 Cor. 13:14; Eph. 5:18–20; 2 Thess. 2:13), but he clearly is not intending to imply that the Father is not "Lord" or "Spirit," that Christ is not God, or that the Holy Spirit is not either Lord or God! Hence, the fact that Jesus is not called God when mentioned alongside "God the Father" cannot have the significance Oneness exponents want to give it.

The fact that Jesus is even titled "Lord" in these contexts further proves the error of attempting to maintain that all these verses are contrasting God with a man. "Lord" (*kurios*) was in Jewish religious contexts as much a title of divinity as was "God" (*theos*). This is why Paul, precisely when he distinguishes Jesus "the Lord" from "God the Father," can go on to ascribe the attributes and activities of deity to him. Christ, for example, is portrayed as preexisting and as being Creator in the same context in which he is distinguished from the Father in 1 Corinthians 8:6 and Colossians 1:13–17. Other authors do the same (John 1:1–3; Heb. 1:1–10).

Hence, the attempt to restrict divinity to the Father, when he and the Son (and the Spirit) are being distinguished, simply fails. A much better explanation for why the Father is usually alone called God when spoken of in the same context as the Son and Spirit—and this constitutes our fourth response to the Oneness argument—is simply that it was customary, as a matter of literary convention, for the New Testament authors to do so.

We find in the Old Testament and intertestamental literature the development of a way of speaking about God that preserved God's transcendence while also emphasizing the reality of his involvement with the world. Authors frequently distinguished "God" from "his Spirit," "his wisdom," "his hand," "his Word," etc., and the central point of making these distinctions was simply to "provide expressions of God's immanence without compromising his transcendence" (Dunn, 130, cf. 132ff.). To speak of any of God's attributes as distinct from himself was simply to speak of God himself involved in the world.[1]

None of this changes when we come to the New Testament, except that here we have a clear revelation that God's "Word" and God's "Spirit" are terms that can be used to refer to two personally distinct ways in which God is God, and not simply different forms of God's activity. These authors no more intend to undeify the Spirit or Word by distinguishing them from God than did the Old Testament or intertestamental authors. Thus, for New Testament authors to refer to "God" (or "Father"), "Jesus" (or "Son" or "Lord"), and "the Holy Spirit" together in the same context (as they do some 65 times in the New Testament [cf. Bowman, Trinity, ch. 9]) is simply for them to refer to the totality of God in his threefold way of existing. It is a way of saying "God/God/God," but in a much richer and more felicitous manner.[2]

A final word must be said concerning how it is that Jesus (and others) can refer to the Father as *his* God (John 20:17; 2 Cor. 1:3; Eph. 1:3; Rev. 1:6). On the face of it, the traditional trinitarian answer to this differs little from the answer Oneness believers would themselves give: namely, it is because of Christ's Incarnation, because of the fact that he was a full human being, that he could not only refer to the Father as *his* God, but also explicitly say that the Father was greater than he (John 14:28). It was, moreover, for this same reason that the Son had to continually pray to God as any human must pray (Mark 1:35; 14:35; etc.).

However, we trinitarians differ radically from Oneness Pentecostals in the way we maintain this truth. To put it simply, we do not ask, as Oneness exponents insist on asking, "Is he [Christ] now taking the part and place of God or is he taking the part and place of man?" (Magee, 14). Such a question is a fundamental denial of the Incarnation itself, for it represents a rejection of the truth that "the Word became flesh" (John 1:14). A belief in the Incarnation means that *everything* Christ went through and did, God went through and did; otherwise, it is really a meaningless belief. The one person of Jesus Christ cannot be split in two, not even for the sake of a (supposedly) helpful "illusion." The Incarnation, if it means anything, means that one cannot answer Magee's either/or question with a straight either/or answer.

Hence, when Christ suffered, God suffered; when Christ wept, God wept; when Christ experienced hunger, God experienced hunger; and when Christ suffered a forsaken death, God suffered a forsaken death. The apostle Paul said that God purchased the church with his own blood (Acts 20:28). The Oneness insistence that it was not as

God, but only as a man, that Christ did these things splits Christ in two and is tantamount to denying the Incarnation altogether! As we shall shortly see, however, the Oneness believers' view of God as an undifferentiated unity and not triune really prevents them from portraying Christ in any other way. Only a belief that God can and does fully exist in more than one way—trinitarianism—can truly affirm that God could really become a man without thereby depleting his own infinite transcendence.

Unbiblical Terminology

The fourth general argument frequently used against the Trinity by Oneness believers is that it employs unbiblical terminology and thus is not biblical. This argument may be dismissed with three considerations.

First, there is nothing in Scripture that prohibits the use of unscriptural language to express what Scripture says. Such a notion, if held consistently, would actually prohibit preaching. Instead, we would have to simply come together and read the Bible (in the original language!).

Second, if we are to address audiences that Scripture does not explicitly address and if we are to answer questions that Scripture does not explicitly answer, the use of new terms to express ourselves is absolutely unavoidable. Whenever someone asks, "What do you mean?" we need to attempt to explain ourselves in new ways to make ourselves clear. It would be of no value if we simply kept on reading a verse over and over again. Christian doctrines are simply shorthand ways in which Christians say to themselves and to the world what they "mean." And they must do so in ways that are understandable to their contemporary world and answer contemporary questions.

Finally, it needs to be pointed out that this criticism is somewhat disingenuous on the part of Oneness Pentecostals, for they, too, invariably and without exception, use unbiblical language to express what they believe. Such language is found throughout their books and tracts. They speak of "the roles," "manifestations," or "modes" of the Father, Son, and Holy Spirit, but the Bible never uses these terms. They (like trinitarians here) frequently speak of "the Incarnation," another word not explicitly found in the Bible. Their writings are full of such terminology as "the Fatherhood of Christ," "the God-Man," "the initial physical evidence," "the one substance of God," and other phrases that are certainly absent from Scripture. And certain Oneness theologians, such as Sabin and Reeves (both of whom are objectors to the Trinity on the basis of its unbiblical terminology) are fond of coining new phrases such as "theocarnationalism," "Omnipresent Spirit Substance," or "Word-Image-Son" to describe their own position.

This is not mentioned to criticize the Oneness position on this basis, for the use of new terminology is unavoidable in expressing and explaining one's position. But it does reveal the inconsistency of those who raise such an objection to the Trinity. It is true that the word "Trinity" and the phrase "God in three persons" are not explicitly found in Scripture—but neither is much of the Oneness terminology. But that is not the issue. The issue is whether or not the terminology expresses a biblical teaching. My contention is that the trinitarian terminology does, while the Oneness terminology does not.

Pagan Origins?

Oneness believers, like Jehovah's Witnesses and other antitrinitarians, frequently maintain that the doctrine of the Trinity originated in pagan religions and/or philosophy and is therefore false. They argue that it crept into the original apostolic faith by means of ungodly leaders who loved philosophical ideas (like the Trinity) more than the pure apostolic message. Four things may be said in refutation of this contention.

First, the claim is simply false; it cannot be sustained with any solid evidence and valid argumentation. This is why no recognized contemporary scholar supports this notion. Indeed, the frequent Oneness portrayal of the early church fathers as sinister philosophers preaching a "seductive philosophy," and therefore seeking to corrupt the apostolic faith with pagan ideas, could not be further from the truth. The earliest Christian fathers cared about nothing more than preserving intact, without any alteration, "the faith that was once for all entrusted to the saints" (Jude 3), as we shall see more fully in chapter 7.

Second, if the Trinity had been incorporated from pagan sources into the Christian faith, there would have been a great deal of resistance and controversy surrounding this "apostasy." There is none. However, there *is* much controversy that erupted when some believers attempted to propogate a new and heretical Oneness view of God in the late second century. This is further proof that the Oneness view does not go back to New Testament times (as we shall again show in more detail in chapter 7). But we do not find any controversy surrounding the trinitarianism of the earliest post-apostolic fathers.

Third, the supposed parallels to the Trinity found in other religions and in some philosophies are not very convincing correlations. Scholars are generally much less inclined to make anything of these than they were a century ago. The Christian doctrine of one God existing fully in three distinct ways ("persons") is simply a radically unique concept. This is not to say that there is not "a certain threeness" in the ways a wide variety of religious and philosophical views have understood ultimate reality. [3] But it is to say that it is a long way from "a certain threeness" to the Christian doctrine of the Trinity.

Fourth, even if one insists that there are parallels to the doctrine of the Trinity outside of Christianity, this hardly proves that the doctrine of the Trinity had its *origin* outside of God's revelation and is therefore false. To be sure, one might even follow the lead of such great Christian thinkers as Augustine and C. S. Lewis and argue that the prevalence of a concept of God or ultimate reality as possessing "a certain threeness" is actually further evidence that the Christian doctrine of the Trinity is true. If indeed the Creator of the world and of humanity is triune, we might expect to find something like a threefoldness in the nature and structure of things. And we might further expect to find human beings who, being made in the image of God, are able to discern this threefoldness, however vaguely, by their own religious and spiritual abilities.

I am not presently arguing that this view is or is not correct.[4] I am only maintaining that the presence of trinitarian parallels outside of

Christianity certainly has no negative bearing on the truthfulness of this doctrine. If anything, it *supports* its truthfulness.

Is the Trinity Illogical?

We saw in chapter 1 that Oneness Pentecostals claim that the belief that God exists in three "persons" is self-contradictory and leads to a number of other absurdities. Four things may be said in response to this argument.

First, one must make a careful distinction between a contradiction and a paradox. A paradox is something that, while being *beyond* reason, is not *against* reason. A contradiction, on the other hand, is something that runs directly against reason. For example, if I assert that a given object is a round triangle, I am asserting a contradiction, for the definition of a circle (being round) is logically incompatible with the definition of a triangle (having three straight sides). An object cannot be both a triangle and a circle at the same time. To say that it is both is to say nothing.

On the other hand, when physicists tell us that light has both wave and particle characteristics, they are asserting a paradox, not a contradiction, for there is nothing that logically prohibits a reality from having both of these characteristics. They are not talking nonsense. If they were asserting that light possessed exclusively wave characteristics and yet also exhibited exclusively particle characteristics *at the same time,* that would be a contradiction, but this is not what they are asserting. Light under certain circumstances exhibits one set of characteristics, in other circumstances another set of characteristics. While we do not understand how this can be the case—it *is* a paradox—there is no contradiction in affirming it.

We who are trinitarians readily admit that the doctrine of the Trinity, like almost everything else about God, is paradoxical. But we have always denied that it is a contradiction. In affirming that there is one God who fully exists in three "persons," we are not saying something nonsensical like "there is one God and three gods." We are not affirming that God is one and three in exactly the same sense. Rather, we are asserting that the one being of God fully dwells in three distinct ways—and there is nothing contradictory about that. There is certainly nothing in the definition of the oneness of God that is logically incompatible with the notion that this oneness dwells in three distinct fashions. To say that there is one God in three "persons" is therefore more like saying that "light has both wave and particle characteristics" than it is like saying "round triangle."

The doctrine of the Trinity, then, is no different from other paradoxical doctrines of the Christian faith, like the doctrine of the Incarnation (which the Oneness Pentecostals do affirm). The doctrine of the Incarnation asserts that Jesus Christ is "fully God and fully man." Is this a contradiction? No. For there is nothing in any Christian's definition of God that rules out his becoming a man, and nothing in the Christian's definition of man that rules out a man also being God. Yes, it is certainly paradoxical, for we cannot understand how it could be. But it is not nonsense.

If the antitrinitarian Pentecostals agree on this point (and they do), why do they then find the Trinity to be so illogical? The Trinity is in truth no more paradoxical than the Incarnation.

Second, we saw in chapter 1 that the Oneness Pentecostals argue that the doctrine of the Trinity leads to the absurd conclusion that Jesus had two divine fathers—for Scripture portrays Jesus as being conceived by the Holy Spirit (Luke 1:35) and yet he prays to "the Father" who, trinitarians insist, is in some sense distinct from the Holy Spirit. This argument makes the same mistake that Mormons make in their understanding of the Trinity; namely, it understands the "Father-Son" language of Scripture far too anthropomorphically. When the Bible speaks about "the Father of our Lord Jesus Christ" and Jesus as "the Son of God," it is not referring to God as the literal progenitor of Jesus, or Jesus as the literal progeny of God the Father. Such crass literalism mistakenly attributes to God the human characteristic of sexuality. Such a view, though common among pagan mythologies, is completely foreign to the biblical revelation.

When we, following Scripture, call God "the Father" and Jesus "the Son," we are speaking analogically, not literally. We are saying that the loving relationship that exists between God and Jesus is *like* that of a father and a son—but, of course, devoid of the physical characteristics that are present in human father-son relationships. When we understand this, we see no problem whatsoever in affirming that the one who miraculously created the human seed that the Word of God became (John 1:14) was the Holy Spirit, even though the Father and the Holy Spirit are distinct "persons" in the Godhead.

Third, we also saw in chapter 1 that Oneness people argue that the doctrine of the Trinity is illogical because it requires the belief that both the Father and the Holy Spirit dwelt in Christ, as well as the belief that there are three omnipresent divine Spirits. These objections, like most Oneness objections, presuppose a very mistaken view of the Trinity. Let us say once again that the doctrine of the Trinity does not divide God up into "thirds." Because God is Spirit, God is unquantifiable and indivisible. Any other view of God is really pagan, anthropomorphic, and materialistic.

Hence, wherever and however God exists—as Father, or Son, or Holy Spirit—*all* of God exists. From this it follows that whatever "person" of the Godhead one is referring to, the other two are fully present. This is known as the "perichoresis" of the three "persons," and was first formulated in the fourth century (Prestige, God, ch. xiv). Hence we ought not to be surprised to find Jesus referring to the Father and to the Holy Spirit as dwelling within himself. "For in Christ all the fullness of the Deity lives in bodily form" (Col. 2:9).

The unquantifiability of God also explains why it is that the Trinity does not require, as the Oneness Pentecostals suggest, the illogical and tritheistic belief that there are three separate Spirits of God. Each "person" of the Trinity is the whole Spirit of God, existing in a distinct fashion. Hence, toward us, God is the transcendent Father, the Incarnate Son, and the indwelling Holy Spirit—God existing in three personally distinct ways—and yet it is the one being of God who is present in each "person." Indeed, as we shall see in chapter 8, even the Oneness Pentecostals admit (when they are being consistent) that the one God can at least *temporarily* fully exist in these three distinct ways. But, once this much is admitted, there is no longer any grounds for claiming that the belief that God eternally exists in these three ways is illogical or tritheistic.

Finally, the Oneness adherents' claim that the Trinity cannot explain how Jesus could depend on and pray to God the Father really reveals a serious weakness in their own theological system. According to many Oneness Pentecostals, the Son must only be the humanity in whom the Father dwelt, not the second "person" of the Trinity and divine in his own right, for otherwise we must suppose that God is depending on God, and God is praying to God, when we see Jesus depending on and praying to the Father. And this, they contend, is absurd.

What they do not realize, however, is that their very objection reveals that they do not truly affirm the Incarnation! As I have already pointed out, to affirm with Scripture that "the Word became flesh" either means that what the man Jesus experiences, God experiences—or it means nothing at all. If Jesus the dependent man is not in fact God experiencing human dependency on the independent Father, in what sense did the Word really become flesh? And if Jesus the praying man is not in fact God as a man praying to God, in what sense did God really become a man? Either God became a man or he did not; if he did, then *everything* that the man Jesus does, God does. This is why Christians have always called him "the God-man." To assert anything less— like *sometimes* Jesus is "acting like" a man and *sometimes* "acting like" God—is to assert something far less than what John 1:14 affirms: "The Word became flesh [not just sometimes!]."

The Oneness Pentecostals, however, do not and cannot consistently affirm John 1:14, for they do not distinguish between three "persons" of the Trinity. To state it bluntly, if their undifferentiated God really did become a man in their theology, there would be no one left to run the universe. So they must instead postulate a God who takes up residence in a man, but who does not become a man. He (the Father) talks to the man (the Son), and the man talks back to him, but he does not *become* the man who talks, and he therefore does not experience dependency and pray as the man. This the man, the Son, does on his own—and this is simply to say that God did not become a man.

Ironic as it is, then, we see that the very group that believes itself to be the sole possessor of the truth of the Incarnation by denying the Trinity is actually the group that denies the Incarnation by denying the

Trinity. For the Incarnation and the Trinity go hand in hand. This has monumental consequences for the Christian life, as we shall see in chapter 8.

Weak Arguments for the Trinity

The final objection examined in chapter 1 that is put forth by Oneness Pentecostals against trinitarianism is that many of the popular arguments used to support the Trinity are really very weak. I previously referred to the arguments for the Trinity on the basis of the word for "God" (*Elohim*) and the word for "one" (*echad*) as examples of such weak arguments. There are certainly others. There really is only one response that needs to be made against this Oneness accusation.

It is true that some of the arguments popularly used in defense of the Trinity are simplistic and weak. But this hardly means that all, or even most, of the arguments used to defend the Trinity are weak. If one is honestly attempting to ascertain the truth or falsity of a theological doctrine such as the Trinity, one ought to examine the strongest, not the weakest, arguments for it. The arguments for the Trinity most frequently critiqued by Oneness authors in their books are rarely, if ever, used by informed trinitarian scholars. This is also why Oneness works invariably do not even present a fair understanding of what the historic doctrine of the Trinity is saying. They present a caricature. Hence these writings simply have the effect of tearing down a straw man in order to convince their uninformed readers about the truth of their own position.

The arguments for the Oneness position vary widely in terms of their persuasive power—though I obviously regard them all as invalid. Nevertheless, in the first chapter of this work I attempted to portray the Oneness position in its *strongest* light, though there are numerous arguments used by certain Oneness people that their own more informed leaders would regard as extremely weak. Hence I pass them by. Conversely, throughout the remainder of this work, I shall be presenting what I think are the strongest arguments *for* the Trinity and the best arguments against the Oneness position. It is these arguments with which I would like Oneness believers to enter into dialogue. To this task we now turn.

3

Is Jesus His Own Father?

In chapter 2 we focused on arguments raised against the Trinity by Oneness Pentecostals. In this and the next four chapters we shall consider arguments used by Oneness theologians to defend the Oneness doctrine. We begin with the Oneness claim that the Bible teaches that Jesus Christ is the Father. To be more precise, Oneness theology teaches that Jesus Christ is God the Father incarnate. This teaching is the cornerstone of Oneness theology.

Jesus and the Father: *Getting the Big Picture*

Before examining the particular arguments used by Oneness Pentecostals to defend their belief that Jesus is the Father, it is important to orient our study in a larger context. We need to stand back, away from isolated prooftexts, and get the "big picture" in Scripture concerning the identity of Jesus Christ.

Consider the way that Scripture generally speaks regarding the Father and Jesus. Jesus is explicitly referred to as "the Son" over two hundred times in the New Testament, and never once is he called "Father." By contrast, over two hundred times "the Father" is referred to by Jesus or someone else as being clearly distinct from Jesus. In fact, over fifty times this juxtapositioning of the Father and Jesus the Son is rendered explicit within the very same verse. Thus, throughout the New Testament we repeatedly find such expressions as these:

> ". . . follow Christ Jesus, so that with one heart and mouth you may glorify the God and Father of our Lord Jesus Christ" (Rom. 15:5–6).
>
> "Praise be to the God and Father of our Lord Jesus Christ . . ." (2 Cor. 1:4).
>
> ". . . by Jesus Christ and God the Father, who raised him from the dead . . . Grace and peace to you from God our Father and the Lord Jesus Christ" (Gal. 1:1, 3).
>
> ". . . at the name of Jesus every knee should bow . . . and every tongue confess that Jesus Christ is Lord, to the glory of God the Father" (Phil. 2:10–11).
>
> ". . . our fellowship is with the Father and with his Son, Jesus Christ" (1 John 1:3b).
>
> ". . . if anybody does sin, we have one who speaks to the Father in our defense—Jesus Christ, the Righteous One" (1 John 2:1).
>
> "Grace, mercy, and peace from God the Father and from Jesus Christ, the Father's Son . . ." (2 John 3).

This typical New Testament way of speaking is, of course, exceedingly strange if Jesus is himself God the Father.

Indeed, if Jesus is in fact the Father as well as the Son, another strange fact about the general pattern of New Testament teaching emerges. As mentioned in the previous chapter, in the Gospels Jesus never refers to "my Son" the same way he refers to "my Father." That is, although Oneness teaching unanimously maintains that Jesus could at different times speak from either his human (Son) or divine (Father) nature, for some reason Jesus *never once* spoke from his divine perspective as Father in referring to the Son whom he himself (supposedly) sent into the world.

Not to be preoccupied with numbers, but one cannot help but be somewhat impressed by the fact that whereas one hundred seventy-nine times Jesus is presented as referring to "the Father," "my Father," or "your Father" in the Gospels as distinct from himself, at no time does he refer to "my Son" or anything of the sort as distinct from himself! Forty times in John's Gospel, Jesus refers to himself as "sent by the Father," but never does he refer to himself as the Father who sent the Son.

Just imagine how clear things would have been, from a Oneness perspective, if Jesus had occasionally—or even once!—balanced all this talk about himself being sent into the world by the Father, about himself being the Son of God, and so forth, with clear talk about himself sending the Son into the world, about himself being the Father of the Son. If Jesus or some inspired author had given us just a few statements to this effect, Oneness exegetes would not have to perform the scriptural gymnastics they use to defend themselves.

But, of course, such language is completely absent from the New Testament. As we shall see, this is why UPCI exegetes have to strain to find such far-fetched cryptic references to Jesus' alleged identity as John 14:18 or Isaiah 9:6. They simply have nothing else to stand on.

The way the Bible does speak, then, is to refer to Jesus as God's Son and to the Father as someone distinct from Jesus the Son. It bears repeating that Jesus Christ—at least two hundred times called the Son, and fifty times in the same verse juxtaposed to the Father whom he and others refer to as distinct from himself more than two hundred times— is *never once* himself called the Father. In the Gospels, Jesus constantly refers to the Father as "my Father" or "the Father who sent me," or the like, but *never once* does he refer to "my Son" or "the Son whom I have sent" or anything of the kind.

In the light of these facts, I think it is small wonder that the Oneness phrase "Jesus is the Father" sounds so "off" to unprejudiced biblically trained ears, just as it did to the biblically astute ears of the early church fathers when modalism first raised its divisive head in the late second century. Given this general pattern of speaking and teaching in the New Testament, could anything really be more natural than to assume that Jesus is in fact "the Father's Son" (2 John 3)? And, conversely, could anything be more *unnatural* by biblical standards than to think that Jesus is also "God the Father," indeed, that he is his own Father?

Had the apostles believed that Jesus was personally identical with the Father, they most certainly would have clearly taught this. After all, their message that Jesus is "the Son of God" comes through loud and clear. Not a trace of ambiguity is involved here. John simply summarizes the theme that we find shouted with crystal clarity throughout the New Testament when he writes, "But these are written that you may believe that Jesus is the Christ, the Son of God . . ." (John 20:31). But whatever happened to their (supposed) message that Jesus was also, in his divine nature, "the Father"? Why are the New Testament writers so remarkably clear in communicating the sonship of Jesus—to the point that no one has ever missed this—yet so remarkably opaque in communicating the (supposed) fatherhood of Jesus—to the point that the vast majority of Bible readers have never even suspected this? Why is the (supposed) fact that Jesus was his own Father so secretively hidden in the New Testament if indeed one's salvation depends on believing this? The UPCI and other Oneness groups certainly have no trouble articulating *their* Oneness faith. No one who paid attention to what they were saying could ever miss their belief that Jesus is the Father. But why, one must ask, is the New Testament so much less clear on this score?

The answer, I believe, is not that the New Testament authors did not know how to communicate effectively, for they communicate that Jesus is the Son of God with perfect clarity. Rather, the opaqueness of the teaching concerning the "Fatherhood" of Christ in the New Testament is due to the fact that no one in the New Testament ever believed that Jesus was himself God the Father. Not only is this teaching opaque in the Bible, it is wholly nonexistent!

Yet, according to most Oneness groups, trinitarians are simply blind to the "Oneness revelation," and indeed far more than 99.99% of all lovers of Christ who have ever lived have died without hope of heaven because they, being trinitarians, failed to pick up on this "secret identity" of Jesus. They lacked "the key" and hence missed out on eternal life. One might say that the "illusion of separation" some Oneness theologians talk about was simply too convincing for these trinitarians. It seems that they took the way Scripture unanimously speaks about the Father and Jesus too seriously!

We shall now proceed to examine the particular texts on which Oneness theology bases its view of Jesus as the Father, but we must examine these in light of the general and clear teaching of the New Testament that Jesus is the *Son* of God the Father, and also in light of the fact that the church throughout its history has found only this teaching in Scripture concerning Jesus Christ. In this light, we must judge that the burden of proof is wholly on the Oneness theologians to overturn this virtually unanimous testimony in order to substantiate their esoteric doctrine. Only if there is undeniable force to their scriptural interpretation can their doctrine be given serious consideration.

Prooftexts for Jesus as the Father

We saw in chapter 1 that the Oneness contention that Jesus is the Father is based on several prooftexts that they believe directly teach this, as well as on a number of cross-referencing arguments that they believe indirectly imply this. We shall first examine the direct prooftexts and then examine the cross-referencing arguments.

Isaiah 9:6:
The "Everlasting Father"

The only verse put forward by Oneness exponents that could conceivably be taken to explicitly identify the Son of God as "the Father" is Isaiah 9:6. Hence it is the single most cited text utilized by Oneness writers to defend this doctrine. Here, Oneness exponents argue, the "son" to be given to Israel is called "Everlasting Father," and this means that the Son of God is also God the Father.

Historically speaking, such an interpretation is wholly without precedent, among either Christians or Jews, and this, in my estimation, must already render the Oneness interpretation most improbable. However, even if we were to concede that such an esoteric interpretation were possible, there are yet several very basic considerations that immediately render it more than improbable.

First, it goes without saying that we ought never to base an entire doctrine on one verse. Such is a clear tactic of desperation, and it is used frequently by cultists to twist the central themes of the Bible. Even if this one verse did teach that the coming Son would in some sense be called "the Father," we should be cautious in making this into a doctrine unless it is substantiated elsewhere (which it is not). The principles of scriptural interpretation that must govern our handling of particular texts are that "the whole must interpret the part" and "the clear must interpret the unclear." Hence we must in this particular case honestly ask ourselves whether Jesus is elsewhere and unambiguously called "the Father." Is this the general teaching of Scripture? If not, then perhaps what one thinks this one verse is teaching is not what the verse is actually teaching.

This is especially true when considering one verse from the Old Testament in regard to a doctrine that is only rendered explicit in the New Testament (the deity of Christ, the fatherhood of God). In light of the progress of revelation, we must allow the New Testament to interpret the Old, not vice versa.

Seen in this light, it becomes clear, as virtually every reputable commentator on Isaiah has seen, that Isaiah's use of "father" (*av* or *ab*) has nothing to do with the formal title of "Father," which develops in the New Testament out of Jesus' unique and revelatory relationship with God. "Father" wasn't even a standard title of God in the Old Testament! In short, this verse does not teach that Jesus is "the God and Father of our Lord Jesus Christ"; it does not, in other words, teach that Jesus is his own Father.

This title, as well as the other titles employed in Isaiah 9:6, denotes the coming Messiah's *character*. This is what the Semitic concept of "name" (*shem*) refers to when it says, "his name shall be called . . ." (Alexander, 203).

There are two ways in which the divine title used here of the coming Messiah might be interpreted, neither of which would make Jesus his own Father. The first understands the expression to mean something like "everlasting Father" (KJV), "father-forever" (Leupold), or "father for all time." In this interpretation, the verse therefore "describes the nature of his rule" and amounts to saying that the coming Messiah, in contrast to all other presently reigning kings, will not be "a despot" (Herbert, 75; cf. Leupold, 186). It describes the coming Messiah's "paternal role" (Mauchline, 114) and is roughly equivalent to "good shepherd" (Young, 334; see Wainwright, 42). The unexpected reign of this king, in other words, will be a reign of paternal love and care. The love and rule of this one is to be like the "rule" of a shepherd over his flock or a loving father over his children (cf. John 10:11–14; 13:33; 1 Peter 2:25).

The second interpretation translates the expression as "father of eternity" or "father of all ages" or the like. According to this interpretation, the coming Messiah is described as eternal in nature, perhaps implying that he is the Creator, the Lord of time and history (Barnes, Isaiah, 193; Bowman, Oneness, 22, 23).

Obviously, neither of these interpretations has anything to do with Jesus' supposed identity as God the Father.

John 14:7–10:
"If You See Me, You See the Father"

Oneness exponents frequently cite this passage in their attempt to prove that Jesus is "the Father manifested in the flesh" (Bernard, Oneness, 68). Here and elsewhere (e.g., John 8:19; 12:45), Jesus claims that if you see (or know or receive) him, you see (know, receive) the Father. Does this mean that Jesus is the Father incarnate, as Oneness Pentecostals suppose?

In a sense, of course, these verses do imply that Jesus is the manifestation or "embodiment" of the Father. The main intent of John 14:7–10 is to assure us that "the Father" is not a different "God" than the God revealed in Christ. One does not, and cannot, look someplace else to "see" and "know" God the Father. One must look only to Jesus Christ, the one Word, image, and expression of God (John 1:1, 18; Col. 1:15–16; Heb. 1:2). For just this reason, "picturing" the Father (and/or Spirit) alongside Jesus—a sort of horizontal tri-embodied Trinity—is prohibited, both by the teaching of this verse and by the traditional teaching on the Trinity.

Nevertheless, it does not at all follow from this that Jesus is personally *identical* to the Father. Indeed, the meaning of the passage under consideration presupposes the distinctness of Jesus from the Father. Let us examine the passage in its entire context.

We first note that Jesus begins this passage by saying "No one comes *to* the Father except *through me*" (14:6, emphasis added). The verse clearly presupposes a distinction between the one believers come *to*, and the one believers come *through*. If Jesus were personally identical to the Father, this distinction would collapse and the verse would be meaningless.

Jesus further explains himself in the next verse, when he teaches his disciples that to know and see him is to know and see the Father. This is not a retraction of the "to" and "through" distinction made in the previous verse, but a restatement of it. It is, he is saying, only through himself that the heart of God is clearly revealed, and thus it is only through himself that believers can come to know the Father (cf. 1 John 2:22–23).

Philip doesn't get the point, however, and so he asks again to see the Father (v. 8), to which Jesus again replies that "anyone who has seen me has seen the Father" (v. 9). Note that Jesus does not here (or anywhere) say "I *am* the Father." He is simply reiterating that it is only through himself as the Son that the Father is made known. It is completely unjustified to interpret this verse to mean that here "Jesus tried to tell them that He was the Father" (Bernard, Oneness, 67). If Jesus was trying so hard to do this, why didn't he simply do it? No, the distinction between the Father and Jesus the Son presupposed in the context of these verses is still very much intact.

This distinctness continues on, and becomes even more explicit, when we hear the Jesus of John's Gospel immediately continue on to say, "Don't you believe that I am in the Father and that the Father is in me? . . . Believe me when I say that I am in the Father and the Father is in me. . . . I am going to the Father. And I will do whatever you ask in my name, so that the Son may bring glory to the Father" (John 14:10–13).

Who is Jesus here? He is the one *in* the Father, and the one *in whom* the Father is. But he is not himself the Father. Christ is the one who is at the Father's side and the one through whom we must go to get to the Father, but he is not himself the Father. He is the Son who brings glory to the Father as he is himself glorified (John 13:31–32; 17:1) and the Word who makes visible ("enfleshes," John 1:14) the love of the invisible Father, which otherwise would not be made visible. But he is not himself the invisible Father.

The Son, Jesus Christ, comes in his Father's name (authority) and does the works of his Father (John 5:43; 10:25; 14:10; 17:26), teaches the teachings of his Father and testifies of his Father (John 7:16; 8:28; 14:24), receives everything he has from his Father and in all things submits to the Father (John 5:19, 30; 8:28–29; 15:10), and now intercedes for us before the Father (1 John 2:1; cf. Rom. 8:34; 1 Tim. 2:5; Heb. 7:25). But all of this presupposes that *Jesus Christ is not himself the Father!* Could the Bible be any clearer?

Everything written in the Gospel of John is written so that the reader might believe that "Jesus is the Christ, the Son of God" (John 20:31). To attempt to render this supreme truth as only "half the story," as Oneness theology does, is to stand this Gospel—and really the whole of the New Testament—on its head.

John 10:30:
"I and the Father Are One"

All that has been said in the preceding section applies, I believe, to the Oneness believers' exegesis of one of their favorite verses, John 10:30. Jesus here proclaims that "I and the Father are one," and this, for Oneness exponents, means that "Jesus was not only Son in His humanity but also Father in His deity" (Bernard, Oneness, 67).

It should be clear by now, however, that this passage, far from collapsing the distinctness of Jesus and the Father, again presupposes their distinctness. Jesus emphatically does not here (or anywhere) say, "I am the Father." And, as the ancient champions of the Trinity pointed out against Praxeas's simplistic exegesis of this passage in the second century, Jesus in this verse uses the first-person plural (*esmen*) to refer to

himself and the Father—he does not say, "I and the Father *am* one."
What is more, he uses the neuter *hen* rather than the masculine *heis*
for "one," thereby suggesting unity of essence rather than a personal
identity (see Bowman, Oneness, 24).

In any case, to be "one" with someone is hardly the same as being
identical with that person. It is God's desire, for example, that the
church would be "one," and even that believers would be "one" with
Christ and the Father (John 17:20–23). But none of this, of course,
implies that our distinct personalities are supposed to be fused together.
Rather, the "oneness" spoken of here refers to a unity of love, joy, and
purpose.

Obviously, Jesus was one with the Father in a much stronger sense
than this, for we elsewhere learn that he is himself fully God. Moreover, the fact that the Jews who heard Jesus speak the words recorded in
John 10:30 immediately thought of stoning him suggests that they
understood the oneness he was speaking about here as a unity of essence,
not just of love and purpose.

But the point nevertheless remains. Far from collapsing the distinctness of the Father and the Son, the unity spoken of in John 10:30
presupposes such a distinctness.

This is why the Jesus who said "I and the Father are one" can also distinguish himself from the Father in the verses immediately preceding
and succeeding John 10:30 (see vv. 25, 29, 36, 38). This is difficult to
explain on Oneness terms. Indeed, it is because Christ's essential oneness
with the Father does not fuse him with the Father that Jesus can elsewhere explicitly refer to himself and the Father as two distinct "persons."
In conformity with Old Testament legal proceedings, which required at
least two distinct persons as witnesses for a judgment to be binding
(John 8:17; cf. Num. 35:30; Deut. 17:6; Matt. 18:16), Jesus says that it
is both he and his Father who sent him that testified to his ministry
(John 8:16–18). So, too, Jesus refers to the Father as "another [*allon*]
witness" to his ministry (John 5:31–32). This language makes absolutely
no sense if in fact Jesus and the Father are "one person."

The only reply that Oneness adherents have at this point is to maintain that the "two witnesses" here are the two natures of Jesus himself

(Bernard, Oneness, 190). But, as Robert Bowman has already pointed out, this notion completely undermines the legal point Jesus is making. The Jewish system requires two *persons* as witnesses. One cannot go into any court of law and say, "I am two witnesses to the crime—my body testifies, and my soul testifies" (Bowman, Oneness, 25). The Oneness reading, therefore, ignores the plain meaning of the text.

John 14:18:
"I Will Not Leave You as Orphans"

Jesus is in this context teaching his disciples about the Holy Spirit who would come after Jesus had departed. In the course of this teaching he tells his disciples, "I will not leave you as orphans; I will come to you." According to Oneness theology, since Jesus refers to himself as the one who would not leave his disciples "fatherless," he must himself be "the Father."

To say that this argument is weak is to be gracious. As with their exegesis of Isaiah 9:6, the Oneness adherents' interpretation of this verse completely confuses Jesus' parental character, which is everywhere taught in Scripture, with Jesus' supposed personal identity with "God the Father," which is nowhere taught in Scripture. Jesus is simply saying, "I'm not going to leave you like abandoned children; I'll be right back" (referring to the coming of his Spirit). He is no more identifying himself as God the Father here than when he elsewhere addresses his disciples as "my children" (e.g., John 13:33). Indeed, the apostle John addresses his audience in a similar fashion (1 John 2:1, 12, 18, etc.), but it is rather unlikely that he is thereby claiming to be God the Father. Of course, Jesus plays a paternal role to believers as God—which John does not—but the point still holds that the language used here is functional, descriptive of a fatherlike role, not an identification of Jesus as the person of God the Father.

The error of this interpretation is further seen from the fact that throughout John 14, as I have already shown, Jesus has been distinguishing himself from the Father (and the Spirit). The Oneness interpretation requires that we, and Jesus' original audience, understand that in this one instance Jesus shifted everything and momentarily spoke *as* the Father, rather than *about* and *to* the Father as he does in all the verses preceding and succeeding John 14:18. We find that the Father is spoken of in the third person by Jesus in verses 2, 6–7, 9–13, 16. And, after this one verse in which he speaks about not leaving the disciples as orphans, he immediately goes back to referring to the Father as though he is distinct from himself in verses 20, 21, 23, 26, 28, and 31. Indeed, in verse 23 he refers to himself and the Father with a "we"!

Yet, because Jesus in one verse calls his disciples "orphans," we are to believe that these fifteen references by Jesus to the Father as a distinct divine "person" in this context are only apparent, a result of an "illusion of separation." In "reality," says Oneness theology, Jesus is the Father.

If this isn't twisting the Scripture, what is?

The Salutations:
"God the Father and the Lord Jesus Christ"

I vividly recall the elitist feeling I had as a seventeen-year-old new UPCI convert when I learned from my pastor "the truth about *kai*." This is "a truth" that is frequently taught by Oneness apologists (Graves, 50–51; Bernard, Oneness, 207–211). *Kai* is the Greek word for "and" that is used in all the New Testament salutations as, for example, when Paul says "Grace and peace to you from God our Father and [*kai*] from the Lord Jesus Christ" (e.g., Rom. 1:7). Of course, this looks as though the Father and Jesus are in some sense distinct "persons"—and all Christians throughout the centuries have always thought this to be the case—but "if you knew the original Greek," Oneness authorities maintain, you would know that *kai* here really means "even" or "who is."

Kai clearly means "even" in some other contexts, as when Paul speaks about "God and [*kai*] our Father" (Gal. 1:4 KJV), or when he speaks about "the mystery of God and [*kai*] of the Father" (Col. 2:2 KJV), for Paul obviously was referring to the same "person" in these passages. And, I was taught by Oneness adherents, so it should be interpreted in all the New Testament salutations. I still own the King James Bible I possessed back then, and next to all these salutations I have penned in cross-references to such verses as Galatians 1:4 and Colossians 2:2. The result of this is that the salutations are interpreted to identify Jesus as the Father rather than to distinguish between them.

Is this argument sound? It turns out to be entirely groundless when put under scrutiny. Of course, *kai* can mean "even," but as the Oneness Greek scholar Brent Graves admits, "the context determines . . . the appropriate meaning" (Graves, 52). We may go further and state that the overwhelming majority of uses of *kai* carry the meaning of "and" rather than "even," so that the burden of proof is on the interpreter to make a case from the context that *kai* means "even" in any given instance. So let us look at the context of these salutations.

In the salutation of Romans 1:7, Paul is, according to Oneness theology, identifying Jesus with God the Father by saying "God the Father, even our Lord Jesus Christ." But a few verses earlier he referred to "the gospel of God . . . regarding *his Son* . . . Jesus Christ our Lord" (1:1–4, emphasis added), and in the two verses immediately following this salutation he thanks "God *through* Jesus Christ" (implying a distinction) and refers to "God," whom he serves "in preaching the gospel of *his Son*" (1:8–9, emphasis added). Indeed, throughout the Book of Romans, Jesus is repeatedly distinguished from the Father, but nowhere identified with him. Is there, then, any compelling contextual reason to translate the *kai* of this salutation as "even," thereby identifying Jesus as the Father? I see none.

The same is true of all Paul's salutations. For example, he supposedly identifies Jesus as God the Father in the salutation of 1 Corinthians 1:3, but he distinguishes between God and Jesus in verses 2 and 4, and refers to Jesus as God's Son and "our Lord" in verse 9. He again supposedly identifies Jesus as God the Father in the salutation of Galatians 1:3, but two verses earlier he had just distinguished between them, saying that God the Father raised Jesus from the dead. Can we imagine Paul vacillating back and forth between the "personalities" or "natures" of Jesus (Son/Father) in the space of these verses—without giving his readers a clue that he's doing so? Can we pretend that the simple Corinthian and Galatian Christians would have naturally made this mental switch without any clue from Paul?

Continuing on, in the salutation of 2 Corinthians 1:2, Paul again supposedly connects Jesus and God the Father with the conjunctive *kai* ("even"), yet in the very next verse Paul blesses "the God and Father of our Lord Jesus Christ." He does this same thing in the opening of his letters to the Ephesians, the Colossians, and the Philippians. Now, if the Father is distinct from Jesus, as he certainly must be in the phrase "Father *of* Jesus Christ," must we not assume that the Father is also distinct in the immediately preceding phrase "Father *and* Jesus Christ"? Could anything be more confusing to Paul's readers than to have Paul changing the "identities" of Jesus from one sentence to the next?

The bottom line is simply this: It is nothing more than a presupposed, misguided theological opinion that leads Oneness exegetes to attempt to force, in such an unnatural way, the epistolary salutations into a Oneness framework. As we have seen, both the immediate and larger context of the salutations dictate that the *kai* be translated as "and," which implies a distinctive (this is called a "disjunctive *kai*"). That this is no novel point I am making is clearly evidenced by the fact that there has never been a recognized translator of the Bible who ever dreamed of translating *kai* in the salutations otherwise. And I believe it is one more testimony to the weakness of their theological system that the Oneness exponents must go against such a reputable tradition to do so.

Revelation 21:6–7: "He Will Be My Son"

In these verses the one on the throne who is "the Alpha and the Omega" says, "He who overcomes will inherit all this, and I will be his God and he will be my son." Now Jesus is elsewhere in the Book of Revelation portrayed as the one who says he is "the First and the Last" and "the Alpha and the Omega" (1:17; 22:13–14). Hence, I have seen it argued, Jesus must be the one who says that each overcomer will be his "son," and therefore Jesus is here portrayed as God the Father.

Several observations quickly dismiss this exegesis of the passage. First, we must concede that if it were an aspect of the clear and uniform teaching of Scripture that Jesus was "God the Father"—indeed, if this were taught with but a minute fraction of the clarity with which it is taught that Jesus is the Son—then perhaps these verses could be read as one further (albeit vague) reference to Christ as "the Father." As we have seen, however, this is simply nowhere taught in the New Testament. And it certainly is not the general view of the Book of Revelation. Throughout this work, Jesus is portrayed primarily as the Lamb of God (showing his sacrificial role) and is clearly distinguished from God the Father.

To sum up the matter briefly, this book opens by referring to "the revelation of Jesus Christ, which God gave him to show his servants . . ." (1:1). Typical of New Testament letters, the salutation is given ". . . from him who is, and who was, and who is to come . . . and from Jesus Christ, who is the faithful witness . . ." (1:4–5) and continues by giving glory to Jesus, who made all believers "to be a kingdom and priests to serve his God and Father" (1:6). Following the general pattern of the New Testament, we see, Jesus and God the Father are consistently distinguished without there being a hint that these two are "really" secretly identical.

This distinction between the Father and Jesus continues throughout the Book of Revelation without qualification. Speaking as the incarnate Son, Jesus (or the Lamb, or Son) constantly refers to God the Father as distinct from himself ("my Father," "my God," see, for example, 3:5, 12). The author portrays Jesus "the Son of God" as saying he would give authority to all overcomers "just as I received authority from my Father" (2:18–27). Jesus the Lamb is elsewhere said to stand next to the 144,000 overcoming believers who bear on their foreheads "his name and his Father's name" (14:1) as they offer up their firstfruits to "God and the Lamb" (14:4). John speaks of the coming of the "kingdom of God and the authority of his Christ" (12:10, cf. 11:15) and John refers to saints as those "who obey God's commandments and remain faithful to Jesus" (14:12). Again, all this unqualified talk about their distinctness is exceedingly misleading if, in fact, the Father and the Son are "really" personally identical.

Finally, Jesus, as the Lamb of God, is portrayed as being at times next to his Father's throne (5:13), as sitting on his own throne alongside the Father who is sitting on his own throne (3:21), or sitting "at the center" of his Father's throne (7:17). Hence the throne is referred to as "the throne of God and of the Lamb" (22:1, 3), just as both "the Lord God Almighty and the Lamb" are portrayed as being "the temple of the city" (21:22, NJB). And, despite the insistence of some Oneness exegetes that all of this "language of plurality," which portrays the Lamb as distinct from the Father, is "illusory," (Sabin, Seminar), never is this "illusory" distinctness negated. Never is there even the slightest suggestion that it is "illusory," that the distinctness of God and the Lamb or the Father and the Son is "really" some kind of "divine sleight of hand."

What is more, never is there any explanation for why it is that only the supposed "human side" of Jesus (the Son, Lamb) bears his name throughout this and every other New Testament book and not the "divine side" (Father) as well. Why does the Book of Revelation never refer to these illusory "two" as something like "the Lamb of God and his Father, Jesus Christ"?

In any case, these reflections must lead us to conclude that the Oneness interpretation of Revelation 21:6–7 is unnatural at best. As is the case with all the Oneness prooftexts, we see that it is "only by isolating . . . verses from their context . . . [that] the Oneness position [can] be maintained" (Bowman, Oneness, 24).

A second argument against the Oneness interpretation of this passage is that we must again distinguish between "God the Father," that is, the "Father of our Lord Jesus Christ," and the paternal role that Jesus (and the Father and Spirit) play in the believer's life. The intent of the passage, as the whole context makes clear, is to contrast the final eternal state of the overcoming faithful with their previous life of hardship (see vv. 4–5) as well as the eternal state of the wicked (v. 8). It is simply saying that God is going to enter into the closest possible relationship with the faithful (like a father-son relationship) as he wipes away every tear from their eyes (vv. 4–7). Hence, even if Jesus is the one who is speaking here, this hardly justifies taking the unprecedented leap of labeling him "God the Father."

Finally, though very little at this point hangs on this, there is really no reason to regard these verses as being spoken specifically by Jesus. The fact that the one speaking here refers to himself as "Alpha and Omega," while Jesus elsewhere refers to himself as "Alpha and Omega," does not prove the point—even though it is also true that there is only one who is "Alpha and Omega" (cf. Isa. 43:10). In contexts that clearly distinguish him from Jesus, the Father is spoken of in similar terms (1:4–5, 8; 11:15–17).

The fact of the matter is that it is the one God who alone is eternal, who alone is "the first and the last," "the beginning and the end." This is true of God regardless of which of his personal ways of existing we are referring to. As the Father, God can say "I have always been"; as the Word or Son, God can say "I have always been"; and as the Holy Spirit, God can say "I have always been." In the traditional trinitarian understanding, God's threefold personal way of existing is as eternal as is God himself, for God is (not just temporarily acts) triune.

Hence, since it is the Father who is the principal speaker from the throne throughout the Book of Revelation, it is more likely that it is the Father who is speaking in this passage. The fact that Christ nowhere else in this book (or anywhere) calls himself "God" (though, of course, the apostles do call him that), and the fact that God and the Lamb are again distinguished several verses later (21:22–23), simply gives further weight to this interpretation. But again, even if it *is* Jesus who is speaking, the passage gives no clear support to the position that Jesus is God the Father.

1 John 3:1–5:
Was Jesus God the Father Appearing on Earth?

There is one final and very popular prooftext argument used by Oneness believers in their attempt to demonstrate that Jesus is the Father, and this is taken from 1 John 3:1–5. John begins this section by referring to "the love the Father has lavished on us, that we should be called children of God!" In the next verse the author concedes that we don't yet know exactly what we shall be like in heaven, but "we know that when he appears, we shall be like him, for we shall see him as he is." Then, in verse 5, John reminds his readers of their hope in Christ by saying, ". . . you know that he appeared so that he might take away our sins."

What Oneness Pentecostals find most significant about this passage is that the only one explicitly mentioned throughout the text is "the Father" in verse 1. So, they argue, the two third-person singular pronouns ("he" in verses 2 and 5) must refer back to the Father. Hence, they reason, it is the Father who is here said to have appeared on earth and who is expected to return again at the end of time.

This is, quite frankly, typical cultic reasoning. Scripture could not be clearer than it is in its teaching that it was Jesus the Son of God who was sent by the Father and who appeared on earth. Scripture could not be clearer than it is in its teaching that it is Jesus the Son of God who alone shall return for his bride (Matt. 16:27; Acts 1:11; 1 Thess. 4:13–18). Not once does the Bible teach anything else! And Scripture could not be clearer and more uniform than it is—especially in 1 John—in its teaching that Jesus Christ as the Son of God is personally and genuinely distinct from the Father.

The fact is that 1 John consistently distinguishes the Father from the Son (e.g., 1:3, 7; 2:1; 3:23; 4:9–10, 14; 5:5, 20). Nothing could be clearer than that the correct scriptural answer to the question "Who is Jesus Christ?" as far as the apostle John is concerned is that he is "the Son of God" (see also John 20:31). Can one find a single verse, in this or any other New Testament book, that clearly teaches that he is "also" his own Father? No. Yet Oneness exegetes are willing to overturn all of this simply because John in this one passage does not specify that he is talking about the Son of God when he refers to the one who appeared before and who shall appear again!

The fact of the matter is that John didn't need to remind his audience that he was speaking about Jesus the Son when he spoke of his appearing, for the point is so obvious. Instead, only someone with a preconceived idea that Jesus is the Father could have ever been confused by the indefiniteness of the reference to Jesus in these passages—which is why, in the entire history of Christian exegesis, no one has ever found anything significant about these third-person singular pronouns until the Oneness movement came along.

Oneness Cross-Referencing Arguments

Having dispelled the notion that there are any passages of Scripture that explicitly identify Jesus as the Father, let us turn to the scriptural parallels that Oneness exegetes construct in their attempt to find some sort of biblical basis for their doctrine. We saw in chapter 1 that Oneness authors attempt to prove Jesus is the Father by piecing together diverse texts that ascribe to both of them similar activities, and we must now call this effort into question.

Beware of Cross-Referencing Arguments!

We ought first to make a preliminary point regarding the Oneness adherents' hermeneutical methodology itself, when used as an attempt to establish their doctrine on this basis. While it is, as an exegetical rule, permissible and sometimes valuable to cross-reference one passage of Scripture with another to illustrate a point, it must also be said that the points made through this method of exegesis are only as strong as the explicit and general teachings of Scripture that back them up. Cross-referencing, we might say, can illustrate a point that can be proven on other grounds, but it cannot itself provide the sole grounds for proving the point being illustrated.

Used alone, in other words, the "paralleling" method of prooftexting, which is so popular among Oneness exegetes, has next to no value. It constitutes fundamentally bad exegesis. Among other faults, this method can really be used to prove almost anything from Scripture, as we shall see (and for this reason is a method frequently used by cults).

As examples, consider two arguments. First, Paul expresses the divinity of Christ in one passage by saying that the fullness of God's being (*theotetos*) dwells in Christ (Col. 2:9). But in another passage Paul also prays in even stronger terms that all believers would be "filled with all the fulness of God" (Eph. 3:19 KJV). Hence, some New Age exponents argue, Paul regards each believer as being (at least potentially) God incarnate, equal to Jesus Christ.

If these were the only two verses in the Bible, or at least the only two verses on the subject of the nature of Christ and the believer, this argument might look half impressive. But, of course, there exists a great abundance of scriptural teaching that demonstrates that "the fullness of God" in Christ is fundamentally and qualitatively different from "the fullness of God" in the believer. Christ was God manifested in the flesh. We are not and never shall be.

Note that this point holds true on the basis of the general testimony of Scripture, whether or not we can actually spell out what the difference between "the fullness of God" in each of these two verses is. One simply cannot legitimately overturn well-grounded scriptural teachings because two verses, when patched together, seem to imply something different.

This patchwork exegesis becomes even more precarious when we are drawing parallels between different authors, for different authors often use words in very different and apparently contradictory ways, without their actual meanings being contradictory. Consider, as our second illustration, this classic problem: Paul argues, as explicitly as can be, that believers are "justified by faith alone apart from works," and he uses Abraham to illustrate this point (Rom. 4:1–16). James, however, is equally as explicit in arguing that "by works a man is justified, and not by faith alone," and he, too, refers to Abraham to illustrate his point (James 2:21–23).

If we assume, with our Lord, that Scripture cannot contradict itself (cf., for example, John 10:35) and if we also assume that we can, without further ado, cross-reference otherwise unrelated passages to produce "biblical" teaching, we have a real problem—for the "biblical" teaching here appears to be contradictory!

The problem lies with the method of exegesis. As exegetes have long argued, Paul and James are simply using the same words ("faith," "works") in different senses. For Paul the word *faith* refers to a whole-hearted love and trust, which naturally produces "fruits"—and hence it "alone" saves people. For James, however, the word *faith* may simply denote intellectual assent (which even the devils have)—and this "alone" cannot justify someone. If, however, it is accompanied by "works" (what Paul calls "fruits"), this is evidence that the faith is not simply intellectual, but is, rather, a wholehearted love and trust in God, the kind Abraham had when he offered up his son (James 2:21).

Hence, even when it looks like two otherwise unrelated passages are talking about the same things and doing so with exactly the same language and even using the same illustrations, one must be extremely cautious in basing anything on "paralleling" such passages together. In no case can the lesson derived from such "cross-referencing" be different from the teaching of either verse taken individually. Moreover, never can such a method be used to prove a doctrine that is not elsewhere explicitly taught in Scripture. And, most emphatically, never can such a method be used to overturn a teaching that is explicitly taught elsewhere in Scripture.

The Oneness attempt to prove that Jesus is the Father by utilizing this patchwork exegesis flagrantly violates all three of these rules.

Jesus and the Works of the Father

Oneness cross-reference arguments in support of the belief that Jesus is the Father basically reason in this fashion: Text "1" here says the Father does this divine work "D"; text "2" over there says that Jesus does the same divine work "D"; therefore, Jesus must be the Father.

For example, it is the general teaching of Scripture that God, or sometimes explicitly God the Father, raised Jesus, the Son of God, from the dead (Rom. 6:4; Acts 2:24; Gal. 1:1). But in John 2:19 Jesus says, "Destroy this temple, and I will raise it again in three days." Verse 21 explains that he was speaking about his body. Does this mean that Jesus is the Father, as Oneness exegetes maintain? A number of considerations count decisively against such a suggestion.

First, since Scripture everywhere explicitly teaches that Jesus is the Son of God, distinct from God the Father, and since it nowhere reverses this teaching by explicitly teaching that Jesus is also his own Father, the very attempt to establish such a notion on a cross-referencing argument such as this must be judged as misguided. Whatever John 2:19 means, therefore, one cannot legitimately use an argument such as this to make it mean what Oneness believers want it to mean.

Second, it is perfectly clear that it is not the intent of John 2:19 to teach that Jesus is the Father, nor is this the intent of those passages that say that the Father raised Jesus from the dead. That is, nowhere in Scripture is the fact that Jesus raises himself from the dead used to prove that Jesus is the Father. Hence, it constitutes fundamentally bad exegesis to derive such a teaching by splicing together such passages.

Third, this interpretation of John 2:19 makes Jesus out to be someone with a multiple-personality disorder. It requires that we view Jesus as switching back and forth between his supposed identities of Father and Son—and doing so between sentences. In 2:19 Jesus is supposedly speaking "as the Father." Yet in his previous sentence (2:16) he clearly spoke "as Son," for he referred to his Father as distinct from himself.

Nothing in the text itself, of course, gives any indication of such a psychological alteration. Nor is there any reason to suspect that Jesus' audience had any clue of such theological subtleties. Finally, to suppose that Jesus could and did switch between identities in this manner has the consequence, as we have seen, of undermining the reality of the Incarnation itself. It thereby transforms the revelation of God into an illusory charade.

How, then, are we to explain that Jesus in this verse attributes to himself an activity elsewhere attributed to the Father? There really is no difficulty here. It is perfectly consistent with the doctrine of the Trinity, which teaches that all three persons of the triune God are involved in every work of God in the world. All acts of God proceed *from* the transcendent Father, *through* his Son or Word or Image, *in the power of* his immanent Holy Spirit. And this is true both during the Incarnation and at all other times, since the way God is and acts while Christ is incarnate reveals the way God is and acts at all times. Hence, the creation itself, for example, also arises from God the Father (Rom. 11:36; 1 Cor. 8:6; Eph. 3:9), proceeds through the Son (John 1:1–3; 1 Cor. 8:6; Col. 1:15–17; Heb. 1:2–10), and was accomplished by the power of God's Spirit (Gen. 1:2; Job 33:4; Ps. 104:30). As such, the act can, in different senses, be attributed to any of the three.

Thus, without attempting to psychologize what it was like for the divine Word to experience a human death—a fruitless question if ever there was one—we may confidently say that the miracle of the resurrection involved something like the same divine operation as all the other miracles surrounding Christ's life. While this and all miracles were ultimately performed through the Son incarnated as the man Jesus, it is also true that the miracle of the resurrection came from the mind and plan of the transcendent Father and was accomplished in the power of the immanent Holy Spirit. Therefore, one can with Scripture say that either the Father, or the Spirit, or even the Son himself, raised Jesus from the dead without thereby collapsing the three into some secret identity.

This response to the Oneness argument for the "Fatherhood of Jesus" on the basis of John 2:19 can be applied to the host of other patchwork arguments the Oneness groups use to buttress their position. We can therefore consider these arguments much more briefly.

We saw in chapter 1 that Oneness writers argue that since Jesus said he answered prayer (John 14:14), while the Father is said to answer prayer (John 15:16), Jesus must be the Father. Even a cursory reading of John 14:13–14, however, reveals the absurdity of this argument. Throughout the immediate context where Jesus supposedly identifies himself as Father, Jesus clearly distinguishes the Father as someone really distinct from himself (e.g., John 14:13, 20, 21, 23). We are again asked by Oneness exegetes to believe that in the midst of all this, for one verse and out of nowhere, Jesus supposedly reversed everything and spoke "from the Father's perspective" by saying, in effect, "This Father I'm always talking about and who I have said will answer your prayer— well, I am really he." And then suddenly in the next breath he is talking from the perspective of the Son again (without telling anyone of his transition) and "asking the Father" (who he himself supposedly is!) to "send the Spirit" (who he also is!) (v. 16)! Rather strained exegesis, is it not?

A much more biblical approach to the question of who answers prayer is simply to point out that both the Father and the Son, in distinct capacities, answer prayer. What was true of the incarnate Son on earth is true of the incarnate Son in heaven; namely, the Father performs all activity through and in him (John 14:10). Just as Jesus could say both that "I work" and "my Father works" (John 5:17–19), so Scripture can say both that "Jesus answers prayer" and "the Father answers prayer." No contradiction whatsoever is created by this.

We find the same straining exegesis accompanying the Oneness argument that because Jesus says at one point that the Father will send the Spirit (John 14:16), he must be speaking as the Father when he attributes this activity to himself (15:26). How I, as a new Oneness convert, delighted in baffling many of my high school trinitarian opponents (and converting several of them) with such tricky maneuvers as this! But I recall being stumped myself once when one of these "opponents" (so I was taught to see them) simply read John 15:26 in its entirety on his own and pointed out that the verse says that Jesus will indeed send the Spirit, but it adds that he will do this *"from the Father."* Now, he innocently inquired, if Jesus is in this verse speaking *as* the Father, which the Oneness interpretation requires, why does it yet say that he will send the Spirit *from* the Father? My embarrassed response was that the verse simply couldn't mean what it explicitly says, but that I had no idea what it "really" meant.

As awkward as the Oneness adherents' exegesis is, however, they really are forced into it by their theology. Once the Oneness position assumes that the Holy Spirit can only proceed from one, then if it in fact genuinely appears that two are sending the Spirit, these two must "really" be one. (Indeed, even the distinctness of the Spirit himself is only an "appearance," according to Oneness teaching). But from whence do they get this unique revelation? Certainly not from Scripture, which, as we have seen, frequently ascribes the same activity, in different senses, to the Father, Son, and Holy Spirit.

Hence, there is no reason not to take Scripture at face value when it says both that the Father will send the Spirit and that the Son will send the Spirit "from the Father"—or even when it speaks of the Holy Spirit as acting as a personally distinct agent (e.g., John 16:7–13; Acts 8:29; 15:28; 16:7, 9). All of this fits perfectly into a trinitarian framework, whereas it does not fit at all into a Oneness framework.

Exactly the same answer can be given to two other patchwork arguments that Oneness groups customarily use to prove Jesus' identity as the Father. Jesus in one spot says the Father draws people unto him (John 6:44), while elsewhere he says he himself draws people unto himself (John 12:32). Hence, they argue, Jesus is the Father. But it certainly is not the intention of either passage to teach that Jesus is the Father, and this is itself enough to dismiss the argument. One simply cannot legitimately splice together texts and get them to mean something neither intends to mean independently.

In keeping with what has already been said, the act of drawing sinners to Jesus Christ is an act that involves all three of the personal ways God is God, and there is nothing terribly contradictory about this. Jesus is in 12:32 referring to himself when he is "lifted up" at his crucifixion. What he is saying is that it is through this loving deed that people will be drawn to him. The love of God manifested on the cross has throughout all time functioned as a sort of magnet to lure individuals lovingly into a relationship with the Father.

But this is not at all incompatible with Jesus also saying with a great deal of frequency that only those whom the Father has set apart and draws can come unto him (John 6:37, 39, 44, 65, etc.). Nor is this incompatible with Jesus and the rest of Scripture elsewhere teaching that it is the Holy Spirit who points sinners to Christ and empowers them to believe (John 16:13–15; 1 Cor. 12:3, 13; 1 John 4:2). The Father decrees the sinner's salvation; Christ dies for the sinner's salvation; and the Spirit makes effectual the sinner's salvation by leading him or her to the cross. The Father saves, through the Son, by the power of the Holy Spirit.

All of this is summed up in the beautiful trinitarian passage of Ephesians 2:18, where Paul writes that "through him [Christ] we both have access to the Father by one Spirit." The trinitarian process by which the Father is revealed to us in the Son by the power of the Spirit is, we see, reversed in the process of salvation as we go to the Father, through the Son, by the power of the Spirit. Hence there is no reason to suspect that Jesus is making an esoteric reference to himself as Father when he says that he will draw all people unto himself.

A very similar response may be given to the Oneness argument that Jesus is the Father who shall raise believers from the dead. How clever I once thought it was to point out to trinitarians that both Jesus and the Father (and the Spirit) are, at different times, said to raise believers from the dead (John 6:40; cf. Rom. 4:17; 8:9–11). I sincerely believed that this clearly proved that Jesus was the Father (and the Spirit). I now see how completely misguided this argument is. The Father, Son, and Holy Spirit are all involved in the resurrection act, in just the senses outlined above. There is nothing incoherent about this suggestion, and one has only to take all Scripture at face value (not twist it in unnatural directions) to accept it.

It is informative to observe how completely selective the Oneness reading of the New Testament has to be in order to argue on this basis. In John 6:40, where Jesus says he shall raise the dead (and thus is speaking "as the Father"), he also says, *in the very same sentence,* "For my Father's will is that everyone who looks to the Son and believes in him shall have eternal life." Hence we must, on the Oneness interpretation, believe that Jesus switched from speaking as a human Son to speaking as the divine Father, all in one sentence.

So, too, we should observe four verses later that Jesus says, "No one can come to me unless the Father who sent me draws him"—clearly manifesting the "human" (Son) voice—but he immediately adds, "and I will raise him up at the last day"—clearly manifesting the "divine" (Father) voice. This multiple-personality Jesus again (we are to believe) switches voices in the middle of a sentence. And, of course, the audience (we are to believe) picked up on all of these smooth mid-sentence transitions. And well they should, for salvation itself depends on this!

We can conclude, therefore, that the cross-referencing arguments furnish no proof for the Oneness position that Jesus is the Father. They do support in a powerful way the conclusion that Jesus is *God*, since they show that Jesus does what only God can do (raise the dead, answer prayer, and the like). But this is exactly what the doctrine of the Trinity has always maintained. Only the trinitarian understanding of God can affirm both that Jesus is God and that he is personally distinct from the Father. And both of these affirmations are demanded by the Scripture texts quoted by Oneness Pentecostals mistakenly in support of the notion that Jesus is the Father.

Did the Son of God
Exist Before His Birth?

We have thus far demonstrated that the stock arguments against the Trinity raised by Oneness Pentecostalism fail (ch. 2), and that it is scripturally impossible to maintain that Jesus is not only the Son of God but also the Father (ch. 3). In this chapter we complete our defense of the trinitarian view of Jesus by refuting the Oneness arguments against the actual preexistence of the Son of God. We will proceed by first examining the New Testament evidence for the preexistence of the Son of God—specifically in John, in Paul's writings, and in Hebrews—and then consider the prooftexts used by Oneness writers to limit Jesus' sonship to his humanity.

New Testament Evidence for Christ's Preexistence

We saw in chapter 1 that, since the Oneness view of God requires that Jesus be himself the Father and the Spirit, the only sense in which Jesus can be distinct from the Father and/or Spirit is in his humanity. This necessitates the view that Jesus, insofar as he is Son, began to exist when he was born in Bethlehem sometime around 6 B.C. And this further requires that all statements concerning Jesus' preincarnate existence must relate either to his preincarnate existence as Father, or to his preincarnate existence as a mere idea or plan in the Father's mind.[1] The Oneness position, I shall now argue, is in error on both scores.

Christ's Preexistence in the Gospel of John
The One Who is "With" God and Who "Is" God

There is perhaps no stronger testimony to the actual distinct preexistence of Christ than the entire first chapter of the Gospel of John. It was, in fact, largely my own study of this chapter that finally convinced me that the Oneness view of the Son of God could not possibly be correct.

New Testament scholarship is in substantial agreement that the first eighteen verses of John are intended to function as a prologue to the rest of John's Gospel, setting the backdrop for all that is to subsequently come. This means that if this passage teaches the actual *personal* preexistence of the Word (as almost everyone except Oneness adherents recognizes), we may expect this to be a central theme throughout John's Gospel (as I shall subsequently argue is in fact the case).

The Gospel begins in eternity past by the author saying: "In the beginning was the Word, and the Word was with God, and the Word was God. He was with God in the beginning" (John 1:1–2).

Modalistic antitrinitarians maintain that here "the Word" (*logos*) is not "a person," but "an expression" or "a concept." Hence the verse simply means that "with God was his thought, concept, envisaging" (Sabin, V, 1; see Bernard, Oneness, 232f.). The Word here, then, is for Oneness believers a thing, not a who. That this depersonalized interpretation of Logos is mistaken, however, is clear from reading the entire context.

First, the Word is explicitly said to be himself God, and God, of course, is not a mere impersonal concept. The Word is *all* that God is, including God's personhood.

Second, the preposition *pros,* translated "with" here (though it has the connotation of "toward" or "facing"), is most frequently used to describe personal relationships. The burden of proof certainly lies on anyone who would wish to argue the contrary. But this is especially difficult to do in this instance since it is most difficult to see what John could have meant by saying that a "concept" or "envisagement" was "with" or "facing" God—and was itself God!

And third, the personhood of the Word is clearly manifested in the fact that personalistic activities are ascribed to him. This Word is said to be the one through whom the world was created (1:3), the one who is the life and light of all men (1:4–5), and the one who came to, but was rejected by, his own creation (1:5, 10–11). He is thus described in strongly personal terms that could not have been said of a mere "thought."

The presupposed personalistic nature of the Logos who always existed "with" God and who was himself God is then rendered as explicit as possible in verse 14, which reads: "The Word became flesh and made his dwelling among us. We have seen his glory, the glory of the One and Only, who came from the Father, full of grace and truth."

This verse is, of course, referring to Jesus Christ and is identifying the Word the author has been speaking of thus far in the prologue with the Son of God who is the subject of the rest of the book. It is important to note that the verse does not say, or even remotely suggest, that the Word became personal or distinct from the Father only when he "became flesh." The Word is spoken of as divine, personal and yet distinct from the Father from the beginning of this chapter on through the end of John's Gospel.

John is in verse 14 talking about the same one Logos he has been talking about all along (vv. 1–13) when he says, "We have seen his glory, the glory of the One and Only. . . ." It is this same Word, Jesus Christ, who John in this verse says came "*from* the Father" (not *as* the Father). Indeed, verse 14 really only repeats what John has already told us of the Word in verses 5, 9–11: the Word came to, but was rejected by, his own creation. John says this in reference to the *preincarnate* Word, showing that he does not bifurcate between a post-incarnate personal Word who is Jesus Christ and a supposedly pre-incarnate impersonal Word, as the Oneness interpretation requires.

The conclusion that John understood Jesus actually and personally to preexist with God and as God prior to his becoming flesh seems unavoidable. Therefore, the Oneness attempt to explain Christ's preexistence as an existence either as the actual Father or as the idealized envisaged Son cannot succeed in this passage.

The One "Before" John the Baptist

John's theme of Christ's preexistence is carried on in the very next verse when he turns his attention to John the Baptist. Here the apostle records the Baptist as testifying to Christ's identity as he cries out, "This was he of whom I said, 'He who comes after me has surpassed me because he was before me'" (John 1:15). And the next day the Baptist repeats his point: "This is the one I meant when I said, 'A man who comes after me has surpassed me because he was before me'" (v. 30).

The reference to Jesus' existing "before" the Baptist, coming right on the heels of the prologue as it does, and given the fact that the Baptist was actually older than Jesus, is an unmistakable reference to Jesus' preexistence as the Word.

That the Baptist goes on to testify that this one is "the Lamb of God" and "the Son of God" (vv. 29, 34) rules out the possible Oneness explanation that he is here referring to Christ's (supposed) preexistence as the Father. But, by the same means, no one can really maintain that the Baptist had in mind some watered-down notion of "ideal" preexistence in these passages either. Indeed, one must wonder what meaning there could be in his saying that Christ was superior to him because he preexisted in God's mind. Didn't even John himself preexist in that limited sense?

The One Who Has Come Down from Heaven

The theme of Christ's personal distinct preexistence and his descent to earth outlined in the prologue (John 1:1–18) is alluded to frequently throughout John's Gospel. Thus, for example, Jesus explains his unique authority to Nicodemus when he says, "No one has ever gone into heaven except the one who came from heaven—the Son of Man" (3:13).[2] Later in this chapter John the Baptist proclaims this same truth when he says, "The one who comes from above is above all . . ." (v. 31). This is precisely what Jesus again teaches the Pharisees when he rhetorically asks, "What if you see the Son of Man ascend to where he was before!" (6:62).

Bernard, we saw earlier, attempts to explain this last passage by arguing that Jesus was referring to his preexistence as the Father (Bernard, Oneness, 183), but the fact that Jesus refers to himself as "Son of Man" rules this out. The context of this saying also rules it out, for throughout this discourse Jesus has been distinguishing between himself and God the Father even while he has been teaching that he "came down from heaven" from a preexistent state. Hence we hear Jesus throughout this chapter saying such things as the following:

"For the bread of God is he who comes down from heaven and gives life to the world" (6:33).

"For I have come down from heaven not to do my will but to do the will of him who sent me" (6:38).

"I am the bread that came down from heaven. . . . No one has seen the Father except the one who is from God; only he has seen the Father. . . . I am the living bread that came down from heaven. . . . Just as the living Father sent me and I live because of the Father, so the one who feeds on me will live because of me. This is the bread that came down from heaven . . ." (6:41, 46, 51, 57–58).

After all this, is one to believe—when Jesus immediately goes on to refer to himself as "the Son of Man" and as ascending to where he was "before" he descended—that he was really referring to himself as Father, that he was actually himself the Father from whom he had just told us six times he himself had come? Is there even the slightest suggestion in the text itself that Jesus intends this? Is it not a good bit more likely that Jesus was in all these verses referring to the same state of distinct preexistence as "the Word" mentioned in the prologue of John's Gospel? Or, to ask it another way, if (for the sake of argument) Jesus had wanted to say that he, as the Son of God, really did exist with the Father before he came down to earth, could he have been any more clear about it than he was here? According to Oneness believers, how should Jesus have spoken differently if he had wanted to say what the trinitarians believe he said?

The Great "I AM"

A similar argument can be made against the Oneness interpretation of John 8:58. Here Jesus says, "Before Abraham was, I am" (KJV), and this is usually taken by Oneness people to be a self-identification of Jesus with the preexistent Father. "That day [Jesus] spoke out of the depths of his divine (father) consciousness" (Magee, 15).

In response to this we must first note that Jesus, just three verses earlier, had distinguished himself as Son from the Father, saying, "If I glorify myself, my glory means nothing. My Father, whom you claim as your God, is the one who glorifies me. Though you do not know him, I know him . . . and keep his word" (8:54–55). Are we to believe that Jesus in the next breath switches voices from the "human Son" to talking here as the "divine Father" who claims preexistence? Is there any reason to think that Jesus taught with such a split personality? There is certainly no indication of this here or in any other text of Scripture. Nor does the general portrait of Jesus and the Father in John's Gospel lend itself readily to this interpretation, for the Father is referred to as distinct from Jesus over a hundred times in this work, while never once is Jesus called anything other than the Son.

The clear impression one therefore gets from John 8:58 is that Jesus is here claiming that it is he *as Son* who is the great "I AM" of Exodus 3:14. The assertion of actual preexistence fits perfectly with the announcement of this theme in the prologue, whereas the Oneness view that Jesus is here speaking as the Father fits with nothing else we learn from this work.

What makes this argument even stronger is the fact that Christ, just previous to this, had explicitly referred to his preexistence with God the Father and his being sent by God the Father. He says, "If God were your Father, you would love me, for I came from God and now am here. I have not come on my own; but he sent me" (8:42).

If this passage doesn't teach that Christ came from the Father (where he had been) in order to get "here"—in order to "become flesh" (1:14)—and that this is what is meant by his being "sent" by the Father, then this verse, so far as I can discern, means nothing. If Jesus had wanted to say that he once existed with the Father but that he came from the Father to exist here on earth, how else would he have said it? This verse is on a par with a host of similar statements of Jesus (or made by John about Jesus) in which it is explicitly taught that Jesus' identity as distinct from the Father did not begin with his human identity.

Hence we read, "Jesus knew that the Father had put all things under his power, and that he had come from God and was returning to God" (John 13:3). And again Jesus says, ". . . you have loved me and have believed that I came from God. I came from the Father and entered the world; now I am leaving the world and going back to the Father" (16:27–28).

Taken at face value, no clearer statement of Christ's existence distinct from the Father prior to his human birth is really imaginable. Jesus "came from God" before he "entered the world." Hence he can refer to his existence as the great "I AM," an existence he had "before the world began" (John 17:5; cf. 1:15; 6:62). And it is for this reason that he can continually refer to himself as having "come down from heaven."

We thus see that the explanation that Jesus is referring to himself as Father when he refers to himself as the "I AM" and as "coming down from heaven" does not work. But there is a less frequent but slightly more sophisticated Oneness explanation for verses such as these. In this newer, revised Oneness view, all verses that speak of Christ's "coming down from heaven" and the like are merely metaphorical statements concerning Christ's heavenly commission. In this view, Jesus "came down from heaven" in just the same sense that "Every good and perfect gift is from above, coming down from the Father . . ." (James 1:17). All such language simply comes to mean that Christ is God's ultimate gift "from heaven" (Sabin, V, 3–4).

Such a reading, however, is impossible for at least three reasons. First, the verses simply don't read like metaphors on this level. "The one who comes from heaven is above all" (John 3:31); "I have come down from heaven" (6:38); "I am from above" (8:23); "I came from the Father and entered the world" (16:28). What is being said about Jesus here is obviously supposed to be considered unique and unprecedented. Christ is one of a kind! He is not like any other gift. He really did "come from above" in a sense in which all other gifts from God do not. This is what John has been telling us from the start (1:1–18).

Second, the language of Christ's descent is directly paralleled with the language of his ascent. So, unless we wish to make his ascent a mere metaphor, we cannot consistently make his descent merely metaphorical. Thus Christ's "coming from" God directly parallels his "returning to" God (13:3); his "coming into the world" parallels his "leaving the world" and his "going back to the Father" (16:27–28); and his being "lifted up" will put him back where he was "before" (6:62; 17:5). Thus, if Christ *really* "returned to God," "left the world," and was "lifted up," we must conclude that he also *really* "came from God," "down from heaven," "into the world" from where he really was "before."

To be sure, since the angels told the disciples that Christ would return to earth "in the same way" he ascended (Acts 1:10–11), this line of Oneness reasoning would land us on the conclusion that Christ is only coming back in a figurative sense—a conclusion I'm quite confident Oneness exponents would rather avoid. Thus, while the purpose, and therefore the form, of Christ's first and second comings are very different, the fact that it is the real Christ who really came and will come again is presupposed in each.[3]

A third refutation of this Oneness line of argumentation is that the descent of Christ is paralleled with the descent of the Spirit in John's Gospel. It is most unlikely that anyone would want to maintain that the Spirit's origin in heaven is a mere metaphor. This theme in John is succinctly expressed when Jesus says, "Now I am going to him who sent me. . . . Because I said these things, you are filled with grief. But I tell you the truth: It is for your good that I am going away. Unless I go away, the Counselor will not come to you; but if I go, I will send him to you" (16:5–7).

Jesus, we see, must return to the one who sent him so that the Father may then send "another" (14:16), the Holy Spirit. Since the sending of the Spirit is real, so is "the going" of Jesus, which preceded it—and so, we must affirm, is the "sending" of Jesus, which preceded that. The two "sendings" directly parallel each other in chapters 14 through 16 in John.

To make this point another way, if the Spirit was not "sent" like a mere earthly prophet (e.g., "commissioned") but really came down from heaven, how can one argue that the Son did not likewise really come down from the Father? Or, to address once again the issue of preexistence, if we accept that the Spirit in any sense existed before his being sent (and who doubts this?), then must we not out of consistency accept that the Son also existed prior to being sent? For again, the "sendings" directly parallel one another.

The Glory of Christ Before Creation

In the light of all of this teaching on the preexistence of Christ, it seems most natural to interpret John 17:5, 24 after the traditional manner as referring to the actual preexistence of the Son. Here Jesus prays, "And now, Father, glorify me in your presence with the glory I had with you before the world began" (17:5). And later, "Father, I want those you have given me to be with me where I am, and to see my glory, the glory you have given me because you loved me before the creation of the world" (v. 24).

Oneness exponents attempt to make these verses refer to the preexistent plan in the Father's mind for his earthly Son, on a par with the ideal preexistence of the crucifixion (1 Peter 1:19–20; Rev. 13:8) or of the church (Eph. 1:4–5; 2 Tim. 1:9) in the mind of God. Unlike their other attempts at idealizing Johannine preexistence passages, the Oneness interpretation of this verse is not wholly without historical orthodox precedent. In my estimation, however, it is nevertheless somewhat improbable.

It is simply very difficult not to take all of the Johannine talk about Christ's preexistence on the same level. Jesus is said to exist from the beginning with God and as God (1:1). John the Baptist testifies to this fact (1:15, 30). Jesus himself refers to this with the divine name (8:58). He is repeatedly said to have been sent by the Father and to have come down from heaven (3:13, 31; 6:33, 38, 41, 46, 51, 56–58; 8:42). He repeatedly talks of ascending back to where he was before (6:62; 13:3; 16:27–28). So, when he now speaks of a glory he had with the Father before creation, it seems most natural to suppose that the same actual distinct state of preexistence is in mind. In any case, if one denies this in these verses it certainly cannot be for theological reasons derived from John's Gospel.

Christ's Preexistence in Paul's Writings

"Ideal" Preexistence in Paul

The Oneness exponents' argument that the preexistence of Christ is a preexistence of foreknowledge and of purpose fits several passages in Paul; and, in fact, their interpretation of these verses fits well with some of the scholarly opinion on the matter. When, for example, Paul places the preexistence of Christ on the same level as the preexistence of the church, as he does in Ephesians 1:4–5 (cf. 2 Tim. 1:9), there is no reason to assume that Paul has an actual preexistence in mind with one (Christ) but only an ideal preexistence in mind with the other (church), though this possibility cannot be entirely ruled out. But it seems most likely that in this context Paul is conceiving of the man Jesus Christ in whom the Word was enfleshed along the same lines as the first-century Rabbis conceived of the Torah. To say that it existed "in the beginning" was one way of saying that it had the preeminence in God's plan for the world.[4]

The mistake that Oneness exegetes make is in supposing that, because certain passages can be interpreted this way, this is the way all such passages speaking of the distinct preexistence of Christ should be interpreted. This is similar to the Jehovah's Witnesses' futile argument that because "spirit" means only "breath" in many passages of Scripture, it must mean this in every passage of Scripture that mentions it. This is simply extremely bad exegesis. We must take each passage on its own merits. When we do this, we find that the Oneness interpretation of preexistence doesn't fit with most of what Paul says on the matter, even if it does fit with some of what Paul says on other matters.

Christ the Creator

In Colossians 1:16–17 we find Paul writing, "For by him all things were created: things in heaven and on earth, visible and invisible, whether thrones or powers or rulers or authorities; all things were created by him and for him. He is before all things, and in him all things hold together."

Some Oneness exegetes take these verses to refer to Christ's preexistence as Father. "These verses describe the eternal Spirit that was in the Son . . ." (Bernard, Oneness, 115–16). This is an incredible explanation, for the simple reason that the verse immediately preceding this one speaks of Christ as "the image of the invisible God, the firstborn over all creation" (v. 15), and the verses before that speak of Christ as the Father's "beloved Son" (vv. 12–14). When Paul continues in verse 16 to say that it is "by him" that "all things were created," he is explicitly referring to *this* person, who is certainly not God the Father. He is "the beloved Son" and "the image" *of* the Father.

What is more, what meaning would there be in saying that the Father created all things "in," "through," and "for" himself? The prepositions presuppose some distinction between the Father who creates and the Son-Image through whom and for whom he creates. The fact that Paul, following his typical style, has already twice explicitly distinguished between God the Father and his Son Jesus Christ in this chapter (1:3, 12–13) only strengthens this point.

Slightly more plausible, however, is the Oneness attempt to explain this verse by maintaining that "God used His foreknowledge of the Son when He created the world" (Bernard, Oneness, 116). Hence this verse comes to mean that the whole creation was "with a view towards" and "for the sake of" the Son, Jesus Christ.

The major difficulty to be found with this interpretation is that Paul here says three things about Christ's role in the creation. He says that all things were created "in him" (*en auto*), "through him" (*di autou*), and "for him" (*eis auton*). It is, I think, impossible to maintain that all of these phrases simply come to mean the same thing—something like "with a view towards" or "for the sake of." Indeed, Paul is explicitly distinguishing between a sense in which all things were created "for the sake of" Christ (*eis auton*) and the sense in which all things were created "in" and "through" Christ.

There is one other consideration that, in my mind, wraps up the issue. Generally speaking, when an ancient author in Greek uses the preposition *dia* followed by a genitive ending, the *dia* is being used in an instrumental sense. It is thus appropriate to translate it as "through," or "by means of." When an author uses *dia* followed by an accusative ending, however, the *dia* is being used with a sense of final causation. It is thus appropriate to translate it as "for the purpose of," or "with a view towards."

When Paul says that all things were created "through Christ," he is using *dia* followed by a genitive case ending (as does John 1:3). If he had wanted to say that all things were created "for the sake of" Christ, as Oneness interpreters want him to say, why didn't he use *dia* with an accusative ending? Indeed, one must wonder why Paul would even want to say here that all things were created "for the sake of" Christ, since he already said just that when he said that all things were created "*eis auton.*"

Hence, while Paul does understand the entire creation to exist *for* Jesus Christ the Son, he also understands the entire creation to have come about *by means of* Jesus Christ the Son. And this, of course, means that the inspired apostle believed that the Son of God really did preexist before creation. This is why he immediately goes on to state, without qualification, that "he is before all things" (v. 17). If this statement is not affirming that the Son of God really existed "before all things," what would a statement that *did* say this look like?

The exact same argument can be used of 1 Corinthians 8:6, which says that "for us there is but one God, the Father, from whom all things came and for whom we live; and there is but one Lord, Jesus Christ, through whom all things came and through whom we live." Paul in this passage also uses *dia* with the genitive and must then be referring to Christ as the preexistent Lord who was, in some sense, the means by which God the Father created the world. This passage thus demonstrates that Jesus Christ actually preexisted and did so distinct from God the Father with whom he is here contrasted.

The Humble Son of God

Another passage that has traditionally been taken to teach the real preexistence of Jesus Christ is the hymn of Philippians 2:5–11. Verses 5 through 7 are the crucial ones for our purpose: "Your attitude should be the same as that of Christ Jesus: Who, being in very nature God, did not consider equality with God something to be grasped, but made himself nothing, taking the very nature of a servant, being made in human likeness." As almost every scholar in church history has seen it, this passage teaches exactly the same thing as John 1:1–14. Jesus Christ was equal with God the Father (see vv. 9–11), he was with the Father, and he was himself "by nature God" (*morphe theou huparchon*). But he did not cling to this divine status but rather "emptied himself" to take on "the very nature of a slave" (*morphen doulou labon*).

Oneness theology, of course, cannot accept this, for it contradicts their idea of "absolute Oneness," and hence some alternative explanation for the passage must be found. The standard explanation, as we saw in chapter 1, is that the verse refers to Jesus Christ as the Father. Commenting on this verse, Bernard says that "Jesus was equal with (the same as) God in the sense that He was God" (Oneness, 221). And again, ". . . in His divinity, He is truly equal to, or identical to God. The word equal here means that the divine nature of Jesus was the very nature of God the Father" (Oneness, 222).

This explanation simply does not work. First, neither in Greek (*isos*) nor in English does the word *equal* mean "identical." There are a number of ways in Greek for saying one thing is "identical to" or "the same as" something else, but Paul does not employ them here. "Equality" is a term of *relationship*, and it therefore implies some type of plurality.

Second, the Oneness interpretation requires us to believe the impossible notion that Paul was speaking of Jesus as Father in one breath (Phil. 2:6–8), and Jesus as Son, in contrast to the Father, in the next (vv. 9–11), and that his first-century audience, without any hint from Paul, would have picked this up (while everyone else in church history missed it!).

Finally, what are we to make of verses 10–11, which seem to speak, as does verse 6, of Christ as divine while also distinguishing him from "God the Father": ". . . at the name of Jesus every knee should bow . . . and every tongue confess that Jesus Christ is Lord, to the glory of God the Father"? Was Paul really saying that the humanity of Jesus is to be confessed as "Lord," while his divinity is to be glorified as "God the Father"? Could Paul as easily have said that every tongue shall confess that the human Son is Lord, to "the glory of Jesus the Father"? Does that not sound a bit strange? Yet, if the Oneness interpretation of the passage is right, that is exactly what Paul is saying.

An alternative and slightly more plausible reading of this passage has been recently offered by at least one influential Oneness spokesperson. Following the lead of several New Testament scholars, Robert Sabin attempts to interpret all of Philippians 2:5–11 as a commentary on the earthly life of Jesus (Sabin, The Man, Seminar). Hence it was the man Jesus Christ who did not grasp after the equality with God he had by virtue of the Incarnation. Rather, to reverse what Adam did by grasping after an equality with God that was not rightfully his, Christ forsook the equality with God that was rightfully his.

This same interpretation, we might here add, is given to 2 Corinthians 8:9, in which Paul says, "For you know the grace of our Lord Jesus Christ, that though he was rich, yet for your sakes he became poor, so that you through his poverty might become rich." The traditional interpretation of this passage has been that Christ was rich in his preexistent glory (cf. John 17:5; 6:62; 8:58), but for our sake he "emptied himself" and became as one of us. By contrast, this verse does not in Sabin's view distinguish between Christ's preexistence and his earthly existence, but between his state of being by nature, and his state of being by choice. He could have been rich (for he was this by nature), but he chose to become poor.

This interpretation, while far superior to the standard Oneness interpretation, nevertheless has a number of objections that, in my mind, count decisively against it. First, it is not clear what the "richness" of the earthly Christ might be. The Oneness interpretation requires, it seems, that there was a time in Christ's earthly life when he chose not to grasp after equality with God and thereby chose not to retain all his riches by divine right. But is there anything in the Gospels to substantiate this point? Was not Christ poor and lowly from the moment of his birth?

Second, Philippians 2:5–11 explicitly contrasts the state of being "in the nature of God" with being "in the nature of a servant" as well as being "equal with God" with being "made in human likeness." This fits well with the view that the passage is contrasting Christ in his preexistent state with Christ in his incarnate state, but it is much more difficult to fit into the Oneness alternative explanation.

One must wonder, for example, how Jesus was not "in the nature of a servant" or "in human likeness" while on this earth (as a Jewish male carpenter!) before he chose to become so. Indeed, one wonders how one could even be a real human being before one is "made in human likeness" and "being found in appearance as a man" (Phil. 2:7–8). Correlatively, one must also wonder what kind of aberrant Christology results when we ponder the sense in which Jesus was not "equal with God" and "in the nature of God" *after* he chose not to grasp after these things. Was not Jesus Christ fully God and fully man from the beginning of his life on through the end (indeed, into eternity)?

Hence, while this Oneness reinterpretation of these passages is not utterly impossible, it is quite unlikely. It only becomes plausible if one has other reasons for thinking that the notion of Christ's distinct and personal preexistence is a notion that Paul (and other biblical authors) could not have entertained. But this, we have already seen, is not at all the case.

The Descending and Ascending Christ

We have dealt with those passages that are generally taken to be the most important texts showing that Paul believed that Jesus Christ existed, distinct from God the Father, prior to his Incarnation. But there are two other passages that add to the cumulative case for preexistence in Paul's theology and hence warrant our brief attention.

In Romans 10:6–7, Paul is arguing against salvation by works (vv. 3–4) by maintaining that faith alone saves a person. Against any notion of salvation by self-effort, then, Paul maintains that "the righteousness that is by faith says: 'Do not say in your heart, "Who will ascend into heaven?"' (that is, to bring Christ down) 'or "Who will descend into the deep?"' (that is, to bring Christ up from the dead)."

The point Paul is making as he here quotes Deuteronomy 30:12–13 is that no amount of human striving could have brought Christ down from heaven or have risen Christ up from the dead. Christ, in other words, came down from heaven on his own. The passage is in some respects similar to John 3:13, and both passages clearly presuppose that Christ existed before he came to earth.

In Ephesians 4:7–10, Paul is celebrating the victory Christ achieved on the cross and the benefit this has for the church. He writes:

> But to each one of us grace has been given as Christ apportioned it. This is why it says: "When he ascended on high, he led captives in his train and gave gifts to men." (What does "he ascended" mean except that he also descended to the lower, earthly regions? He who

descended is the very one who ascended higher than all the heavens, in order to fill the whole universe.)

Predictably, the standard Oneness explanation of this passage is that it refers to Christ as the Father. This, however, can easily be dismissed by observing that the verses immediately preceding clearly distinguish, in Paul's customary fashion, between God the Father and the Lord (vv. 5–6; cf. 1:2–3; 2:18; 3:9–11, 14; 5:20), and by noting that Christ is called the Son of God several verses after this passage (vv. 12–13). Nor could it here be argued that this "descent" is figurative, since the ascent with which it is paralleled is clearly literal. Hence this verse most likely is to be taken as yet another testimony to the distinct preexistence of Christ in Paul's thought.

Christ's Preexistence in Hebrews
Hebrews 1:2–3

As we saw was the case with Colossians 1:16–17, 1 Corinthians 8:6, and John 1:3, Hebrews 1:2 teaches that it was through the Son, "the radiance of God's glory" (v. 3), that God made the universe. The standard Oneness reply, we should by now expect, is that this verse means that all things were created "with a view towards" or "for the sake of" the Son. God made the world with the Son in mind. But this interpretation is rendered most unlikely for the same reason the Oneness explanation of the other creation passages is unlikely; namely, the Greek simply doesn't say this. The author here again uses *dia* followed by a genitive, indicating the instrumental sense of the preposition. Hence, all things were created *through* the Son—implying that the Son was there at the time!

This interpretation is further substantiated by the fact that the author has just previously said that the Son had been appointed "heir of all things," which says almost the same thing as that the world was created "for the sake of" the Son. So why would the author simply repeat himself? What is more, the author quickly reiterates his opinion that the Son was actually involved in creation when he attributes to the Son as God (see v. 8) the Psalm that reads: "In the beginning, O

Lord, you laid the foundations of the earth, and the heavens are the work of your hands" (Heb. 1:10; cf. Ps. 8).

Hence it can, I think, be taken as established that Hebrews 1:2 teaches that the Son of God was instrumentally involved in the work of creation.

Hebrews 7:1–3

In this passage the author is utilizing a Rabbinic method of interpretation to maintain that the priesthood of Christ has superseded the Levitical priesthood. He attempts to establish his point by noting that the priesthood of Christ is after the order of Melchizedek, while the priesthood of the Levites is after the order of Abraham, and Melchizedek was superior to Abraham (Heb. 7:2–3). At any rate, in the course of this Rabbinic argument he describes Melchizedek as being "without father or mother, without genealogy, without beginning of days or end of life, like the Son of God he remains a priest forever" (v. 3).

While there are a number of issues that surround the interpretation of this difficult passage, one thing at least is clear: The author believes that the Son of God has always existed and will always exist. Melchizedek is Jesus' prototype because, at least as far as the Old Testament describes him, he is "without beginning of days."[5]

Hebrews 10:5

As a means of discussing the atoning significance of Jesus' sacrificed body, the author of this verse records Jesus as saying, "Sacrifice and offering you did not desire, but a body you prepared for me." This, clearly, cannot be the Father talking, since the one talking is talking to the Father and is talking in the passive voice. But just as clear is the fact that the one talking existed before "the body" was prepared for him. The most obvious conclusion, it seems, is to admit that Jesus Christ existed before he existed as a human being.

One possible out for the Oneness adherent is to maintain that what we have here is the ideal Son speaking to the real Father (Sabin, Battle). God is, as it were, conversing with himself and thus attributing personality to what is really simply yet an idea in his mind.

While this interpretation is not unprecedented in New Testament scholarship, I think there is very little to be said for it. There is certainly nothing in the text itself to suggest such a reading. Indeed, it seems that the only thing that can be said on its behalf is that it does not violate Oneness doctrine. But this is hardly a good reason for maintaining it.

Is Jesus' Sonship Tied to His Humanity?

I have attempted to demonstrate in this chapter that the New Testament teaches that Jesus existed as God prior to creation, and that he did so in a manner personally distinct from the Father. But we have not yet explicitly addressed the several texts used by Oneness exegetes to argue that Jesus' sonship is temporal, and the refutation of the Oneness position is not complete until this is accomplished. To this task, therefore, I now turn.

Luke 1:35

In this passage the angel proclaims to Mary: "The Holy Spirit will come upon you, and the power of the Most High will overshadow you. So the holy one to be born will be called the Son of God." From this, Oneness believers argue that the reason Jesus is the Son of God is because, quite literally, he had no human father. His fleshly existence was directly "fathered" by God. Hence, the sonship of Christ, they argue, is a temporal, earthly affair.

This interpretation of the passage is, in my estimation, too narrowly focused and quite anthropomorphic. I find nothing to suggest that Luke was thinking in primarily biological terms when he records the angel as connecting Jesus' divine conception with his title of Son of God. The title "Son of God" was primarily a moral and theological title throughout the ancient Semitic world, and throughout Scripture. And, heard in this context, it is clear that the angel was simply telling Mary that she was going to miraculously conceive a supremely holy child who will be called the Son of God. Nothing more can be read into this.

Still, even if one persists in this biologically orientated interpretation of the verse, this could only be shown to give us *one* of the New Testament reasons Jesus is called the Son of God. It cannot be used to prove the *only* reason Jesus is the Son of God.

Hebrews 1:5–6

This passage is frequently cited by Oneness apologists in their attempt to argue that there is no eternal Son of God (Magee, 33; Bernard, Oneness, 105). Here the author applies the coronation hymns of Psalm 2:7 and 2 Samuel 7:14 to Christ as he compares his divinity to that of the angels by asking, "To which of the angels did God ever say, 'You are my Son; today I have become your Father'? Or again, 'I will be his Father, and he will be my Son'" (Heb. 5:5).

What Oneness exegetes find most significant about this passage is its temporal claims. "Today"—not eternally—"I have become your Father." And again, God "will be" the Messiah's Father, and the Messiah the Father's Son. Such language, it is argued, positively excludes the eternal sonship of Christ. It locates the sonship of Christ as beginning with his human birth.

One does not have to look far, however, to see that something is askew with this interpretation. After all, the same author who penned verse 5 also penned verse 2 of this chapter, in which, we have seen, he declares that the Son was in some instrumental sense involved in creation. This same author, moreover, penned verses 8 and 10, in which he calls the Son "God" and "Lord" and says that "In the beginning, O Lord, you laid the foundations of the earth. . . ." Hence whatever meaning verse 5 has, it cannot legitimately be used to date the beginning of the Son's existence at Bethlehem.

The correct meaning of this verse, however, is not difficult to discern. The Old Testament passages the author is quoting speak of an ideal king's relationship to the God of Israel and have nothing whatsoever to do with the biological birth of the king. Rather, they simply speak of God's openly declaring (probably during the coronation ceremony) his special covenant relationship to the king, and through the king, to all of Israel.

That is why this very same Old Testament passage can be applied to Jesus after his resurrection (see Acts 13:33). The logic that would use Psalm 2 to date the beginning of Christ's sonship at Bethlehem would thus also have to date it as beginning at his resurrection. Indeed, this sort of logic would also require that we date Christ's sonship at his baptism and/or transfiguration (Matt. 3:17 and parallels, and 2 Peter 1:17–18). However, if these later conclusions are unacceptable (as they certainly are for both trinitarian and Oneness believers), then so is the former.

On the other hand, when we understand the text in its proper context, no difficulty is created by any New Testament application of this verse. Christ began to be known (not was initially *constituted*) as the Son of God at his birth, and he was openly declared to be such at his baptism, transfiguration, and resurrection (cf. Rom. 1:4; Acts 2:36). But just as Acts 13:33 does not rule out Jesus' being the Son of God before his resurrection, so Hebrews 1:5–6 does not rule out his being God's Son before his birth.

Jesus as a Begotten Son

The remaining texts that Oneness exegetes attempt to utilize to show that the title of "Son" refers only to the temporal humanity of Christ speak of Christ as "the only begotten" Son of God (KJV—John 1:18; 3:16, 18; 1 John 4:9) who was "born of a woman, born under law" (Gal. 4:4). The fact that the Son is "begotten," it is argued, rules out his being eternal.

Two considerations quickly dismiss these arguments, however. First, as is widely recognized by contemporary biblical scholarship, the Johannine Semitic phrase "only begotten" (*monogenes*) is not a biological term. Rather, the term specifies uniqueness. *Mono* means "one," and *genos* means "kind." Jesus is, therefore, not God's only born Son (in contrast to all of his nonbegotten sons?); rather, he is, as the NIV rightly translates it, God's "one and only" Son.[6]

Concerning Paul's statement that God sent his Son "born of a woman," we need only point out that this clause most readily refers to the conditions of the Son's sending, not to the nature of the Son himself. The verse does not say that God "created" his Son by having him be born of a woman. It merely says that God sent his Son, born of a woman.

There is nothing in this that is at all in tension with the truth of Christ's real preexistence—something we have already seen Paul elsewhere affirm. The human birth of Christ is simply an aspect of "the very nature of a servant" he voluntarily assumed in "being made in human likeness" (Phil. 2:7). "The Word became flesh" (John 1:14; cf. 1 Tim. 3:16), but he did not begin to exist with this enfleshment.

Conclusion

The biblical case for the distinct personal preexistence of Jesus Christ is, we have shown, exceedingly strong, while the modalistic arguments against this doctrine are essentially groundless. It is not without reason that the church has from its infancy found the truth of Christ's eternal preexistence to be a firmly grounded teaching of Scripture. Therefore, the insight that the triune relationality of God revealed to us must have some correspondence to who God eternally is within himself was not simply an insight the church arrived at by its own reflection. It is, in fact, a true insight, but the church was guided in its thinking by Scripture. Indeed, the inspired authors of Scripture were themselves led to this conclusion. If Jesus was indeed the "Word," "image," "form," "Son," and "expression" of God the Father *in time*, so he must in some sense *always* have been. The loving triunity of God revealed to us cannot be an artificial device, mask, or "illusion" that God temporarily assumes simply for our sake. Rather, it manifests what is deepest, truest, and most authentic about God. As such, the doctrine of the Trinity lies at the heart of the Christian faith and impacts everything else that is distinctly Christian.

That the UPCI and other Oneness groups deny this so vigorously not only renders their theology radically unbiblical—it also tragically puts a wall of artificiality between their faith and their God. This, we shall see in chapter 6, has drastic negative implications for their understanding of salvation.

5

Is Jesus the Holy Spirit?

esides maintaining that Jesus is the Father, it is, as we have seen, also essential to Oneness theology that Jesus be understood to be the Holy Spirit. Oneness adherents maintain that whatever distinctness there might be between Jesus the Son and the Holy Spirit (or between the Father and the Holy Spirit) can only be a difference in activity. In the end, Jesus is the one "person" who is the Father, and the Son, and the Holy Spirit. Having refuted their claim that Jesus is the Father and that, as Son, Jesus is not eternal, we now need to turn to their claim that he is also himself the Holy Spirit.

After making one preliminary observation, we shall carry out this analysis by examining the general way in which the New Testament speaks about the Spirit and then proceed to examine the particular biblical arguments that Oneness apologists attempt to use to ground their modalism.

The "Implicit" Distinctness of the Spirit

However much Oneness theologians might insist on the "absolute identity" of Jesus and the Spirit, they too must concede that there is a distinct way of existing that distinguishes the Spirit from the Son. That is to say, even when they say that the Holy Spirit who is himself Jesus dwells inside of believers, they don't mean to say that the actual incarnate Jesus (the Son) dwells inside of believers.

Thus, even for them, the "Jesus" living in the believing heart is really distinct from the Jesus who has a glorified body "up in heaven." Yet they, along with trinitarians, would want to confess both that "the fullness of the Godhead" dwells in the incarnate Son (Col. 2:9) and that the Holy Spirit is fully God.

The point here is that, in spite of their insistence on the absolute Oneness of God, even Oneness theologians assume that there are at least *temporary* distinctions within the Godhead. While they rightly insist that God cannot be quantified and divided up into sections—this results in polytheism—even Oneness believers understand the Holy Spirit to be fully God in a manner quite distinct from the way the incarnate Jesus is fully God. And yet they (of all people!) must agree that this distinction does not in any way lessen the divinity of God as incarnate Son or God as Holy Spirit.

In admitting this much, however, it seems that Oneness believers have greatly undermined their most basic rationale for rejecting the doctrine of the Trinity: They are implicitly agreeing that there is nothing tritheistic or contradictory about affirming that God fully dwells in three distinct ways. Indeed, making the distinction between the Son and the Holy Spirit out to be only temporary and, worse still, only "apparent," as Oneness theology does, only increases the mysteriousness of the Trinity. For it implies that the *real* undifferentiated eternal God is somehow concealed behind the three revealed temporary "manifestations" of God. The true God, in other words, is never truly revealed. In trinitarianism, the threefoldness of God's revelation *is* the very eternal innermost heart of God. I shall have more to say on this point in chapter 8.

The Holy Spirit As the Third Person

We have already mentioned the established biblical principle that the explicit and general teaching of Scripture must always interpret the nonexplicit and particular teaching of individual passages of Scripture. One common denominator of all cultic theologizing is that it systematically overturns this principle. Thus, as we did in our examination of the Oneness claim that Jesus is the Father, we shall begin our refutation of the Oneness claim that Jesus is the Holy Spirit by briefly examining the general teaching of Scripture on the Spirit.

Is the Spirit Distinct from the Father and Son?

We noted in chapter 3 that "the Father" was spoken of as being distinct from Jesus over two hundred times in the New Testament. The various arguments utilized by the Oneness Pentecostals to prove otherwise could not dent such an impressively uniform witness. It must now be said that the testimony of the real distinctness of the Holy Spirit is almost as impressive. And, we shall see, the arguments to the contrary by Oneness believers are just as impotent in overturning this general witness.

Like the references to the Father as distinct from the Son, the Holy Spirit is distinctly referred to over two hundred times in the New Testament. Only in two passages is it possible to argue that the Spirit is in some sense identified with Christ (2 Cor. 3:17; Rom. 8:9–11), and only in a handful of other instances is it possible to produce an indirect case through cross-referencing that Jesus and the Spirit are one and the same "person."

We shall subsequently see that these few passages used by Oneness groups in an attempt to prove their position cannot legitimately be interpreted in this fashion. But what is important for us to note presently is that the general tendency of the New Testament is to speak of the Holy Spirit as being distinct from the Father and Son. And since the general teaching of Scripture must always interpret the particular, this fact alone should be enough to render the Oneness identification of Jesus with the Spirit as highly suspect.

Is the Holy Spirit a "Person"?

What is even more impressive than the numerical frequency of the distinct portrayals of the Holy Spirit is the manner in which the Holy Spirit is distinctly portrayed, for he is portrayed not as a distinct "aspect" or "power" of God, but as distinct in a personal way. It is true that early on in the progress of God's scriptural revelation, the Spirit was for the most part conceived of in less personal terms. It is also true that the Holy Spirit is at times spoken of in less than personal terms even in the later stages of God's revelation.[1] But this by no means negates the fact that the definitive final biblical teaching on the Spirit is that he is personal and distinct from the Father and Son. While some of the biblical language about the Spirit falls short of describing the Spirit as personal, nowhere does the Bible deny that he is personal.

We learn from Scripture that the Holy Spirit is a distinct "person" when we hear that it was he who personally called and guided certain individuals to certain mission fields in the church's infancy (Acts 8:29; 10:19–20; 13:2; 20:28; 16:7, 9). The Holy Spirit, we further learn, can be lied to (Acts 5:3), blasphemed against (Matt. 12:31–32), tested (Acts 5:9), resisted (Acts 7:51; 1 Thess. 5:19), and grieved (Eph. 4:30), things that obviously could only be said about a person (see Wainwright, 200ff.).

The Spirit's distinct personality is further evidenced by the fact that he is said to have personally instructed Paul as to what he should teach (1 Cor. 2:13), and is said to be the one who spoke through God's prophets (Acts 1:16; 1 Peter 1:11–12; 2 Peter 1:21). It is, moreover, the Holy Spirit who is said to convict individuals (John 16:7–11), to teach the church (John 16:13), to guide the church in its decisions (Acts 15:28), to comfort believers (John 6:6–7; Rom. 8:26), to point to and glorify Christ (John 15:26; 16:14), to sanctify the church (1 Cor. 6:11; Rom. 15:16), and to give gifts to the church according to his own will (1 Cor. 12:4–11). These are all activities that clearly presuppose that the Holy Spirit is to be thought of as something like a conscious, feeling, and willing agent—a "person."

The Personal Distinctness of the Spirit in John's Gospel

What is of utmost importance for us to realize in all of this is that there is no suggestion in any of the above cited passages that the personal identity of the Spirit is "really" identical with the personal identity of the Father and the Son, as Oneness Pentecostals attempt to argue. There is, in other words, no suggestion that the Holy Spirit is "really" only the person of Jesus operating in a different capacity.

A sampling from Jesus' discourse on the Holy Spirit found throughout John 14 through 16 makes this point very clear. Jesus in this passage emphasizes both the real "personhood" of the Spirit and the Spirit's distinctness from himself and the Father, referring to the Spirit consistently in the third person as "he" (e.g., John 14:16–17, 25–26; 15:26; 16:12–15). It is also exceedingly difficult to know what Jesus might mean in this discourse by referring to the Spirit as *"another* Counselor" if this Counselor was really himself. Indeed, it seems most misleading to refer continually to the Holy Spirit (and the Father) as a distinct "he," a distinct "person," and even go on to ascribe to this "other" personal activities distinct from oneself, if in fact it is all-important (a matter of salvation!) that one's audience understand that one is "really" talking about oneself! If Jesus does not intend to distinguish the Spirit as a distinct way in which God personally exists as God—a distinct "person" of the triune Godhead—by using all of this language, then what on earth is he trying to do? Why speak this way if it is not true? If Jesus is here again simply "using the language of plurality" or "separation," it is all too convincing!

Indeed, it is not apparent what meaning is even left in these passages if we assume a "secret identity" between the three apparent "persons," for everything that is said about the activity of the Spirit here (and elsewhere) is said in relation to the Father and Son. The Spirit is "sent by" and "comes out of" the Father and Son "in the name of" the Son; the Spirit speaks according to the will of the Father, he always testifies of the Son, and so on. If the Spirit is, in fact, personally identical with the Father who is, in fact, identical to the Son, all this language is not only "illusory"—it seems blatantly nonsensical!

The Spirit in Paul's Theology

What is succinctly brought together in the above-cited Johannine discourse is also manifested throughout Paul's writings. Hence we find Paul attributing personal characteristics to the Spirit, while also distinguishing him from God the Father, when we hear him teach that "the Spirit intercedes for the saints in accordance with God's will" (Rom. 8:27). Clearly, the Spirit who intercedes (a personal activity) on our behalf is in some sense personally distinct from the transcendent Father with whom he intercedes.

This personal distinctness comes out again when Paul informs us that "the Spirit searches all things, even the deep things of God" (1 Cor. 2:10). Clearly, some real distinction is being made between the immanent Spirit who through us searches (a personal activity) the depth of God, and the transcendent God whose depth the Spirit searches. This is essentially no different from what we have already learned about the Father/Spirit relationship in John's Gospel.

What is even more remarkable, however, is the manner in which Paul presupposes the personal distinctness of the Spirit from God the Father and the Lord Jesus Christ while also demonstrating his divinity when he speaks of all three in the same context. The personal distinctness of the Spirit is part and parcel of Paul's generally trinitarian way of thinking and speaking about God. The following passages are representative (emphases have been added):

> "There are different kinds of gifts, but the same *Spirit*. There are different kinds of service, but the same *Lord*. There are different kinds of working, but the same *God* works all of them in all men" (1 Cor. 12:4-6).

> "May the grace of the *Lord* Jesus Christ, and the love of *God*, and the fellowship of the *Holy Spirit* be with you all" (2 Cor. 13:14).

> "Because you are sons, *God* sent the *Spirit* of his *Son* into our hearts, the Spirit who calls out, 'Abba, Father'" (Gal. 4:6).

> "For through *him* [Jesus] we both have access to the *Father* by one *Spirit*" (Eph. 2:18).

"There is ... one *Spirit* ... one *Lord* ... one *God* and Father of all
..." (Eph. 4:4–6).

"... *He* [God] saved us through the washing of rebirth and renewal
by the *Holy Spirit*, whom he poured out on us generously through
Jesus Christ our Savior" (Titus 3:5–6).

Similar statements are found throughout Paul's writings (e.g., Rom.
15:16, 30; 2 Cor. 1:21–22; 3:3; Gal. 3:11–14; Eph. 2:22; 3:14, 16–17;
5:17–21; Phil. 3:3; Col. 1:6–8; 2 Thess. 2:13). The Oneness contention that these three "persons" of the Trinity are "really" only different roles or functions that God (who is Jesus) plays simply does not
stand up in the light of such passages as these. The pervasiveness of
this triadic pattern of speech in Paul's writings suggests that this threeness is no incidental feature of God's being and activity. While it would
certainly be too much to read into these passages a fully developed
and formalized doctrine of the Trinity (as in the Nicene Creed), it is
nevertheless clear from these passages that Paul's general train of
thought about God is far removed from the sort of modalism taught by
Oneness Pentecostalism.

There is in these passages simply no suggestion that "the Lord Jesus"
is "really" the one referred to by all three titles, "Father," "Son," and
"Spirit." If this were the case, why, we again ask, would Paul always
and only associate Jesus with the second supposed "office" or "role"
(Lord, Son), and never the first (God the Father) or the third (the
Spirit)? Why would he in all of these passages contrast the Lord Jesus,
the Son, with the Father and the Spirit? And if Paul believed that Jesus
was more than the Son of God, why have so incredibly few believers
(let alone scholars) picked up this belief in his writings throughout
church history?

No, the threefold distinction that is found throughout Paul's letters
is no mere distinction of activity. Rather, these passages suggest that
Paul had come to accept that God himself fully and personally exists and
operates in three genuinely distinct ways. His experience of God's grace
through the risen Lord Jesus and the power of God in the Holy Spirit

had driven Paul, as well as his believing contemporaries, to accept this remarkable conclusion.

God remains, for Paul, the transcendent Holy One of Israel, the Father of the Lord Jesus Christ (2 Cor. 1:3; Eph. 1:3). But Paul also came to see that this same one God dwelled fully as the Son of God in Jesus Christ (Col. 2:9; Titus 2:13) without thereby ceasing to be Father, and also dwelled fully as the Holy Spirit in the church (1 Cor. 3:16; 6:19; 12:13) without thereby ceasing to be Father and Son. And, finally, Paul (with John and the other early Christians) came to believe that this threefoldness did not conceal, but rather revealed, the very inner being of the eternal God. The one true God was eternally triune and thus is revealed as such to us.

It would, of course, take several hundred years of believers and opponents asking questions to iron out all the implications of this belief. This is what ultimately produced the fully developed doctrine of the Trinity in the early fourth century. But that Paul had already arrived at the essence of this doctrine is clear from an unbiased reading of his writings.

The Spirit in Other New Testament Writings

The words of Jesus in John's Gospel and the theology of the apostle Paul are not the only places where one finds a portrayal of the Spirit as being personally distinct from the Father and Son. Nor are Paul and John alone in exhibiting the tendency to speak about God in a triadic manner, placing God the Father, the Lord Jesus, and the Holy Spirit in close proximity to one another while still maintaining their distinctness.

We might first refer to the Gospel recollection of Jesus' baptism, in which the Spirit is represented by a descending dove upon Jesus while the Father confirms Jesus' sonship from heaven (Matt. 3:13–17; Mark 1:9–11; Luke 3:21–22; John 1:31–34). It was the clear threefoldness of events such as these that ultimately led the church to come to its trinitarian understanding of God, and with good reason. For either these passages show us that God can be truly God as transcendent

Father "in heaven" while at the same time being God in the Son and as the Spirit, or this event deceives more than it reveals.

If, as Oneness exegetes have always maintained, Jesus is "really" the one "person" who is both the Father speaking from the sky to himself and the dove descending upon himself—even though Jesus certainly *appears* to be only the Son of God in the river being baptized—then, it seems, Jesus is really a sort of divine ventriloquist (and a very effective one at that, judging from the number of sincere believers who have been fooled by him!). This was actually the explanation that I, as a Oneness questioner, was given regarding this passage by my pastor. The heavenly voice, the dove, the man—all are in fact one "person," simultaneously wearing different masks and acting and speaking through them.

Things are, it seems to Oneness apologists, never as they appear in the Gospels. The God of Oneness theology is a "master of illusion" who is so convincing that the overwhelming majority of those who have ever loved and trusted in Christ have lost out in eternity for not recognizing this!

This same revelatory threefoldness runs throughout the rest of the New Testament. First, we should note that Jesus tells his disciples to "make disciples of all nations, baptizing them in the name of the Father and of the Son and of the Holy Spirit" (Matt. 28:19). If Jesus was "really" intending to refer to himself in this passage, as Oneness exponents insist, it is difficult to imagine a less effective way of doing it!

Along the same lines, the author of Hebrews warns any who "trampled the Son of God . . . and who . . . insulted the Spirit of grace" that they have "only a fearful expectation of judgment and of raging fire that will consume the enemies of God" (Heb. 10:27–29). What coherence does this verse have if the Son of God who is "trampled" and the Spirit of grace who is "insulted" are in fact the same "person"? Only persons can be trampled and insulted, and the fact that the author distinguishes between the one who is trampled and the one who is insulted reveals that he believes the Holy Spirit and the Son are different "persons."

To continue along the same lines, we find this same author utilizing the traditional triadic manner of speech about God when he writes, ". . . This salvation, which was first announced by the *Lord*, was confirmed to us. . . . *God* also testified to it by signs, wonders and various miracles, and gifts of the *Holy Spirit* distributed according to his will" (Heb. 2:3–4, emphasis added).

Similarly, Peter opens his first epistle by addressing the elect "who have been chosen according to the foreknowledge of *God* the Father, through the sanctifying work of the *Spirit*, for obedience to *Jesus Christ* and sprinkling by his blood" (1 Peter 1:2, emphasis added). And, finally, Jude closes his epistle by encouraging his readers, saying, ". . . build yourselves up in your most holy faith and pray in the *Holy Spirit*. Keep yourselves in *God's* love as you wait for the mercy of our *Lord Jesus Christ* . . ." (Jude 20–21, emphasis added).

It should be evident from all these Scriptures—and this is but a small sampling of the triadic passages in the New Testament—that the Holy Spirit was conceived of in personal terms on the one hand, and yet that the Holy Spirit was conceived of as really distinct from the personal Father and the personal Son on the other hand. The distinctness of the Son and the Father, which I demonstrated in the previous chapters, we now see is explicitly paralleled by the distinctness of the Spirit from both the Father and Son.

There is, of course, yet no reflection as to *how* the one true God could fully exist in each of these three ways. Indeed, this theological problem (which both trinitarians and Oneness believers share) yet remains with us, for we inevitably think in quantitative terms. But it seems evident that the early disciples became increasingly aware of this triune reality as they reflected upon their experience of Jesus and the Spirit.

To force on all these passages a modalistic grid that would reduce the distinctness of the Spirit to a mere role, while relocating the relationality of the Father and the Son to a temporary relationship between distinct "natures," would be to fly in the face of the natural meaning and obvious implications of these texts as well as the general testimony of the Word.

Oneness Arguments for Jesus as the Holy Spirit

Having demonstrated that the general portrayal of the Holy Spirit in the New Testament is against the Oneness apologists' understanding of the Spirit, we must now proceed to refute the particular arguments they use to buttress their position.

2 Corinthians 3:17: "The Lord Is the Spirit"

As explained in chapter 1, this passage is the classic prooftext employed by Oneness Pentecostals to establish their identification of Jesus with the Spirit. Do they prove their point? I think there are four interrelated considerations that show conclusively that they do not.

First, one must note that the text does not say that "Jesus is the Spirit." If it *had* said this, the Oneness case would perhaps be stronger than it is, but as it stands the Oneness interpretation must simply assume that the reference to "the Lord" here is a reference to Jesus Christ.

Second, we must note that "Lord" is used by Paul in two senses in the context of this passage. Immediately after referring to the Lord *as* the Spirit, we find Paul referring to this Spirit as "the Spirit *of* the Lord." In the next verse, however, he again calls the Spirit "the Lord." Paul, we see, is clearly making some distinction between "the Lord" and "the Spirit of the Lord" who is also "Lord."

Third, it must be noted that Paul, in keeping with his general theological and literary style, has just distinguished between Christ and the Spirit a few verses prior to 2 Corinthians 3:17 (see 3:3–6). It would be most odd for Paul now to equate them without giving his readers any clue that he is doing so.

Finally, and most decisively, when read in its entire context, verse 17 of chapter 3 is most easily understood as being an explanatory note on Paul's usage of Exodus 34:34 in verses 7–16, and this understanding rules out the Oneness interpretation of this verse. Throughout this passage Paul is contrasting the old covenant of the law ("the letter"), which "kills," with the new covenant of the Spirit, which "gives life" (vv. 3–6). Paul finds it significant, however, that even the condemning covenant of the law "came with glory," as evidenced by the fact that Moses' face temporarily radiated after receiving the Lord's foundational instruction for this covenant (v. 7). For this reason he had to place a veil over his face to protect the eyes of the Israelites. When he would himself be in the presence of the Lord, however, his veil would be lifted (v. 16, quoting Exod. 34:34).

From this fact Paul makes two points. First, if the covenant of the letter came with that much glory, "the ministry of the Spirit" cannot fail to possess "even more" glory (v. 8). Second, whereas the glory of the Lord was concealed under a veil in the covenant of the law, this glory is to be openly proclaimed and manifested on the face of each believer with the new covenant (vv. 12, 13, 18). As was the case with Moses, the veil is lifted "whenever anyone turns to the Lord" (v. 16, cf. Exod. 34:34).

It is immediately after this that Paul adds his explanatory note: "Now the Lord is the Spirit, and where the Spirit of the Lord is, there is freedom" (v.17). What point is Paul making here? Is Paul intending to identify Jesus with the Spirit? Not at all. Coming on the heels of verse 16 as it does, Paul is clearly saying that "the Lord" *to whom he has just referred*—"the Lord" spoken of in Exodus 34:34, the one in whose presence Moses and all believers have the veil lifted—"is the Spirit"—namely, the Spirit he has been talking about throughout this entire chapter (vv. 3, 6, 8).

The episode with Moses, in other words, symbolizes for Paul the abiding contrast between the covenant of the law and the covenant of the Spirit. The glory of the former was veiled; the greater glory of the latter is unveiled. The former had an external legal authority and was killing; the latter is written on the heart, is life-giving, and is freeing (vv. 3, 6, 16, 18). All this becomes clear when we understand that "the Lord" to whom Moses turned is the same Lord, the same Spirit, to whom believers today turn to have the veil lifted. The Oneness reading of this passage completely misses this point. It reads into the text an agenda that Paul never had.

Romans 8:9–11: Christ and the Spirit of Christ

This is the second of the two passages in which Oneness exponents feel that Christ is explicitly equated with the Holy Spirit. The passage seems to equate "the Spirit," "Spirit of God," "Spirit of Christ," "Christ," and "the Spirit of him who raised Jesus from the dead" (i.e., the Spirit of the Father) by using these terms seemingly interchangeably, thereby serving as a perfect prooftext for the Oneness contention that all these titles refer to one and the same "person."

In response, it can hardly be denied that Paul is here using these terms more or less interchangeably, but it can and must certainly be denied that this has the significance of revealing that Paul thinks of Jesus and the Spirit as being in every sense one and the same "person"— and hence that the dozens of other passages where Paul clearly distinguishes between them (including twice just preceding this verse [8:1–4]) are really only "distinctions of activity."

A closer reading of this passage is all that is needed to square it with Paul's general theology of the Spirit. Romans 8:9 reads as follows: "You . . . are controlled . . . by the Spirit, if the Spirit of God lives in you. And if anyone does not have the Spirit of Christ, he does not belong to Christ." While there is in this passage no discernable distinction between "Spirit of God" and "Spirit of Christ" dwelling within the believer, the passage does require some real distinction to be made between "the Spirit of Christ" and the "Christ" to whom we belong because of his Spirit. The former dwells within us and sanctifies us; the latter is incarnate and his death atones for our sins.

Paul is, I believe, saying that unless one has the Spirit who produces faith in Christ and produces Christ's character—"the Spirit of Christ"— he or she is not a part of the body of the One who died for our sins and rose for our salvation. He or she is yet controlled by "the sinful nature."

This distinction is then broadened to include the Father in verse 11 when Paul writes: "And if the Spirit of him who raised Jesus from the dead is living in you, he who raised Christ from the dead will also give life to your mortal bodies through his Spirit, who lives in you." This verse clearly distinguishes between the *Father* who raised Jesus up, the *Spirit* by whom Jesus was raised up, and *Jesus* who was raised up. There is simply no getting around the real, personal, threefold distinction embodied in this passage. That Paul in the previous verse refers to the

Spirit of Christ as "Christ in you" cannot legitimately be used to qualify this. In this pre-polemical environment, this informal use of language has no more significance than simply revealing how closely together Paul associated the Spirit with Jesus. The Spirit is indeed the presence of Christ himself (see Acts 16:7, 9; 2 Cor. 13:5; Eph. 3:17). But far from being denied in this passage, the distinctness between the Spirit and Jesus (and Father) is actually presupposed throughout this passage.

Cross-Referencing Oneness Arguments

If we keep in mind the relative informality of the pre-polemical language of the New Testament and the precariousness of basing any doctrine on cross-referencing alone, we shall have little difficulty in dismissing the host of other cross-referencing arguments employed by Oneness adherents to establish their doctrine.

For example, in John 5:21, 25 and 6:40, Jesus declares that he shall raise believers up from the dead on the last day. In Romans 8:11, however, believers are portrayed as being raised up by the Holy Spirit. Oneness believers conclude from this that Jesus must himself be the Holy Spirit.

This is really simply a variation of the argument that futilely attempted to use these same verses to argue that Jesus is the Father (see ch. 3). Our answer is similar and may, therefore, be succinctly stated.

In the Johannine passages, Jesus explicitly tells us that he received this authority to raise the dead from the Father, that he gives this gift of immortality "just as the Father raises the dead," and that it is the Son of God (namely, himself) who has received this authority (cf. 5:19–27). How then can anyone fly in the face of this explicit statement and say that Jesus is here speaking "as the Spirit" (or "as the Father")? He identifies himself as the Son and speaks of the Father as distinct from himself!

In contrast, the classical doctrine of the Trinity has no difficulty in letting these verses say what they clearly say, for in trinitarian theology the Father, the Son, and the Spirit can individually be said to raise the dead because, as God, each one does raise the dead. All activities of

God flow *from* the Father, *through* the Son, and are carried out *in the power of* the Holy Spirit. The act is one act, performed by one God, but involving all three ways in which God is God.

The trinitarian understanding of God also has no trouble accommodating the fact that Scripture can alternatively speak of both Jesus and the Spirit "abiding in" (Matt. 28:20; John 14:16, 18; Acts 2:38; 2 Cor. 13:5), "comforting" (John 14:16, 18), and "sanctifying" (Eph. 5:26; 1 Peter 1:2) believers. Only by a most forced form of exegesis can these passages be made to mean that Christ and the Holy Spirit are in every respect one and the same. It certainly is not the intent of any of these passages to teach such a thing, and thus we must be very suspicious when someone pastes them together with one another in order to wring such a meaning out of them.

It is far less intrusive to these texts to understand that the Holy Spirit, while being distinct from Christ, is nevertheless the very presence of Christ here on earth. Hence, Jesus can throughout John 14 through 16 refer to "another Counselor" who will come to his disciples, or he can alternatively say, "I will come unto you." Christ is not here implying that there is no real distinction between him and the Holy Spirit (rendering the other 22 third-person references to the Spirit in these three chapters "illusory" or "poetic"). Rather, he is simply teaching that all that he is shall be present in the "person" of the Holy Spirit. This is exactly what trinitarian theology would expect, since, as we have said, all of God is involved in each personal way in which God is God.

These passages are proclaiming that believers can experience the very love, joy, peace, and holiness of Jesus himself when they experience the indwelling Holy Spirit whom he and the Father have sent to us. Hence, too, we can understand that it is Jesus himself who through his Spirit abides in us, comforts us, will never leave us or forsake us, and sanctifies us by his grace.

Indeed, so intertwined and completely indivisible is the threefold way in which God is God that Jesus can even refer to the coming of the Spirit as the coming of the Father and the Son together: ". . . *we* will come to him and make our home with him" (John 14:23, emphasis added). This use of the first-person plural is entirely inexplicable on

Oneness terms—I, as a Oneness proselytizer, avoided it like the plague!—but on trinitarian terms it makes perfect sense and proclaims something wonderful.[2] The verse implies that the very same loving sociality that eternally characterizes the triune God has been implanted in the believer's heart by the indwelling Spirit. God's internal dynamic of love has been "opened up," as it were, to include undeserving creatures such as us, who apart from God's grace want only to be at war with God (cf. John 17:21–26; 2 Peter 1:4). Their preoccupation with "the absolute Oneness" of God prevents Oneness Pentecostals from appreciating this most glorious aspect of the Good News.

There are other cross-referencing arguments attempting to show that Jesus is identical with the Holy Spirit, but their misguided logic is virtually the same and our reply is the same. Thus, Oneness exponents frequently ask, "How can Jesus say that he shall provide his disciples with what they should say in Luke 21:15, while the parallel in Mark 13:11 attributes this to the Holy Spirit?" Or, "How can both the Spirit and Jesus be portrayed as intercessors for believers?" (Rom. 8:26; Heb. 7:25).

Such questions, I hope it is now clear, are based on an unsound hermeneutics. The Lord simply did not give us the Bible to treat like some jigsaw puzzle, the correct completion of which is a condition for salvation! There are no "secret" keys that unlock the "hidden mysteries" of "who Jesus really is." Cults of all sorts flourish on just such an esoteric concept, and it gives these groups a certain elitist, exclusivistic twist. But, for just this reason, they distort the clear teaching of God's Word.

No, while there are indeed some passages in Scripture that are "hard to understand" (2 Peter 3:16), certainly the proclamation of who Jesus is and God's beautiful plan of salvation ring through with crystal clarity:

> "For God so loved the world that he gave his one and only Son, that whoever believes in him shall not perish but have eternal life" (John 3:16).

> "But these are written that you may believe that Jesus is the Christ, the Son of God, and that by believing you may have life in his name" (John 20:31).

Baptism, Salvation, and The Name

We have thus far demonstrated that the Oneness view of God and of Christ and the Oneness rejection of the Trinity are unbiblical. However, while the antitrinitarianism of Oneness Pentecostalism constitutes its most blatant and fundamentally damaging heresy, its denial of the Trinity is hardly its only heretical belief. This is really quite typical. Historically speaking, heresies have almost always "come in packages."

No Trinity—No Salvation by Grace

More specifically, groups that have denied the doctrine of the Trinity, opting either for a modalistic or for an Arian view of the Father, Son, and Holy Spirit, have almost always held to a number of other

131

esoteric and unhealthy beliefs, particularly in regard to the doctrine of salvation by grace.

The theological reason for this is that the doctrine of the Trinity, far from being a "merely speculative" piece of church theologizing, is intrinsically connected with everything else that is distinctly Christian. As we shall see in chapter 8, without this doctrine the reality of God's eternal love and self-sufficiency, as well as the authenticity of God's self-revelation, God's sacrificial love on the cross, and thus of God's grace, is undermined. It is not a coincidence, then, that antitrinitarian groups as otherwise diverse as (for example) the Jehovah's Witnesses, the United Pentecostal Church, and the Worldwide Church of God all arrive at a sub-Christian view of God and an aberrant, legalistic view of salvation.

To speak specifically concerning the United Pentecostal Church and related Oneness Pentecostal groups, the denial of the Trinity results in an understanding of salvation that exchanges the perfect security and the total sufficiency of the work of Christ on the cross for the "security" of a precise baptismal formula ("Jesus' Name baptism"), the "security" of a momentary and sometimes questionable experience (speaking in tongues), and the very shallow "security" of one's own ability to keep a prescribed set of rules (the standards). Oneness adherents claim that if any of these so-called prerequisites for salvation are absent or are altered, one cannot hope to be saved.

We do well to note the extremity of the chasm existing between these two distinct sources of security and the difference between the two views of God they entail. The God of orthodox Christianity is a God who loves undeserving, vile sinners with an unconditional love, a God who voluntarily suffers on the cross the hellish nightmare that the sin of these sinners produces, in order that they might share in the heavenly dream he has for them. This is a God who sent his own eternal Son and gave his own eternal Spirit to envelop these sinners with his own eternal love and cause them to share in the eternal joy of this eternal triune fellowship.

But, in Oneness theology, this beautiful relational God of the New Testament has been traded in for a nit-picky God of solitude who is compulsively obsessed with prescribed baptismal formulas and modes and who will eternally damn any of his "children" who don't get it right! He has been exchanged for a God who would hold back the "gift" of salvation for months or even years (sometimes entire lifetimes) while sincere believing individuals "seek for the Holy Ghost with the evidence of speaking in tongues"—trying desperately to find out what flaw in their life is preventing the Holy Spirit from coming and hence preventing them from speaking in tongues and being saved! And the God of unconditional love and grace has here been rejected in favor of a God who may instantly withdraw his love and salvation in a moment, even after these first two conditions are met, if the tentative candidate for heaven (one is never more than that) does not obediently follow the meticulous rules for holy living that this God has purportedly commanded!

The depth of error involved in these misconceptions of salvation can hardly be exaggerated and (I speak from experience) can be extremely damaging at a spiritual and psychological level. It is certainly difficult to holistically and genuinely love a God who is so capricious, especially one who would hang all eternity on points so minute and so ambiguous that the great majority of Christians who have ever loved God and his Word have (supposedly) completely missed them.

Indeed, the thought that such a being might actually be in charge of the universe is, I think, a truly terrifying notion. And, in my estimation, the most fundamental reason why such a scary and radically unbiblical view of God and salvation was ever arrived at was that Oneness theology divorced what they think God "really is" (namely, "absolutely one") from who God "appears to be" in the New Testament. In a word, the doctrine of the eternal Trinity was rejected in Oneness theology. God here "plays the role" and "wears the masks" of Father, Son, and Spirit; God creates the appearance, the "illusion," of the Father loving the Son and suffering over the sacrifice of "his one and only Son." But "really" these are simply different "modes" and "natures" *appearing* to interrelate, act, and feel. God is three *temporary things* to us *humans*, but the "who" of God remains hidden.

It is, then, not surprising that the Oneness view of salvation has replaced the traditional Protestant exclusive trust in who God is and what God has accomplished for us through Jesus Christ with a view of salvation that requires individuals to place their trust ultimately in what they think *they* can and have done for God, rather than the other way around. They have, they suppose, pleased God with their baptism and with the correctness of the formula used in baptism. They have "purified themselves" enough to merit receiving the Holy Spirit and have proven this to other Oneness believers by speaking in tongues. And they have attempted to keep God from rejecting them by keeping the rules that are to set God's people apart as holy. But it is difficult to imagine a theology that could be much further from the religion of Paul, Luther, and the entire Reformation!

When one cannot derive one's total worth and wholeness ("salvation") from trusting Jesus alone—and the Oneness view of God has just this effect—one must futilely attempt to derive this needed wholeness from other religious ideas, activities, or experiences. One is thus forced to make idols of such things as baptism, tongues, and idiosyncratic rules. *When one's God is hidden, one must grab onto gods more tangible.* Hence, in the end, antitrinitarianism and legalism are intrinsically related. Historically, they have almost always gone hand in hand.

The Oneness View of Baptism

Directly related to both the Oneness view of salvation and the Oneness denial of the Trinity is the Oneness view of baptism. In the remainder of this chapter we will look, first, at the Oneness teaching that baptism is a prerequisite for salvation, and second, at the Oneness teaching that baptism must be administered using the formula "in Jesus' name."

Baptismal Regeneration

Oneness Pentecostals teach that baptism in water is an absolute prerequisite for salvation. This position is commonly called "baptismal regeneration" because it holds that one is "regenerated" only

when he or she is baptized. It is not unique to the Oneness movement. It is also taught by the Catholic Church and by the hard-line
wing of the Church of Christ.

There are several passages that baptismal-regenerationists use in
an attempt to substantiate their position. In Acts 2:38, the classic
prooftext for the Oneness view of salvation, Peter responds to the
Jews' question about salvation by saying, "Repent and be baptized,
every one of you, in the name of Jesus Christ, for the forgiveness of
your sins. . . ." Again, Ananias is reported to have told Saul, shortly
after his conversion, to "Get up, be baptized and wash your sins away
. . ." (Acts 22:16). Along the same lines, Peter seems to suggest that the
manner in which Noah's ark saved his family "through water" is a
symbol of the "baptism that now saves you" (1 Peter 3:20–21). This,
it is further maintained, is no different from what Jesus meant when
he told Nicodemus that "no one can enter the kingdom of God unless
he is born of water and the Spirit" (John 3:5), the water here referring
to baptism. And Paul, it is argued, reveals that he sees baptism as
mandatory for salvation when he tells the Romans that "all of us who
were baptized into Christ Jesus were baptized into his death. We were
therefore buried with him through baptism into death . . ." (Rom.
6:3–4; cf. Gal. 3:27; Titus 3:5). According to the United Pentecostal
Church and most other Oneness groups, then, unless we are baptized, we have not died with Christ and our sins are not forgiven.

Let it first be acknowledged that the passages used by Oneness
Pentecostals (and other baptismal-regenerationists) in defense of their
position *do* show that baptism was regarded as being an essential
aspect of the ordinary saving experience of early believers. In the
strongest possible terms, baptism is associated with one's being united
with Christ (Rom. 6:4–5), with one's "putting on" Christ (Gal. 3:27),
with the forgiveness of sins (Acts 2:38), and, paralleling the Old Testament practice of circumcision, with one's becoming a member of
the New Covenant community (Col. 2:11–12). There is nothing to
indicate that this act was perceived as being in any sense peripheral to
the gospel. It was in ordinary cases (with some possible exceptions,

cf. 1 Cor. 1:15–17) the first thing Christians did after responding in faith to the gospel message (see Acts 2:38; 8:34–38; 10:45–48).

This is not, however, the same as saying that salvation was ever seen as being directly contingent upon baptism. The continual insistence in the New Testament that it is faith, and faith alone, that saves a person is itself enough to prove this (e.g., John 3:15, 36; 5:24; Acts 2:21; 10:43; 15:9; 16:31; Rom. 1:17; 3:22–30; 4:3, 5; 5:1; 9:30; 10:9–13; Acts 15:9, etc.). At least sixty times in the New Testament, eternal salvation is explicitly tied to faith and/or repentance with no mention of baptism. Relatedly, Paul, who conceives of baptism as paralleled with Old Testament circumcision (Col. 2:11–12), explicitly argues that Abraham was justified by God *before* he was circumcised (Rom. 4:9–12). As important as circumcision was, it was for Abraham a "sign" and "seal" of the righteousness he had by faith. This seems to be how Paul thought of baptism. The fact that the thief on the cross could be saved without being baptized further corroborates this point (Luke 23:42–43; cf. 18:9–14).

The passages adduced by the Oneness Pentecostals do not prove the contrary. First, the fact that Peter commands the Jews in his Pentecost sermon to be baptized "for [*eis*] the forgiveness of sins" does not entail that the forgiveness of sins comes as a direct result of baptism. The preposition *eis* in Greek can simply mean "with a view towards," "in connection with," or "in the light of." If this interpretation is meant, Peter is in this passage simply saying that baptism should follow the repentance that has brought about the forgiveness of sins (cf. Acts 15:9). The act of divine forgiveness renders baptism important and significant.

This further makes sense out of the fact that in Peter's next two recorded sermons to unbelievers in Acts, he directly associates the forgiveness of sins with repentance and faith in Christ without even mentioning baptism (3:17–26; 4:8–12). Paul preaches in a similar fashion (Acts 16:31). Indeed, Paul tells us that he rarely baptized people at all, since this was not his calling (1 Cor. 1:15–17). It would, I think, be quite impossible to see how this could be if he or anyone else believed there was a direct causal relationship between baptism and divine forgiveness. How could an apostle of Christ not be called to bring people into a forgiven relationship with the Father?

The Oneness understanding of baptism is also difficult to square with the fact that the Holy Spirit, we learn from Acts, is sometimes given in a dramatic fashion *before* individuals are baptized in water (Acts 10:44–48). Is one thus to suppose that God poured out his Spirit in this fashion upon people whose sins he had not yet forgiven? This reversal of the Acts 2:38 baptism-Spirit order is, I think, enough to tell us that we should not take Acts 2:38 as a sort of ironclad formula to which God is bound. It is also enough, I believe, to teach us that the remission of sins is not causally connected with water baptism.

What closes the case on this, however, is the recognition that Luke and Mark use this exact same phrase, "for [*eis*] the forgiveness of sins," in relation to the baptism of John the Baptist (Luke 3:3; cf. Mark 1:4). Yet John's baptism clearly did not, in any literal sense, wash away people's sins. Why else would his disciples need to believe on Jesus for the forgiveness of their sins and be rebaptized (Acts 19:4–6)?

The parallel passage in Matthew says that John's baptism was a baptism "with water for [*eis*] repentance" (Matt. 3:11; cf. Acts 19:4), and this seems to be equivalent with the phrase "for [or unto] the forgiveness of sins." The act of being baptized certainly didn't *bring about* repentance. Rather, baptism was the result of repentance, and it derived its significance from the act of repentance. In just the same way, the act of being baptized, both for John and Christ's disciples, didn't literally bring about the forgiveness of sins. Baptism was the *result* of the forgiveness of sins that had already occurred, and the act derived its significance from this divine act.

The other passages used by baptismal-regenerationists are no stronger in proving their case. In fact, far from showing the regenerationist view of baptism, 1 Peter 3:21 can most easily be read to show the opposite. The entire passage reads:

> . . . In it [the ark] only a few people, eight in all, were saved through water, and this water symbolizes baptism that now saves you also—not the removal of dirt from the body but the pledge of a good conscience

toward God. It saves you by the resurrection of Jesus Christ, who has gone into heaven. . . . [1 Peter 3:20–22]

The author is here drawing a double analogy: The water of the flood is to baptism what baptism is to our present salvation. That he is here talking symbolically is clear not only from the fact that he explicitly says he is talking symbolically, but also from the fact that he goes on to clarify that he is not talking about any literal washing or "removal of dirt from the body," as though the water had any efficacy in itself, but about baptism as a "pledge of a good conscience toward God." The reality that brings forth baptism is the act of repentance and the forgiveness of sins that produces the saint's "good conscience."

Turning to John 3:5, there is simply no decisive reason to think that Jesus is referring to baptism when he says that one must be "born of water." It is certainly difficult to suppose that Nicodemus would have understood "water" as referring to the not-yet-existent ritual of Christian baptism. What is more, the subject matter of this entire passage is the activity of the Holy Spirit in contrast to the flesh, and it would be most awkward for Jesus to disrupt this train of thought midstream with a reference to a still-future ritual. Hence it seems most likely that "water" is being used as a metaphorical synonym for "Spirit" in verse 5.

What further supports this conclusion is the fact that Jesus speaks in a similar manner, but with a different analogy, three verses later. Here being "born of the Spirit" (no mention of water this time) is likened to the wind blowing (John 3:8). But, clearly, being born of the Spirit and being born by the wind are not two different things. Then why think being "born of water" and being "born of the Spirit" are distinct?

In keeping with other sections of John and of other New Testament writings, it seems most reasonable to assume that water here symbolizes the life and purification ("washing") that the Spirit brings, just as the wind symbolizes the freedom by which the Spirit moves (cf. John 4:10–15; 7:38; 1 Cor. 6:11; Eph. 5:26; Titus 3:5; Rev. 22:1).

In fact, this religiously symbolic use of water was common in ancient Near Eastern thought, and Nicodemus would have readily picked up on this.

The general teaching of Scripture, then, is that those who believe on the Lord Jesus Christ shall be saved. Baptism, obedient living, a transformed life, and many other aspects of the Christian life will ordinarily in due time result from this saving faith. But salvation is not itself the result of any of these things. And the few references that some have supposed to teach the contrary, I have shown to be mistaken.

The Baptismal Formula: "In Jesus' Name"

It should be pointed out that, historically speaking, the Oneness belief that baptism should be performed "in Jesus' name" or "in the name of the Lord Jesus Christ," rather than with the traditional trinitarian formula, actually preceded the Oneness doctrine of God. The "New Issue" that ultimately resulted in a split between the trinitarian and nontrinitarian Pentecostals in the second decade of this century was originally an issue only over the correct baptismal formula. Indeed, the belief that baptism should be done "in Jesus' name" was the principal factor that ultimately led to the belief that Jesus is himself the Father, Son, and Holy Spirit.

In an attempt to harmonize Matthew 28:19, in which Jesus commands his disciples to baptize "in the name of the Father and of the Son and of the Holy Spirit," with the Book of Acts, which, it was thought, always employed the formula "in the name of Jesus Christ [or 'the Lord Jesus']" (Acts 2:38; 8:16; 10:48; 19:5), certain enthusiastic and very uninformed believers in the early Pentecostal movement concluded that the name of the Father, Son, and Holy Spirit must be Jesus. "Father," "Son," and "Holy Spirit," it was pointed out, are not proper "names," but only titles. But "Jesus" is a proper name and hence must be *the* proper name referred to by all three of these titles. Indeed, it was reasoned, why else would "the name" of Matthew 28:19 be singular? These are still the basic arguments used by Oneness Pentecostal groups today (Bernard, New Birth, 170–80; Graves, 143f.; Fauss, ch. 2; #105; #6109; #6146).

Hence, it was and is argued, the singular "name" of the Father, Son, and Holy Spirit is "Jesus Christ." A variation of this argument is the contention that the titles "Father," "Son," and "Holy Spirit" respectively correspond to the formula "Lord Jesus Christ," since "the Father was always called 'Lord'; the Son was called 'Jesus'; and the 'Holy Ghost' means the anointed of God, or the 'Christ'" (#6111). In any case, the Oneness view is that Jesus is ultimately referring to himself in Matthew 28:19, and from this it follows that he must himself be the Father, Son, and Holy Spirit.

Several other passages are frequently utilized to prove that the only valid baptism is baptism administered "in Jesus' name." In 1 Corinthians 1:13 Paul asks the divisive Corinthians, "Is Christ divided? Was Paul crucified for you? Were you baptized into the name of Paul?" The implication, it is argued, was that the Corinthians were not baptized in the name of Paul, but in the name of the one who was in fact crucified for them, namely, Jesus Christ.

Another often-quoted verse to substantiate the necessity of Jesus' Name baptism is Acts 4:12, in which Peter tells us that salvation is found only in Jesus, ". . . for there is no other name under heaven given to men by which we must be saved." Only the name of Jesus has power to save, it is argued, and thus only the calling out of this name during a person's baptism is efficacious in saving that person (Bernard, New Birth, 160; Fauss, 29). In the Oneness view, baptism in the trinitarian formula is invalid and thus unsaving.

What is more, Paul says that "whatever you do, whether in word or deed, do it all in the name of the Lord Jesus . . ." (Col. 3:17). Since water baptism is clearly a "deed," it is frequently argued, it should be performed in Jesus' name.

Our first response to the Oneness view of the baptismal formula is to recall what has been demonstrated in the first five chapters of this book: namely, that there is absolutely no reason to suspect that Jesus is himself God the Father and the Holy Spirit of God as well as being the Son of God. Hence, if Jesus is in fact referring to himself alone in

Matthew 28:19 as Father, Son, and Holy Spirit, this is the only place in the entirety of Scripture where he or anyone else does so, and he would be doing so in contradiction to everything else that is said about the distinctness of the Father, Son, and Holy Spirit.

This renders it a most unlikely supposition that the disciples understood him to be referring to himself with this command and that they therefore baptized in his own proper name. The fact that no one else in church history interpreted Jesus' command in this fashion confirms this opinion. Thus, even if the earliest disciples did in fact baptize "in Jesus' name," it should at least be very clear that they did not do so with the "Oneness" significance that Oneness Pentecostals attach to it.

A brief word about church history may be in order here. The more informed Oneness Pentecostals like to argue that Jesus' Name baptism was practiced not only in Acts but in the second and third centuries as well. And, indeed, there does exist a small amount of evidence to this effect. The *Shepherd of Hermas*, the *Didache*, and the gnostic-tending *Acts of Peter* and *Acts of Paul* all mention baptism "in the name of the Lord" or "in the name of Jesus," and this may (or may not, as we shall see) denote a formula used during baptism in these second- and third-century works (see, for example, Bernard, New Birth, ch. 10; Chalfant, ch. 5).

But, even if this is granted, in none of these works does this formula have anything like the theological significance that Oneness Pentecostals attach to it. Far from equating Jesus with the Father, the *Shepherd of Hermas* tends to subordinate Jesus to the Father and even at times to make him out to be an angel. The *Didache* not only mentions "baptism in the name of the Lord" but also prescribes pouring water on a person's head three times (showing that the author certainly did not think of the three titles as referring to one name) when baptizing them "in the name of the Father, Son, and Holy Spirit" (*Didache* 7:1–3). Similarly, both the third-century *Acts of Peter* and the *Acts of Paul* refer to the trinitarian formula or mode for baptism alongside the supposed "Jesus only" formula, and both works, though not fully orthodox, are clearly trinitarian in their general thrust.

For good reason, then, no scholar has ever suspected these works of being modalistic because of their baptismal formula. The point is that even if the phrase "in Jesus' name" is taken to be some sort of baptismal formula in these works, it carries no Oneness significance. What is more, the fact that it is used alongside the trinitarian formula shows that no real importance was placed on it. Either the phrase "in Jesus' name" is a formula that was at times used in place of, or alongside of, the trinitarian formula, or, more likely, the phrase is not to be taken as a formula at all.

The final thing to be said about this is that even if the "Jesus' name" formula was occasionally used in the second and third centuries, no recognized scholar disputes that from the beginning of the second century on, the *dominant* formula for baptism was the trinitarian one of Matthew 28:19. But if in fact the original formula had been "in Jesus' name" and saving significance was attached to this, this could not have been the case. One must, at the very least, expect that the introduction of a "new" formula would have caused a good bit of controversy. Yet, as a matter of fact, there is not one shred of evidence to this effect. The early church quibbled about a good many issues, but the use of the trinitarian formula was not one of them.

Returning, then, to the Matthean passage, Oneness writings have always placed much emphasis on the fact that "the name" in Matthew 28:19 is singular, for, they argue, this suggests that there is only *one* name, *one* person, to whom the three titles "Father," "Son," and "Holy Spirit" apply. This argument is found in virtually all Oneness tracts on baptism and is one of the most effective and frequently used arguments in evangelizing uninformed trinitarian Christians. Is there anything to this argument? In my estimation, there is none.

If the concept of "the name" is understood in its original first-century Jewish milieu, no theological significance can be attached to its singularity in the Matthean formula. The phrase "in the name of" was a common one in Jewish religious circles and had a wide variety of applications. It could mean simply "in relationship to," as when a slave who was being set free would be ceremonially immersed "in the name of freedom." Obviously "freedom" is not here a proper name.

The phrase could also mean something like "with respect to its intention," as when an offering would be slaughtered "in the name of . . . the offering . . . the offer . . . God . . . the altar fires . . . and the sweet savour." Note that the singular "name" is followed by a multitude of things, including God. Does this singularity mean there is one person to whom all these things apply? Of course not.[1]

Again, the phrase "in the name of" could simply mean "with an obligation towards" or "in the authority of," as when the Samaritans would circumcise their young men "in the name of Mount Gerizim," or when a disciple would teach or do a work "in the name of" a principle of behavior, a truth, or perhaps his master or rabbi.[2]

The bottom line is that there need be nothing theologically significant about the singularity of "the name" in Matthew 28:19. There is, then, absolutely no historical or biblical justification to interpret this verse the way the Oneness groups do. When Jesus commands us to baptize "in the name of the Father and of the Son and of the Holy Spirit," he is not cryptically making some esoteric self-reference that must be decoded for believers to be baptized correctly and therefore saved. He is simply saying that Christian baptism should be done "with a view towards" or "in the light of" what the Father, Son, and the Holy Spirit have accomplished in salvation history and in their individual lives.

It was the Father's sending the Son and coming to us by the Spirit that made salvation possible, and the power of the Holy Spirit enables us to go through the Son to the Father and experience salvation (Eph. 2:18). Hence, the act of baptism, which proclaims this salvation and initiates us into the community of believers, should be done "in consideration of," "in appreciation of," "in the light of," and thus "in the name of" the Father and the Son and the Holy Spirit.

The Oneness Pentecostals *are* right about one aspect of their interpretation of Matthew 28:19: namely, that there is no indication that Jesus intended his baptismal command to be taken as a precise liturgical formula. To perform an act "in the name of" someone (or something), we have seen, does not mean that one must verbally repeat the name of this person (or thing) when doing the act. Oneness Pentecostals fail, however, to apply this same insight to their interpretation of the baptismal passages of Acts.

Because the Semitic phrase "in the name of" could have such a wide variety of meanings, there is no more reason to take the Acts phrase "in the name of Jesus" as an audible liturgical formula than there is to think that the Matthean formula was to be taken like this. When Paul says that the Christian is to do everything "in the name of the Lord Jesus" (Col. 3:17), does he mean that we must pronounce his name before each and every one of our activities? Of course not.

Consistent with this, there are actually a great number of Scriptures that speak of a person's doing something "in the name of" another. Hence, for example, we read in Matthew that Jesus said:

> "He who receives you receives Me, and he who receives Me receives Him who sent Me. He who receives a prophet in the name [*eis onoma*] of a prophet shall receive a prophet's reward; and he who receives a righteous man in the name of a righteous man shall receive a righteous man's reward. And whoever in the name of a disciple gives to one of these little ones even a cup of cold water to drink, truly I say to you he shall not lose his reward." [10:40–42 NASB]

Here the phrase "in the name of" clearly only means something like "on behalf of" or "by the authority of." It has nothing to do with a magical formula said during an act. So it is in a multitude of other passages and, indeed, so it most likely is in Acts. When it is said that certain believers were baptized "in the name of the Lord Jesus," this need mean nothing more than what is meant by giving a cup of cold water to someone "in the name of a disciple." It merely means that baptism "for the forgiveness of sins" derives its significance and beauty from the person of Jesus Christ to whom it centrally points.

Further evidence that we are not dealing with a rigid formula invested with saving significance in the Book of Acts is to be found in the flexibility with which the supposed "formula" is identified. Literally, Acts 2:38 has "on [*epi*] the name of Jesus Christ"; Acts 8:16 and 19:5 have "into [*eis*] the name of the Lord Jesus"; and Acts 10:48 has "in [*en*] the name of the Lord," with some manuscripts adding "Jesus Christ" or simply "Jesus." This hardly sounds like a fixed formula upon which all eternity hangs![3] There is simply no evidence before the fourth century that the words spoken over a candidate at baptism were any big deal. Thus, to take the phrases in Acts and make them into a magical incantation upon which God's forgiveness rests is to grossly misunderstand the phrase and, consequently, grossly misportray the kind of God whom Scripture reveals.

Beyond all this evidence, however, what has to constitute the strongest objection to the Oneness understanding of baptism is the incredible view of God that it presupposes. This view, I would argue, really presents a return to a form of paganism in which it is believed that deities can be manipulated to behave in certain ways by the utilization of certain incantations and formulas invoked by devotees. In this view, saying the correct formula somehow causes God to forgive your sins; saying a different formula, however, prevents God from forgiving your sins.

In other words, the God presupposed in this theology will damn a person on a technicality. Love is not enough for this God! The work of the cross is not enough for this God! Thus his own grace and righteousness are not enough for his people! Salvation here hangs not on what God has done for someone who accepts him, but on the technical correctness of a procedure that the believer performs for God!

In contrast to everything the Reformation stood for, salvation among Oneness Pentecostals cannot be understood as an unconditional, loving, divinely established relationship that cuts through all the sin and failings of otherwise hopeless sinners. Rather, it consists of a relationship that will never even be started until certain technically right words are pronounced and certain technically right deeds are carried out. In the Oneness view, salvation is not a relationship between a passionately loving Father and his undeserving children. It is more like a relationship between a meticulous, perfectionistic employer and his fearful employees.

In my estimation, therefore, the God of Oneness Pentecostalism is an intensely compulsive God who wagers the eternal salvation or damnation of a soul on a "truth" so obscure that all the great saints and scholars throughout church history have completely missed it. And this, I believe, is not even close to the gracious God revealed in the Son of God, Jesus Christ.

7

Was the Early Church Oneness?

hroughout this work we have seen that the Oneness doctrine of God does not square with Scripture. This ultimately is the ground upon which the error of any theological opinion must be exposed. But, while this is the decisive consideration in the judging of any theological opinion, it is not the only consideration. I want now to submit that the teachings of those Christian leaders who immediately succeeded the apostles are also very relevant to this affair.

The reasoning here is simple: Religious traditions take time to change. Indeed, from the study of world religions we learn that religious traditions, once established, are among the most stable aspects of all human culture. They are inherently conservative and resistant to change. Hence it may be safely assumed that the less time the tradition of the apostolic teaching had to be corrupted, the less likely it is that it *was* corrupted. This assumption is especially warranted in light of

147

the fact that the early post-apostolic Fathers were all self-consciously trying to preserve and protect the apostolic teachings.[1]

An examination of the teachings of the earliest post-apostolic Fathers, therefore, should provide for us very relevant information as to whether or not the Oneness Pentecostals are correct in claiming that the original apostolic teaching was that Jesus is himself the Father, Son, and Holy Spirit. For, if the apostles did teach this, it is virtually inconceivable that Christian leaders in the two following generations would have, or could have, intentionally or unintentionally failed to teach this. Yet that is exactly what one is required to believe if one is to accept the Oneness adherents' claim that they possess the "original" New Testament teaching on the Godhead. For, I shall show, it is indisputable that none of the earliest Fathers were at all close to holding the Oneness doctrine.

Indeed, what is perhaps even more damaging to the Oneness view is that there is not even a trace of anyone's arguing for or against modalism until the late second or early third century. Hence, to accept the Oneness claim, one must accept that not only was this doctrine lost (or overthrown) within one or two generations after the apostolic church, but that this occurred *without anyone's noticing it or raising one objecting voice against it!* If this conclusion is unacceptable— and it certainly is—this provides yet one more proof that the Oneness view of God is in error.

As a personal aside, let me say that it was just this study of the early Fathers that, more than anything else, initially caused me to call radically into question my Oneness view of God. I originally began my study of these theologians at Yale Divinity School in an attempt to find further proof of the Oneness view. To my surprise, however, I concluded my study a year later as a trinitarian.

A relatively cursory review of what the early post-apostolic Fathers taught is all that is required to prove that they did not hold the Oneness view. Following the pattern of the New Testament, never is Jesus once called "Father," and in only a few controversial instances is it possible to argue that he may be referred to as the "Holy Spirit."

Specifically, there are five passages in the earliest Christian writings that some have taken to identify Christ as the Spirit. Two are found in the *Shepherd of Hermas* (59:5; 78:1), two in *2 Clement* (9:5; 14:4), and one in Justin Martyr's *First Apology* (60:6–7). It is a matter of scholarly debate as to the extent to which these passages reflect a theology that identifies Christ with the Holy Spirit or simply reflect a loose way of referring to Christ's preexistence. In any case, in all of these works the Son of God is always elsewhere distinguished from the Holy Spirit, and in none of these works is he ever identified with the Father. Hence, even if these works are not consistently trinitarian, they are at least binitarian, and they certainly are not modalistic monarchian or Oneness!

On the other hand, and again closely following the pattern of the New Testament, Jesus is called the "Son of God" dozens and dozens of times. Many more times in this literature he is called such things as "God's child," "the Word of the Father," "the mouth of the Father," the "image of God," the "scepter of God's righteousness," and the like. And, as such, Jesus is with great frequency mentioned alongside of the Father and/or the Holy Spirit.

If, then, the identification of the Father and Spirit with Jesus was of central importance to the apostles, they apparently did a marvelous job of concealing this fact from those whom they taught.

1 Clement

Turning to the specific writings of the earliest post-apostolic authors, we may first note how the author of *1 Clement* presupposes the commonality of trinitarian language in his day when he declares an oath by saying, "For as God lives, and as the Lord Jesus Christ lives, and the Holy Spirit (Who are the faith and hope of the elect) . . ." (58:2).[2] So, too, Clement rhetorically asks his congregation at one point, "Do we not have one God and one Christ and one Spirit of Grace poured out upon us?" (46:6). The incidental nature of this trinitarian language demonstrates just how established this sort of speech had become. Indeed, in this last statement Clement is arguing against any who would bring disunity to the church body (cf. 46:5), thus showing that this trinitarian language and faith was one of the most fundamental things his congregation shared in common. Around this they could be unified.

There is, therefore, nothing innovative about Clement's theology. One does not take oaths, or ask rhetorical questions, or attempt to bring unity to a congregation, with innovative language. What is especially noteworthy here is that in the case of *1 Clement* we are actually not yet even out of the first century, since it was probably written in A.D. 95 or 96!

Ignatius

In similar fashion to Clement, we hear Ignatius just a short time later (about A.D. 110) noting in passing that Jesus Christ was "before the ages . . . with the Father and appeared at the end of time" (*Mag.* 6:1). According to Ignatius, then, the distinctness of Christ from the Father was not, as Oneness Pentecostals contend, something that began with the Incarnation. The fact that Ignatius makes this point in passing, without arguing for it, shows that he was not making a novel point.

Ignatius further presupposes a faith in the distinctness of Christ from the Father when he writes: "Let all run together as to one temple of God, as to one altar, to one Jesus Christ, who came forth from one Father and remained with the One and returned to the One" (*Mag.* 7:2; cf. 8:2). Ignatius further prays that his hearers may prosper "in whatever you do . . . physically and spiritually, in faith and love, in the Son and Father and in the Spirit, in the beginning and in the end" (*Mag.* 13:2). Scholars have noted how the trinitarian, triadic element in this passage (Son-Father-Spirit) breaks up the otherwise diadic rhythm of the passage (physically-spiritually, faith-love, beginning-end). This is significant in that it shows just how established the triadic manner of speaking about God had already become. It was more natural for Ignatius to break up the rhythm of a diadically structured passage to include the trinitarian statement than it was for him to alter the trinitarian statement.

Also significant is the manner in which Ignatius goes on in this same passage to exhort his readers to "be subject to the bishop and to one another . . . as Jesus Christ in the flesh was to the Father, and as the apostles were to Christ and to the Father" (*Mag.* 13:2). So, too, he further informs his readers that "the Spirit itself was preaching, saying these words [through prophecy] . . . 'Become imitators of Jesus Christ, just as he is of his Father'" (*Phil.* 7:2). And he describes the process of our salvation in strongly trinitarian terms when he says: ". . . you are stones of a temple, prepared beforehand for the building of God the Father, hoisted up to the heights by the crane of Jesus Christ, which is the cross, using as a rope the Holy Spirit . . ." (*Eph.* 9:1).

While Jesus is commonly referred to as "God" by Ignatius, nowhere is Jesus' distinctness from the Father ever qualified. Indeed, Christ is frequently called "God" right next to God the Father, as when he says, "For our God, Jesus Christ, was conceived by Mary according to God's plan, both from the seed of David and of the Holy Spirit" (*Eph.* 18:1). Similarly, Ignatius opens his letter to the Romans by noting how they have found "mercy in the majesty of the Father Most High and Jesus Christ his only Son . . . in accordance with faith in and love for Jesus Christ our God . . ." (*Rom.* prologue). And he soon goes on to state, "for our God Jesus Christ is more visible now that he is in the Father" (*Rom.* 3:3).

Clearly, and in good trinitarian fashion, Ignatius finds no difficulty whatsoever in calling Jesus Christ "God" while at the same time acknowledging his distinctness from God the Father. According to Oneness theology, however, Jesus can only be distinguished from the Father in terms of his humanity. Ignatius was no modalist!

With this, it should again be reiterated that there is not in Ignatius's writings the slightest shred of evidence that Jesus is, as Oneness Pentecostals maintain, "really" himself the Father as well as the Son (or, we might add, the Holy Spirit). These common trinitarian distinctions are never qualified. Hence we must take at face value such trinitarian-sounding passages as the ones I have raised here and must understand Ignatius to be confessing a trinitarian-like faith in the Father, Son, and Holy Spirit. (I say "trinitarian-like" because, of course, Ignatius and the rest of the second-century church did not use all of the formal language of the Trinity developed in the third and fourth centuries; but the essential elements of their belief were the same.) And here we are dealing with a man whose life span overlapped the apostles!

Despite this evidence, some Oneness Pentecostals have claimed that Ignatius was in fact a Oneness believer. Chalfant, for example, confidently maintains that Ignatius was "a one God preacher," "a Christian leader who was . . . what we might call 'oneness' or 'Monarchian,'" and Chalfant maintains that Ignatius's letters "show no evidence of any teaching on a trinity" (Chalfant, 16–17). The above-cited *Magnesians* 7:2 is quoted as evidence of Ignatius's "modalism," as is the fact that Ignatius calls Jesus "God," but none of the other trinitarian-structured passages are considered by Chalfant.

The man who is perhaps the most prolific published writer for the UPCI today, David Bernard, also maintains that Ignatius "emphasized the doctrines associated with Oneness" (Bernard, Oneness, 237; New Birth, 267, 273). Unfortunately, Bernard does not in his published works supply any evidence from Ignatius to substantiate this claim, nor does he discuss any of the sorts of passages we have thus far examined that seem to run clearly against his thesis.[3]

The only other significant published UPCI historian now in print is Thomas Weisser, who is also impressed with the fact that Ignatius calls Jesus Christ "God" and thus agrees with the position of Bernard and Chalfant that Ignatius was Oneness in his theology. But, again, no discussion of the above-cited passages is to be found (Weisser, Heresy 16–17). Nor is there any explanation offered by any of these authors as to how Ignatius can call Christ "God" alongside of God the Father.

To conclude that the case against the traditional trinitarian reading of Ignatius by Oneness historians is unconvincing is, in my estimation, generous.

The real value of these Oneness revisions of early church history is, I believe, that they clearly reveal that these men realize that *if* their doctrine were true, Clement, Ignatius, and all the other second-century expositors of the Christian faith *should* be Oneness. And, if they were not, one should at least be able to detect all sorts of cries of "heresy" at this time for their radical departure from the faith.

To the misfortune of these Oneness revisionists, however, it can quite easily be shown that none of these ancient Fathers embraced such a notion, and yet no one at this time ever thought they were believing anything different from what the apostles or the church at large had from the beginning believed.

Polycarp

Our case against the Oneness position is further strengthened as we extend our investigation beyond Clement and Ignatius. Chalfant (and Bernard, following him) makes much of Polycarp as a true heir of the apostolic faith and a disciple of John. He portrays Polycarp as a staunch Oneness believer who, just before his death, testified that "he worshiped Christ alone" (Chalfant, 18ff., cf. Bernard, Oneness, 237; New Birth, 273).

Polycarp is, it must be agreed, an important witness to the faith of the early church. But it is not clear where Chalfant (or Bernard) gets his "Oneness" information. He does cite one passage, *The Martyrdom of Polycarp* 12:2, but the reference to "worshiping Christ alone" that he gives is nowhere to be found (Chalfant, 21). However, what we do find two paragraphs later is significant. Here one finds the author of this mid-second-century work attributing to the dying Polycarp a prayer in which he says:

> O Lord God Almighty, Father of your beloved and blessed Son Jesus Christ . . . I glorify you, through the eternal and heavenly High Priest, Jesus Christ, your beloved Son, through whom to you with him and the Holy Spirit be glory both now and for the ages to come. Amen. [14:1–3]

In a similar fashion, we find Polycarp praying in his letter to the Philippians (usually dated about A.D. 110):

> Now may the God and Father of our Lord Jesus Christ, and the eternal High Priest himself, the Son of God Jesus Christ, build you up . . . and may he give to you a share and a place among his saints, and to us with you, and to all those under heaven who will yet believe in our Lord and God Jesus Christ and in his Father who raised him from the dead. [*Phil* 12:2]

Do these sound like the prayers of a "Oneness preacher"? I know from experience that such talk as this would be regarded as utterly heretical in contemporary Oneness churches. The UPCI church I attended, for example, forbade a song to be sung because it was entitled "Jesus, He is the Son of God"! Yet, the fact that trinitarian language such as this was used in a prayer and doxology in the second century clearly demonstrates that such language was regarded as "normal" for early-second-century Christians.

The Early Church on Genesis 1:26

Equally significant is the manner in which the early-second-century *Epistle of Barnabas* affirms not only Christ's personal distinctness from the Father, but his eternal preexistence as Lord as well. Though this document could not have been written later than A.D. 132 (a date close to the turn of the first century is more likely), the author puts forward, in a perfectly incidental manner, a trinitarian exegesis of Genesis 1:26. He asks,

> . . . if the Lord submitted to suffer for our souls, even though he is Lord of the whole world, to whom God said at the foundation of the world, "Let us make man according to our image and likeness," how is it, then, that he submitted to suffer at the hand of men? [5:5]

One should note that the question the author is asking assumes that the audience knows of and accepts as commonplace the pluralistic interpretation of the Genesis passage. This means that the author was not attempting to come up with a new doctrine or new interpretation of Genesis 1:26. This is what the communities of believers in his time believed. And he was writing sometime between A.D. 70 and 132!

We should not, then, be surprised when we find this same exegesis of Genesis 1:26 popping up all over the place in the second century. We find it, for example, in the early-second-century *The Shepherd of Hermas* (whom Chalfant and Bernard claim was Oneness) when he writes, "The Son of God is far older than all his creation, with the result that he was the Father's counselor in his creation" (*Sim.* 89:2). In similar fashion the apologist Justin explains the plural in Genesis 1:26 by saying that God "conversed with someone who was numerically distinct from Himself, and also a rational Being" (*Dial.* 62). He is referring, of course, to Jesus Christ who "was with the Father before all the creatures, and the Father communed with Him" (ibid.). And the very same tradition is found throughout the *Epistle to Diognetus* (7:1–4; 9:1).

Irenaeus, whom Bernard says was "certainly . . . not a believer in the doctrine of the trinity" (Oneness, 239; cf. 267), simply carries on this established tradition when he writes: "Now man is a mixed organization of soul and flesh, who was formed after the likeness of God, and moulded by His hands, that is, by the Son and Holy Spirit, to whom also He said, 'Let Us Make Man'" (*Heres.* IV. preface). And again: "For with Him were always present the Word and Wisdom, the Son and the Spirit, by whom and in whom freely and spontaneously, He made all things, to whom also He speaks, saying, 'Let Us make man after Our image and Likeness'" (ibid., V.20.1).

What must be reiterated concerning this exegesis is that there is nothing in any of these ancient authors to indicate that they understood themselves to be advocating any new idea in this trinitarian exegesis. They think they are simply passing on the apostolic tradition! And, judging from the total lack of resistance on the part of anyone to all this early trinitarianism, we can safely assume that they were doing just that.

The Early Church on the Preexistence of Christ

This trinitarian exegesis of Genesis 1:26 is not at all surprising, since all the evidence indicates that the notion of Christ's distinct preexistence was a widespread notion in the early church from the start. Indeed, one of the dominant themes in the *Epistle of Barnabas* is precisely the distinct preexistence of Christ. And no one disputes the fact that the concept is to be everywhere found expounded upon in Justin the second-century apologist, Theophilus, and Athenagoras.

But perhaps its most developed and eloquent expression occurs in the second-century work the *Epistle to Diognetus*. One sampling from this eloquent work showing the concept of Christ's distinct preexistence will have to suffice. In paragraph 7 the author writes:

> . . . the omnipotent Creator of all . . . established among men . . . the word from heaven and fixed it firmly in their hearts, not, as one might imagine, by sending to men some subordinate . . . but [the Father sent] the Designer and Creator of the universe himself, by whom he created the heavens . . . he sent him in gentleness and meekness, as a king might send his son who is a king; he sent him as God; he sent him as a man to men. . . .

Again, the question that cries out for an explanation by the Oneness exponents is how these ordinary Christians and all these ordinary Christian churches, which immediately succeeded the apostolic community, could so easily and nonpolemically advocate this very trinitarian concept of Christ and think they were simply "handing down" the truth they received from the apostles—if in fact the apostles had ever held to the Oneness view of the Godhead. How did the "trinitarian heresy" take over so quickly, so thoroughly, and so quietly as to go entirely unnoticed by the generations of Christians immediately following the apostles?

One might simply note, by way of contrast, the tremendous uproar that the "Oneness" or modalist doctrine caused when *it* was (for the first time) advocated around the beginning of the third century, in the face of the church's traditional trinitarianism. We find a significant amount of vigorous writing against it, as we would expect to find against any tampering with "the rule of faith." The debate this caused in the third and fourth centuries is the well-known "modalistic monarchian" or "Sabellian" controversy.

The obvious question, however, is this: Why didn't the supposedly novel and heretical trinitarian doctrine cause a similar uproar in the second century when it was (supposedly) proposed against the "original" Oneness doctrine? Or, to state it in slightly different terms, if the Oneness doctrine was in fact the original apostolic doctrine, why didn't it cause so much as a whimper "fading away" (in one generation!) while it caused such an incredible uproar "coming back"?

There is, I submit, simply no good answer unless we assume, as all recognized church historians do, that the Oneness doctrine in fact never "faded away" at all. It did not exist as a significant movement until the late second century!

Amazingly, though, Oneness writers claim that Oneness was the *majority* viewpoint in the second-century church. So David Bernard writes, "Oneness was the only significant belief in the early second century with regard to the Godhead. Even when forms of binitarianism and trinitarianism began to develop they did not gain dominance until the latter part of the third century" (Bernard, Oneness, 238, 47, 70; see also Weisser, Heresy, 16–21; Chalfant, chs. 1–4).

The only evidence that can be cited in favor of this position is a passage found in Tertullian's writing *Against Praxeas* (ch. 3) in which he remarks, "All the simple people . . . who are always the majority of the faithful . . . shy at the economy. . . ." By "economy" here Tertullian is referring to the trinitarian distinctions in "persons" amidst the unity of God.

Several items need to be kept in mind concerning this passage, however. It is a well-known fact that Tertullian's rhetoric is frequently hyperbolic and ironic. One must then be cautious in taking him as always providing us with accurate history. Moreover, to the extent that his statement does reflect the popularity of Praxeas's teaching, it can only be taken as referring to his province, Rome. We do know from Hippolytus and others that modalism did flourish for about a

generation in Rome. Finally, Tertullian explicitly states that "Praxeas
. . . was *the first* to import to Rome out of Asia this kind of wrong
headedness" (ch. 1, my emphasis), and he defends the faith in the
distinctness of the Father, Son, and Holy Spirit as part of the "Rule
[which] . . . has come down from the beginning of the Gospel, even
before all former heretics, not to speak of Praxeas of yesterday." This
is important, for it is Tertullian's assumption that "whatever is earliest
is true and whatever is later is counterfeit" (ch. 2). Praxeas is thus an
innovator and does not represent what the majority have traditionally
believed.

Justin Martyr

We have in passing referred to the Apologists, but we might do
well to conclude our investigation of the early church by briefly examining their thought in a bit more detail. For here we find the most
developed form of trinitarian theologizing in the second century. As
such, we also find here perhaps the clearest testimony to the prevalence
of trinitarian-like faith in the second century.

Justin Martyr, we might first mention, is as explicit as can be in
repeatedly describing Christians to his unbelieving culture as those
who regard as "numerically distinct" the Father, and the Son, and the
Holy Spirit (*Dial.* 128.4). Hence we read, "We bless the Maker of
all through His Son Jesus Christ, and through the Holy Ghost" (*1
Apol.* 67). And in four other contexts we find Justin repeating the
formula "in the Name of the Father, and of the Son, and of the Holy
Spirit" or some derivative (*1 Apol.* 61:3, 13; 65:2; 67:2). We find
Justin's trinitarianism further articulated in a most emphatic manner
when he writes, ". . . we reasonably worship [Jesus Christ], having
learned that He is the Son of the true God Himself, and holding Him
in the second place, and the prophetic Spirit in the third" (*1 Apol.*
13). This last passage reflects Justin's well-known tendency towards
subordinationism and, perhaps, even tritheism. This sort of language,
in any case, would two centuries later be banned as unorthodox by the
Council of Nicea.

But this tendency only serves to strengthen the point we are making. One can clearly see that the question one ought to have regarding the Apologists is not whether or not they thought of God as possessing a triune nature, but whether or not they pushed their understanding of the threeness of God *too far!* So far are the Apologists and the second-century Christians they represent from being modalists that they at times erred (by later Nicene standards) in emphasizing the distinctness of the Father, Son, and Spirit too much!

But if post-Nicene trinitarians find Justin's type of trinitarianism too radical, what would the second-century church as a whole have thought of these trinitarian apologists if, as the Oneness historians would have us believe, the majority of the church were yet at this time "Oneness believers"? Yet one cannot detect any objections to this sort of theology, nor is there the slightest indication that the Apologists were novel in their theology. Rather, all the evidence we have suggests that this sort of theology was quite representative of what the church on the whole in the middle of the second century believed.

It should be mentioned here that Chalfant finds evidence of an early Oneness group in Justin's reference to:

> ". . . those who maintain that this power [Christ] is indivisible and inseparable from the Father, just as they say that the light of the sun on earth is indivisible and inseparable from the sun; as when it sinks, the light sinks along with it; as the Father, when He chooses, say they, causes His power to spring forth, and when He chooses, He makes it return to Himself." [*Dial. Trypho* 128, quoted in Chalfant, 29]

In reply, one need only point out that this characterization hardly squares with anything we know about the modalism of the early church. Indeed, in the verse immediately after the place where Chalfant's quote ends, Justin adds that this sect teaches that "in this way, they teach, He made the angels." This (and the entire passage) characterizes much better gnostic emanation and angelic speculation than it does anything else.

Even more remarkably, Chalfant maintains that Justin is referring to modalists in *1 Apology* 63, for he here refers "to those who affirm that the Son is the Father" (Chalfant, 27). One cannot help but suspect that the primary text has not here been consulted, for Justin explicitly states in the verse immediately preceding the one Chalfant refers to that he is speaking about "the Jews." Indeed, he says this throughout this whole chapter. And the point he is making is simply that, though Christians know that it was Christ the Son of God who was always speaking in the Old Testament, the Jews think it was the Father, and hence they "affirm that the Son is the Father."

There is, therefore, no good evidence for the existence of an explicit modalistic version of Christianity prior to the end of the second century.

Athenagoras

Another apologist, Athenagoras, develops, while also balancing somewhat, the trinitarianism of Justin. Like Justin, he describes Christians as those who worship the Father, Son, and Holy Spirit (*Plea.* 10). With a degree of theological sophistication that was ahead of his time, he writes: "We affirm that God and His Word or Son and the Holy Spirit are one in power . . ." (*Plea.* 24). And again, "We believe in a God who made all things by His Word and holds them together by the Spirit that comes from Him" (*Plea.* 6). Along similar lines, Athenagoras declares that the Christians of the mid-second century are not atheists, but "hold the Father to be God, and the Son God, and the Holy Spirit, and declare their union and their distinction in order" (*Plea.* 10).

But what is perhaps Athenagoras's most remarkable statement on this subject occurs when he describes the "one aspiration" that urges Christians on in life as being "the desire to know the true God and the Word that is from Him—what is the unity of the Son with the Father, what is the fellowship of the Father with the Son, what is the Spirit; what is the unity of these mighty Powers, and the distinction that exists between them, united as they are—the Spirit, the Son, and the Father" (*Suppl.* 12).

One must observe that, as is true for all the Apologists, Athenagoras is simply describing his perspective of what Christians in general are like to non-Christians. He has no motive to distort and twist his representation of what Christians believe. Nor is he attempting to propound some new doctrine. And yet he characterizes the believing community as trinitarian to the core! If the apostolic rule of faith did not ground this trinitarianism, where did it come from, and when did this "pernicious false teaching" (Chalfant) overthrow "the truth" (the Oneness teaching)?

To be sure, the language and categories that Athenagoras and the other Apologists utilized to communicate the Christian community's faith to their surrounding milieu was borrowed, as it had to be, from that milieu. Hence they employed Stoic and Platonic categories when possible to help express their faith. But one can by no means account for the Apologists' thinking on the triunity of God on the basis of the thought-forms they borrowed to express it, as Oneness historians attempt to do (see Chalfant, 30ff.; Morehead, Foundations, 54ff.). The basic content of the Christian life and faith is provided for the Apologists by the church's tradition, and they have no interest in altering it, only in expressing it.[4] And what is most interesting about their expression is the unanimous way they portray, in a very incidental manner, a trinitarian faith as being basic to what it meant to be a Christian in the second century.

Whence the "Apostasy"?

Were it necessary, we could easily carry our analysis of the trinitarian foundation of the early church's faith through the latter part of the second century and into the third and fourth centuries. But we would only find an increasing sophistication in articulating the sort of trinitarianism we have already found.

Hence one finds in such figures as Origen, Tertullian, Irenaeus, and Hippolytus an unqualified trinitarianism that structured everything about their faith. And each of these figures understood himself to be simply passing on the faith that had been handed down by the apostles from the beginning. When anything "new" was proposed—such as the modalistic teachings of Praxeas or the teachings of the Gnostics—they were the first to stand up behind the church tradition.

We can therefore close this brief investigation by reiterating the question that has throughout our exposition been hounding us: If the apostolic community was originally Oneness, as the Oneness historians must maintain, where on earth did this thoroughgoing second-century trinitarianism come from? And how could this trinitarian language and the trinitarian nature of the Christian faith have taken such a foundational and permanent root in the church so quickly and so decisively? Finally, even if such an overhaul of apostolic doctrine were possible, how could it occur without leaving one shred of evidence of anyone's objecting or even questioning it?

The only conclusion that is possible, I submit, is that the original apostolic doctrine of God was not at all the same as what Oneness groups now claim it to be.

The Inescapable Trinity

n the preceding chapters I have set forth the Oneness position (ch. 1), responded to the general Oneness arguments against the Trinity (ch. 2), refuted the Oneness view of Christ (chs. 3–5) and of Jesus' Name baptism (ch. 6), and shown that the second-century church was fundamentally trinitarian and not Oneness (ch. 7). In this concluding chapter I will present a theological refutation of the Oneness doctrine and provide a theological defense of the Trinity. It is hoped that this material will provide the reader with a theological foundation and appreciation for the central significance of the church's doctrine of the Trinity.

The Exclusivistic Implication of the Oneness Truth-Claim

In examining any claim to truth, it is always good to consider what the implications of the given truth-claim are. If these implications are impossible or unacceptable, this is a fairly good initial indication that the truth-claim from which they follow is false.

What, then, are some relevant implications of Oneness Pentecostalism's claim to possess the one true doctrine of God? To begin with, to accept the claim that the Oneness doctrine of God was in fact the understanding of God held by the apostles, one must also accept that this understanding was completely lost, forgotten, or distorted by the generations that immediately succeeded the apostles. This, I argued in the previous chapter, is impossible to maintain.

A related and equally unacceptable implication of the Oneness view is this: According to almost all Oneness Pentecostals, a belief in the Oneness doctrine and a denial of the Trinity is "at least a partial requisite for salvation" (Sabin, III, 1). Therefore, to accept the Oneness truth-claim requires one to accept that all the hundreds of millions of orthodox Christians who lived up until this doctrine was created in the second decade of this century are lost! Indeed, with the possible exception of a few oddball nontrinitarian believers like Praxeas, Servetus, and Swedenborg (though in all likelihood even these individuals weren't baptized "correctly" and didn't speak in tongues—two further "prerequisites for salvation"), nobody in church history up until this century has been saved! All the lives spent in total service to Christ—including such heroes of the faith as Jonathan Edwards, David Livingstone, Billy Graham, and Mother Teresa—all of them have lost out with God! Heaven will indeed be a very small place, if the UPCI and other Oneness Pentecostal sects are correct.

There is a large saying written all across the vestibule wall of the UPCI church I used to attend that is representative of the Oneness view of trinitarian Christians. It reads, "To view him incorrectly is to miss him completely," referring, of course, to Jesus Christ. And, of course, according to Oneness adherents, it is trinitarians who understand Christ "incorrectly" and thus completely miss him.

It is not hard to understand why Oneness believers hold that trinitarians are not saved, for the Trinity they believe in is usually thought to constitute "the most diabolical religious hoax and scandal in history" (cited in Enroth, Guide, 15). The Trinity is variously portrayed as being a remnant of the pagan religion of Babylon, Mithraism, the "Greek carnal mind," Gnosticism, and other "hollow and deceptive philosophy," which Paul warned about in Colossians 2:8. According to the Oneness historian Chalfant, it was primarily the second-century Apologists who performed "the evil task" of seducing true Christianity into a compromise with these diabolical influences (Chalfant, 35). The likes of these are the "grievous wolves and perverse men" (Acts 20:29–30) who caused all of Christendom to backslide (ibid., 11ff.). Hence, to accept the Oneness position, one must accept that all trinitarian believers throughout the ages—basically all believers up until the Oneness movement of this century—have been under the deception of Satan and thus lost. The "gates of Hades" did indeed prevail against the church (cf. Matt. 16:18)!

Counting heads, of course, is no reliable indicator of truth. But, on the other hand, one cannot dismiss the testimony to the work of Christ evidenced in the lives of the heroes of faith that run throughout church history. Nor can one dismiss Christ's promise that the "gates of Hades" would not overcome the church and "the faith that was once for all entrusted to the saints" (Jude 3). The unacceptability of such implications as these already counts decisively against the common Oneness notion that only *they* have the keys of salvation, which had been lost until they found them seventy-five years ago.[1]

Oneness Concessions to Trinitarianism

We have seen that the UPCI and other Oneness groups vehemently deny that God is essentially triune; that is, they deny that God eternally exists as three "persons," Father, Son, and Holy Spirit. This doctrine, they argue, is self-contradictory and tritheistic. They pride themselves on not believing such a "mystery" (e.g., Bernard, Oneness, 65, 288–289; Sabin, III, 1–2). Indeed, according to standard Oneness theology, one cannot even be saved if holding to a trinitarian view of God, and only Oneness believers possess the saving truth about who Jesus really is.

Despite their rejection of the Trinity as self-contradictory and tritheistic, however, it seems to this author at least that most Oneness believers make major concessions to trinitarianism in their thinking. When they are at all consistent in articulating what they believe, they cannot correlate their doctrine with the whole teaching of the Bible without affirming something quite a bit like the doctrine of the Trinity. This, I think, is really inevitable in that it is virtually impossible to affirm *consistently* the deity of Christ and of the Holy Spirit without making some kind of fundamental threefold distinction within the Godhead. Thus, Oneness Pentecostals end up affirming a God of three "manifestations." And, as we shall see, to the extent that the Oneness view is developed consistently, it involves essentially the same mystery as the traditional affirmation that God is basically triune. However, to the extent that the Oneness position attempts to avoid this mystery, it simply trades in legitimate biblical mystery for unbiblical and incoherent nonsense.

The Threefoldness of God's Activity

The trinitarian concessions of Oneness theology are rooted in the teaching of the earliest Oneness preachers who, despite their antitrinitarianism, nevertheless spoke of a "threefold manifestation" of God (Haywood, 12), of God's being "three-in-one" (N. Urshan, Consider, 18), and even of God's being a Trinity (cf. Reed, 244). Although contemporary Oneness authors never speak positively of God as a Trinity, they do make substantial concessions to trinitarian doctrine. Kenneth Reeves, for example, articulates the nature and logic of the Oneness "threefoldness," even though he is arguing against the Trinity, when he writes:

> The One God doctrine of the Christian Monotheist [that is, Oneness believer] does not deny the Father, Son and Holy Ghost; but rejects such Tritheistic ideas expressed and implied by the adduction of such terms as: Three Separate and Distinct Persons in the Godhead, as God the Father, God the Son, and God the Holy Ghost. . . . The Oneness view includes God in His Omnipresence, His particularity in Christ and His impartation to Believers, as the Holy Ghost. [Reeves, Godhead, 52]

Bernard articulates this same Oneness view of the threefoldness of God when he writes concerning 1 John 5:7 (which is almost certainly not part of the original text), "God has recorded Himself in three modes of activity or has revealed Himself in three ways. He has at least three heavenly roles: Father, Word . . . and Holy Ghost. Furthermore, these three roles describe one God: 'these three are one'" (Bernard, Oneness, 141).

And, finally, Reeves speaks more specifically about God's threefold life as Father, Son, and Spirit when he writes:

> The Father is God as the source. The Father is that huge and infinite reservoir from whom smaller amounts of God proceed. The Lord Jesus Christ is the Word-Image Aspect of God targeted for the virgin birth. The Holy Ghost is an area of God He shares with mankind as a residing gift and manifestor of gifts. [Reeves, Dimensions, 53]

The end result is that we have "God in the universe, God in Christ, and God in the church. . . . one God in . . . three spheres" (Reeves, Godhead, 18).

What this shows, I believe, is that even Oneness believers must acknowledge that God can and does act and even (at least temporarily) exist in three distinctly different ways. God exists in his infinitude and omnipresence as "source," as "Father"; God exists in his "particularity," his revelatory aspect, as "Word" or "Son"; and God exists as "residing gift," immanent within believers' hearts, as "Holy Spirit." And, if reflected upon *consistently,* I maintain, this threefold affirmation implies the essence of the mystery of the Trinity.

What is more, in spite of the crude quantitative language that runs throughout Reeves's works (e.g., speaking of God as "huge," or being distributed in "smaller amounts," etc.), Reeves and other Oneness exponents would concede that each of these divine "ways of existing" ("spheres") are fully God. They among all believers would insist that God cannot be divided up into "thirds" (they repeatedly accuse trinitarians of doing this). God is indivisible as to his existence (Bernard, Oneness, 134). It is, therefore, not the case that a "part" of God exists as Father, another as Son, and so on. The totality of the Godhead is fully present in each of his "spheres" or "roles."

Moreover, while some of the later (late third century) modalists in the early church apparently believed that the Father, Son, and Holy Spirit were successive "masks" (*prosopon*) that God wore in the history of redemption, contemporary modalists such as UPCI believers maintain that God plays these three "roles" *simultaneously*. Hence, all of God acts and (at least for now) exists fully as omnipresent Father, fully in and as the incarnate Son, and fully within the believer as the Holy Spirit—and he does all of this at the same time!

Finally, Oneness believers must (and usually do) concede that, because the One indivisible God exists fully in each of these "ways of existing," God exits *personally* in each of these ways (Reeves, Godhead, 18–20; Magee, 27; Reed, 250f.). That is, the personal God who fully exists "outside" of Jesus is as personal as the God who fully exists "inside" of Jesus, and this, of course, is true for this same God when he exists fully "within" believers. Each "mode" or "sphere" can, therefore, be referred to as "he." God can personally act, speak, or manifest himself from either one or all three of his personal ways of existing (as, for example, in the baptism of Jesus, Matt. 3:13–17; Bernard, Oneness, 172f.).

Indeed, some (though not most) Oneness exponents who are particularly consistent go so far as to concede that the Bible teaches that communication can and does occur within God between each of these personal ways of existing. To cite Reeves again, in response to the question, "Is there any internal communication within the Godhead. . . ?" he writes:

It would not be surprising that this should be found true. . . . The intercession of the Spirit within believers (Rom. 8:26–27) indicates some form of communication. . . . God in a particular place can speak, and God in all places may speak. [Reeves, Godhead, 37–38; cf. Supreme, 112; Dimensions, 97]

Hence, in this view, the same one indivisible God who fully and personally exists in one "sphere" (say, indwelling Spirit) can communicate to himself as he fully and personally exists in another sphere (say, transcendent Father). Only with such a supposition could one account for a passage such as Romans 8:26–27. And, I maintain, this view makes enormous concessions to classical trinitarianism. To say that God can fully, and therefore personally, exist in three distinct ways is almost indistinguishable from saying that God exists in three "persons." The only remaining issue, now, is whether the "persons" are essential to *who God is* or are they, rather, just facets of *what God does?*

Is a "Trinity of Activity" Less Mysterious Than a "Trinity of Being"?

I am by no means trying to make trinitarians out of Oneness believers. The Oneness view differs radically from the traditional trinitarian view in that it reduces each of God's threefold "personal ways of existing" to a threefoldness of temporary roles, while also maintaining that Jesus is the personal identity manifested in all three of these roles, not just in the second. These moves constitute fundamental differences with trinitarianism and, I shall subsequently demonstrate, they undermine much of what is essential to the Christian faith.

The point I am presently making, however, is simply that despite their vast differences from traditional trinitarians, and despite their endless railing against the Trinity as a logical and biblical monstrosity, Oneness believers must, in the end, affirm a doctrine that is just as mysterious as the one that trinitarians affirm. They must at least concede that the one indivisible God can and does exists in at least *three distinct ways,* that he does so *fully,* that he does so *personally,* and that he does so *simultaneously.* And this is truly mysterious! Indeed, to this extent, the Oneness doctrine affirms exactly the same mystery expressed in the doctrine of the Trinity.

Therefore, the mystery of the Trinity is unavoidable—whether or not one labels each "sphere" a "distinct person" (even many contemporary trinitarians reject the term "person," as we shall see); whether one maintains that this threefoldness is eternal or merely temporary; and whether one maintains that Jesus is the "one personality" shining through each "manifestation" or whether one maintains that he constitutes the second "person" alone.

One basic fact remains: It is in one sense as mysterious to maintain that a unipersonal God *temporarily* exists fully, personally, and simultaneously in three distinct ways, as it is to maintain that a tripersonal God *eternally* exists fully, personally, and simultaneously in three distinct ways. For both views of God, God is in some sense "unquantifiable" and hence "incomprehensible." Calling each manifestation a "person" and making each temporary distinction "eternal" does not create the mystery, which is how the whole of God could completely exist in this threefold way at all! And both the Oneness and the trinitarian view of God have this mystery in common.

The Oneness view of God, then, to the extent that it is consistent, escapes none of the mystery of the doctrine of the Trinity it so vigorously repudiates. It unknowingly concedes the very same mystery it proudly proclaims to overcome—a mystery that trinitarians have always willingly confessed. But what is most damaging to the Oneness view, as we shall see, is that, because it concedes this mystery only inconsistently and inadvertently, it completely misses all of the benefits that the trinitarian doctrine brings to our understanding of God. In fact, as I will show, the Oneness doctrine itself creates a multitude of insuperable difficulties that the doctrine of the Trinity completely avoids. Thus, there is in the end simply no good reason for embracing the Oneness position.

The Rejection of the Word "Person"

As we have seen, the driving force behind Oneness theology is its conviction that only *its* view of God and Christ is consistent with the foundational biblical truths that there is only one God, and that Jesus Christ is God. From this, Oneness Pentecostals unanimously conclude that God is "one single divine Being or Person" (Urshan, Life, 248; Chalfant, 19) and that this "person" is Jesus Christ. This is the essence of Oneness theology.

From this perspective, all talk about there being "three eternal persons" in the Godhead must be rejected as constituting a direct assault on both of these foundational truths. The distinctness of the "Father," "Son," and "Holy Spirit" can neither be a distinctness of "persons," nor can it be "eternal." We have already addressed this argument in general terms in chapter 2, but now we must concern ourselves more directly with these claims.

The Oneness Caricature of the Trinity: What Do We Mean by "Three Persons"?

Perhaps the most fundamental objection to the doctrine of the Trinity on the part of Oneness exponents is that, according to them, this doctrine teaches that God consists of "three separate and distinct persons" (e.g., Urshan, Almighty; Reeves, Godhead, *passim*; Dimensions, 141f., and *passim*). This designation is assumed to imply that God necessarily has three separate consciousnesses, three separate minds, three separate wills, and perhaps even three separate spiritual forms or bodies. Indeed, the general Oneness portrayal of the Trinity is a rather crude portrait of three separate people in heaven. And this, Oneness Pentecostals rightly maintain, constitutes virtual tritheism.

There is only one problem with this portrayal of the Trinity: It has little to do with what the church has traditionally believed about the Trinity. First, while every trinitarian would agree that the three "persons" are *distinct*, I don't know of any, ancient or modern, who has wanted to maintain that they are *separate*, or even hypothetically separable. Indeed, the church has always believed in the indivisibility (or "simplicity") of God, and hence the inseparability of the three "persons." The traditional doctrine of the perichoresis or "mutual indwelling" of the three "persons" was meant to express and guard just this point. This doctrine maintains, in a nutshell, that none of the three "persons" can exist or even be conceived of apart from the other two, and indeed that each "person" completely dwells within the other two. It is a shorthand way of reminding us that God is unquantifiable and thus wherever God is, *all* of God is. Hence, much of the Oneness antitrinitarian literature that attacks the three "separate" divine persons is directed at nothing more than a straw man.

Relatedly, the Oneness literature is largely attacking a straw man when it maintains that the phrase "three persons" implies that God literally has three separate consciousnesses, three separate wills, and (perhaps) three separate bodies, and that it is therefore tritheistic. Regrettably, there are some popular renditions of the Trinity where this charge of tritheism to some extent applies, and these crude misrepresentations of the traditional teaching are what largely fuel the Oneness Pentecostals' antitrinitarianism. The UPCI and other Oneness groups rightly come against any attempts to picture the Godhead as though there were three incarnate or embodied divine beings instead of one (John 1:14–18); as though there were three "images," "forms," or "expressions" of God instead of one (Phil. 2:6; Col. 1:15; Heb. 1:3); as though the Father (and Spirit) could even be conceptualized apart from Jesus Christ (John 14:7–10); as though God could be horizontally conceived of as some sort of committee. This is clearly against Scripture, and is rightly branded as tritheism. But for just this reason the UPCI and related groups are missing the point when they attack *this* crude view of the Trinity.

What Does the Word "Person" Mean?

As numerous contemporary historians and theologians have argued in recent years, the original Greek and Latin words that were used in the earliest trinitarian creeds and from which the term "person" is derived (*hypostasis, persona*) were much less specific than the term "person" today. While not denying the personal nature of what they designated, these terms did not necessarily connote any sort of separate consciousness or will. They were not, in other words, synonymous with the term "individual" as the word "person" is today. Indeed, this individualized nuance to the term "person" is a relatively recent post-Enlightenment development. The ancient confession of "God in three persons" was thus not equivalent to "God in three individual people."[2]

Because the word "person" has become far more individualized, many well-respected trinitarians feel that it is misleading and should actually be dropped from contemporary trinitarian creeds. It should be replaced, they argue, by a phrase such as "mode of being" (Barth) or "manner of subsistence" (Rahner), which, they contend, are better translations of the original *hypostasis* and *persona.*

Others (such as myself) feel that these modern translations are generally too cumbersome and impersonal for practical use, and hence they call for a less radical solution. These maintain that we should continue to utilize the term "person," but we should do so with caution, making sure through teaching that the church understands that we are not using the word literally, but analogously.

This is, in fact, what the church has always done. Even long before the word took on its modern, individualized nuances, theologians such as the Cappadocians, Augustine, Aquinas, and Calvin all used it reluctantly and with much qualification. In his work *On the Trinity,* Augustine admitted that he used the word "person" (*persona*) to speak of God's threeness "not that it might be spoken, but that it might not be left unspoken." There is simply no better term available. The Cappadocians, Aquinas, Calvin, and many others all define the concept of "person" as applied to the Trinity as something like "a real subsisting relation." The distinct personalness of the three ways God is God was always maintained, but without the radically individualistic connotations associated with the word "person" today.[3] It is for this reason that I deem it expedient to put the word "person" in quotes, reminding the reader that we are using the word in a unique, nonliteral sense.

In any case, whether or not the term "person" is retained, trinitarians have always agreed that the doctrine of "God in three persons" cannot be understood to legitimize (say) picturing God as three literal divine "people" in heaven who are so distinct that they have to (as it were) vote on what activity they might perform—as though their wills and minds were indeed separable! God is not a committee! Such an understanding of the Trinity is simply a misapplication of the creedal language.

The Trinity, the church has always held, is not inconceivable by analogy (for example, the unity of God is *like* the loving unity of three human persons), but it is "unpicturable" in literal terms.[4] Only in the incarnate person of Christ does deity become in any sense "picturable," for here alone we find the one literal, visible, divine manifestation—the one "Word," "Form," "Image," and "Incarnation" of God. "No one has ever seen God, but God the One and Only, who is at the Father's side, has made him known" (John 1:18).

It should therefore be clear that the doctrine of the Trinity that Oneness Pentecostals (and most other antitrinitarian groups) are attacking is by and large a literalistic, and hence tritheistic, caricature of what the traditional doctrine really means. As such, their attacks really do not even touch the correct orthodox teaching of the church.

Is an "Absolute Unity" Less Mysterious Than the Trinity?

A final word concerning the term "person" is in order. We have seen that Oneness believers maintain that God is "absolutely one" (Sabin, Seminar; Bernard, Oneness, 289) and that he is, in contrast to the trinitarian teaching, only one "person." It is assumed by Oneness authors that this understanding of the unqualified Oneness of God— that God is one person—is perfectly clear. No further explanation is needed (or ever given). Indeed, so obvious and clear is the Oneness of God that Oneness authors seem to assume that the very suggestion that there is a mystery within the Godhead is heretical. Hence Bernard, for example, writes that "the only mystery relative to the Godhead is the manifestation of God in flesh, and even that has been revealed to those who believe . . . we can understand the simple truth that there is one God. . . ." And he continues:

> The Bible never says that the Godhead is an unrevealed mystery or that the question of plurality in the Godhead is a mystery. Instead, it affirms in the strongest terms that God is one. Why resort to an explanation that the Godhead is an incomprehensible mystery . . . when Scriptures plainly give us a simple, unambiguous message that God is absolutely one? *It is wrong to state that the Godhead is a mystery.* . . .
> [Bernard, Oneness, 289, emphasis added]

The Godhead, we see, is not a mystery for Bernard, for God is one in just the same way that a person is one.[5] In supposed contrast to the trinitarian mystery, Oneness exponents proclaim the supposedly self-evidently clear truth that God is "one single divine Being or person" (Urshan, Life, 248; Chalfant; 19; Sabin; Seminar; Magee, 28).

But is it the case that the unity, the "oneness," of a person is all that clear in contrast to the "mysterious" unity-amidst-plurality suggested by trinitarians? Is describing God as "one person" the same as describing him as an "absolute unity"? I think not, for the unity of a person is, in fact, a *relational* unity. A person is not at all an undifferentiated monad. As psychologists universally recognize, and as anyone can discern from introspection, a human person is really a highly complex being. In fact, many psychologists believe that the human person embodies a (sometimes tenuous) unity of a multiplicity of "selves." The unity of a self-conscious human person, therefore, involves a genuine *internal plurality.* This internal relationality is manifested every time we think about or talk to ourselves.

The analogy that has been most frequently employed for understanding the Trinity throughout church history has been one that likens the Trinity to the inner constitution of *a single human person!* This analogy is called the "psychological model" of the Trinity, for it is based on the psychology of a person.

In this analogy, the distinctness in union of the Father, Son, and Holy Spirit is thought of as being something like ("analogous to") the distinctness, say, of a person's intellect, heart, and will within the unity of the one person (St. Augustine). Each "aspect" of the person is distinct, yet inseparable from the others, and together they constitute the single personality of that person. Or, another version of this model suggests that the Father, Son, and Holy Spirit are something like the self's relationship to its own self-image (Jonathan Edwards). The very act of thinking, it is pointed out, requires a type of plurality within the one self (e.g., who is talking and who is listening?). So does the act of loving or hating oneself (who is loving and who is being loved?). The "fellowship" of the three divine "persons" is something like this, according to this model.

The point being made here is that while Oneness authors assume that the meaning of their concept of "Oneness" is self-evidently clear, this simply is not the case. The great selling point of the "Oneness" doctrine is, supposedly, that it is so much less "mysterious" than the doctrine of the Trinity—it supposedly isn't mysterious at all! Yet the model (one human person) used by Oneness teachers to make their view of the "Oneness" clear has already been used by trinitarians for centuries to make the triune unity of God clear! Moreover, the internally relational unity of a human person is an analogy much better suited to clarify the trinitarian understanding of God than it is the Oneness understanding.

In a sense, however, one cannot fault Oneness adherents for using the ill-suited model of a single human person to conceptualize their position, for as inappropriate as this model is for their position, there really is nothing better for them to use. Indeed, as a great number of philosophers throughout history have recognized, the very idea of an "absolute" or "undifferentiated" unity is incoherent. It is really equivalent to complete nothingness.[6] "Being" is thus synonymous with "being in relation."

In short, there is simply no analogy for something that is wholly devoid of internal relations. Such an entity (really a *non*-entity) is utterly inconceivable as well as unpicturable.

It is not, then, the view of God that holds to a relationality within God that is incoherent, but any view that would deny this! Once this is understood, any suggestion that an affirmation of a plurality within the Godhead is an assault to "pure monotheism" can be recognized for being the complete nonsense that it is. The doctrine of the Trinity *completes* "pure monotheism"; it does not in the least abrogate it.

To summarize our findings thus far, we have seen that, though they may proudly pretend this is not the case, adherents to the Oneness view of God, no less than the trinitarians, are faced with the mystery of how God can fully exist in a plurality of distinct personal ways at the same time. We have furthermore seen that the view of the Trinity they attack as tritheistic is really only a caricature of the historic orthodox position. Finally, we have seen that Oneness exponents—by claiming that their view of God, which denies internal relationality in God, is unmysterious and clear—have succeeded only in papering over the mystery. In so doing, they have only traded in the mystery of the Trinity for the nonsensical notion of God as an undifferentiated unity.

We might conclude, then, that when Oneness theology is at its best in being at all consistent (by affirming a plurality of distinct "spheres" of divine existence), it comes closest to trinitarianism; and when it is trying the hardest to separate itself from trinitarianism (by denying internal relationality in God), it is at its worst, sinking down into total incoherence.

Are the Three "Persons" Eternal?

The Oneness view of God, we have seen, differs from the trinitarian view by regarding the Father, Son, and Holy Spirit as three temporary manifestations of one undifferentiated God, rather than three eternal "persons" in God. This latter view, Oneness exponents insist, is tritheistic.

I have shown, however, that their understanding of these "three manifestations" is unable to escape the same mystery expressed forthrightly in the trinitarian understanding of "three persons." Moreover, I have argued that their concept of a God who is "absolutely one" is far more mysterious than the view that God has internal relationality.

But what about the eternality of these "three persons"? Is it truer to "pure monotheism" to limit the concepts of Father, Son, and Holy Spirit to apply only to what God temporarily does, as Oneness believers do, rather than apply them to who God eternally is, as trinitarians have always done? While this may initially appear as a rather speculative abstract question, in truth the central message of the gospel hangs on this issue, as we shall see.

Why Not?

If one concedes, as Oneness adherents must, that God does at least *temporarily* fully exist in at least three distinct, personal "ways," "spheres," or "roles," and if it is not tritheistic to accept this, then on what grounds could one maintain that it is tritheistic to accept that God exists *eternally* in just such a threefold manner?

Surprisingly, the Oneness author Kenneth Reeves brings home this point rather well as he argues against his Oneness colleagues concerning the real preexistence of "the form" of God: "If we can perceive that God has a body now, and can also conceive now that God is an Omnipresent Spirit, why is it difficult to perceive that God had an image, shape, or form before He resided in the man Jesus Christ?" (Reeves, Supreme, 106).

The point Reeves is making is that it is no more difficult to conceive of God as possessing a diversity of "ways of existing" (for Reeves, as infinite Father, finite image) in eternity than it is to conceive of him as so existing in time. With this I agree. If God can fully, and therefore personally, exist simultaneously as Father, Son, and Holy Spirit in time, what is so impossible about him doing so in all eternity? If the one indivisible God can exist and act in this threefold way toward us in time, why would it be an assault on his unity if he existed in just this fashion within himself throughout eternity? In a word, if it is not tritheistic to exist three ways in time, why does it become so in eternity?

The Theological Flaw of Ancient Modalism: The Problem of Revelation

It seems, then, that the one God can as easily exist in "three personal ways" from eternity as he can in time. Nothing is gained in terms of affirming the unity of God by denying the essentiality and eternality of these distinctions. But not only is nothing *gained* by this denial, a great deal is actually *lost* by it.

The early Fathers who first had to battle this modalistic heresy believed that there was much at stake in this issue. One cannot read the writings of Tertullian, Novatian, Hippolytus, or Epiphanius without sensing that for them the battle for the eternal Trinity was no mere abstract squabble about numbers. Neither was this only a dispute over how to interpret certain passages of Scripture, though it certainly was this too.

Rather, these Fathers clearly understood that what was at stake in this battle was the authenticity of God's self-revelation. They understood that if the relationality found throughout the New Testament between the Father, Son, and Holy Spirit was something that God merely *assumed* in time for the purpose of our salvation, as the modalists maintained, then even when we come to know God in this threefoldness, we do not come to know God as he truly is. For what God is "truly" like, according to both ancient modalists and contemporary Oneness believers, lies in the supposed "undifferentiated Oneness," which is hidden behind the three (or more) "masks" he wears in time.

In other words, in Oneness theology the three temporary "roles" of God do not arise out of God's essential eternal being. God "plays" Father, Son, and Holy Spirit. But in his heart of hearts—whoever he is—he is not these three.

The big question, then, was whether the history of salvation was to be thought of as a sort of stage where God merely acts out certain roles that are otherwise foreign to his essential self, or whether this history reveals the innermost heart and internal depth of the eternal and infinite Godhead. Does God simply wear masks before us, or does he lovingly envelop us into the very depths of his essential and eternal being? The early Fathers, thankfully, perceived that the latter was the truth.

The reputable church historian G. L. Prestige sums up well the nature and dual error of ancient modalism (Sabellianism) when he writes:

> It presupposes first that in one vital respect the Gospels, the foundation documents of Christian evidence, are consistently unreliable. . . . There is not a hint anywhere that the apparent duologue [of the Father and the Son] is sustained by a single impersonator . . . and secondly that, when God in person came into the world to reveal Himself to His elect, He lied to them by making Himself out quite other than He really was. . . . They [the modalists] were wrong in making the distinction between them [Father, Son, and Holy Spirit] into a transient illusion; illusion and transience are not the attributes of God. [Prestige, Fathers 80, 91]

Hence, Prestige points out, against the modalists Athanasius had to insist "that the personal distinctions in the Godhead, which have been revealed in temporal history, are permanent and authentic features of the personality of God who has revealed them" (Prestige, Fathers 92).

What was at stake in the church's battle with ancient modalism? The very thing that is at stake today: namely, the authenticity of God's self-revelation. When we perceive God's interacting with us and within himself as Father, Son, and Holy Spirit, do we or do we not have displayed to us God as God eternally is in the innermost depth of his heart? If Oneness theology is correct, we do not.

The "Illusion" of the Father and Son

What was true of ancient modalism is true today. The "real" God of Oneness believers is lost somewhere in his supposed "pure unity" behind the plurality of masks he wears before humankind. Hence the God manifested in time is not one and the same as the eternal God—God as he is in his own essence. "All visible projections of God to the eyes," writes Reeves concerning Jesus and the Holy Spirit, "are manifestations of God, and not God's original nature that is seen" (Reeves, Dimensions, 37). Yet, one must wonder how anything can be a genuine "manifestation" of God if it is not a manifestation of his "original nature." Where *is* the original God? Unless the God revealed is the original eternal God, the eternal God really is not revealed. More specifically, unless the "manifested" Father, Son, and Holy Spirit correspond to an eternal Father, Son, and Holy Spirit, the "manifested" threefoldness does not truly manifest the eternal God.[7] This is axiomatic.

This air of "transient illusion" (as Prestige calls it with respect to modalism) comes out especially in the Christology of Oneness theology. All references to the Father and the Son are interpreted by Oneness exponents to refer to the two natures of Jesus, not to two "persons" within the eternal Godhead (Bernard, Oneness, 289). The Father and the Son, then, are "really" one person, Jesus Christ.

But what does this do to all the apparent personal interaction that occurs between the Father and the Son throughout the Gospels? Since the two are in no sense distinct "persons," the interaction, it seems, simply cannot be genuine. Everything that is said about the personal interaction of the Father and the Son, though it clearly appears to be indicative of a personal relationship, is "really" about Jesus interacting with himself. Hence, as Prestige noted above, the "dualogue" is illusory! It is "sustained by a single impersonator"!

The more consistent and thorough Oneness exponents are with the terms of their theology, the more this illusory aspect comes out. And few Oneness spokespersons are as logically consistent and theologically thorough as Robert Sabin, the highly esteemed founder of Oneness Ministries. He is most explicit on this aspect of Oneness Christology when he writes concerning Christ's work of redemption:

> God cannot propitiate himself. To meet his justice requirement, a member of the human race must be offered while God appears to be remote. Thus *apparent separation* [his italics] must exist between the judge and the advocate, between the lamb and the creator-God. But this separation is only apparent. We might say it is only illusory. In reality, God and Christ are interpenetrating genders, identities, are one in the absolute sense. . . . [Sabin, Gender]

And again:

> The *language of separation, the language of plurality,* is made necessary because God alone can acquit, forgive, absolve, forget. . . . Because of the need for the human Christ to be a fit mediator, there are occasions when expressions or representations seem to show separation of the Father and the Son. In truth, the Father and the Son can never be separated. [Sabin, Gender]

Note the contrast between what *appears* to be the case and what, according to Sabin, is "in reality." All "expressions or representations" of the Father being other than the Son, of the Father and Son being two interacting "persons" (which, Sabin concedes, happens on occasion!) are really illusory. "In reality," Jesus is himself both.

Sabin, again with admirable consistency, goes on to describe how there is "the illusion of separation" between God on the throne and the Lamb next to the throne in Revelation 4 and 5. These are, he says, really "two roles performed by God, the role of creator, and the role of redeemer" (ibid.). Appearances are indeed deceiving! Moreover, Sabin notes at other points how Jesus, "on occasion," *projects* the Father *as though* he were distinct from himself and "in heaven." But again, such is of course not really the case, since "in truth" Jesus and the Father are "one in the absolute sense." According to Sabin, then, Prestige was apparently wrong—"Illusion and transience" *are* "the attributes of God"!

But one has to begin to get suspicious. After all, the distinction between the Father and the Son in the New Testament is hardly an "occasional" distinction. Jesus himself is recorded to have referred to his Father or "the Father" as though he was a "person" distinct from himself over one hundred seventy times in the Gospels (almost eighty times in John alone!). For good reason, then, the church has always interpreted the Father/Son distinction with their loving relationship as not only being real, but as being at the very heart of the New Testament proclamation.

Calling this "illusory," then, is no minor matter. When so many Scriptures must be reinterpreted as illusory in order to communicate what they really say, one can't help but begin to suspect that maybe the so-called illusion is in the reinterpretation, and that what the texts *appear* to say is what the texts *in fact* say!

What this Oneness method of interpretation does is cast an air of unreality on everything we read about the Father and the Son in the Gospels. Instead of the dynamic, loving interaction of the Father and the Son, which forms the very heartbeat of the gospel, we have only the illusory interaction of two abstract "natures" of one person.

Hence, we must ask, did Jesus really personally interact with the Father when he heard, learned, and received all things from the Father (Matt. 28:18; John 3:35; 8:26; 8:40; 15:15)? It certainly appears so, but according to Oneness theology this is *only* an appearance, for in reality Jesus *is* the Father. If any interaction occurred, it could only be the interaction of two "natures," two "its." Or again, did Jesus personally look up and pray to the Father (Luke 6:12; 9:28; John 5:19, 30; 8:28; 17:1–2)? Did Jesus and the people witnessing his baptism really hear the Father's personal confirmation of Christ's sonship (Matt. 3:16–17; Mark 1:10–11; Luke 3:21–22)? Again, it certainly appears so, but according to Oneness theology, this, too, is "transient illusion," for "in reality" Christ and the Father are not personally distinct. Rather, Christ was "projecting" himself as the Father in heaven—as though he were a Father distinct from himself. He was acting as a "divine ventriloquist," for he was in fact talking to himself! This supposed impersonation, we might add, was very successful, for everyone but a handful of modalists during the past two thousand years has thought it was reality—and probably missed out on salvation because of it!

The Love Between the Father and Son

Perhaps the most tragic implication of reducing the Father/Son personal distinction to a mere distinction of natures (or even outright "illusion") is that it completely undermines the genuineness of the Father's personal love for the Son and the Son's personal love for the Father spoken of so poignantly throughout the New Testament. Bernard specifically addresses the issue of this apparent loving relationship between the Father and the Son when he writes:

> John 3:35, 5:20, and 15:9 state that the Father loves the Son [forget the numerous other texts!], and John 17:24 says the Father loved Jesus before the foundation of the world. In John 14:31 Jesus expresses love for the Father [again, one verse!]. All of these statements do not mean separate persons. . . . What these verses express is the *relationship between the two natures of Christ.* The Spirit of Jesus loved the humanity and vice versa. . . . Remember, the Son came to the world to show us how much God loves us and also to be our example. *For these two objectives to be achieved,* the Father and the Son *showed* love for each other. [Bernard, Oneness, 186, emphases added]

We have already seen that, according to Oneness theology, it was for the purpose of redeeming us that God created an "illusion of separation," acting *as though* the Father were personally distinct from Jesus the Son. So here, Bernard tells us (and, again, he is only being consistent with Oneness Christology), the love of the Father for the Son was not really a love between two "persons." There was nothing interpersonal about it. It was, rather, the "love" of one of Jesus' *natures* for the other *nature* of Jesus (how two abstract natures, two "its," can love is not at all clear).

Moreover, this "love" is not intrinsic to God as he really eternally is. Rather, it was only to achieve the objective of showing us how much God loves us, and giving us an example of how much we are to love God, that God (the "Spirit of Jesus") loved the Son (the "humanity of Jesus") and vice versa. In this view, the Father and Son "on occasion" *showed* and *expressed* love to one another *for our sake*—note how objective and detached the language is. They [really "he"] did this [really "appeared to do this"] not because they ["he"] really love each other [two "natures"], but only for a "show," an "example," a helpful illusion.

This Oneness position almost inclines us to think of two people who stay married and act in love "for the children's sake." But the situation is actually worse, because in the case of God there are really not even two "persons" to act! What was really going on, we are to believe—and only the "Oneness key" can open up this revelation for us—is that Jesus was simply loving *himself*. The interpersonal display was only a (supposedly) helpful illusion.

Therefore, in beholding the love of the Father for the Son and the love of the Son for the Father, we are not seeing anything that concerns the eternal heart of God himself. God could just as well have done without this pseudo-interpersonal "projected" love. Since the two "persons" are projected, and the love is expressed only for an example, none of this can tell us how God really is, how God really feels, what God is really like. In the Oneness view, we only know that God is "absolutely one," so whatever he is like, he is not like he appears when the Father and Son are portrayed as distinct and as perfectly loving one another. And thus in the end the Incarnation shows us, not what God is (compare John 1:14, 18), not even what God is like, but only what we human beings should be like!

The Father's Sacrifice of the Son

The Oneness denial of the personal distinctness and loving relationship of the Father and Son further leads them to minimize the New Testament theme of the Father's pain in sacrificing his "one and only Son." Indeed, it is not uncommon to hear and read Oneness authorities belittling the trinitarian understanding of the Father's sending of the Son. Sabin, for example, sarcastically asks, "What would it be for Him [God] to say, 'Go save them son'?" (Sabin, VI, 4). And he is continually proclaiming that "God did not send a deputy, He came Himself" (ibid., *passim*).

What would it be? he asks! At least according to the New Testament, it would be everything! Is there a theme that is more basic to the entire New Testament and more moving within God's Word than that the Father delivered up the Son? Jesus, for one, tells us "what it would be" as he tells the parable of a vineyard in which the landlord, after sending three servants who were killed by the tenants of his land, finally and tragically sent his well-beloved son (Mark 12:1–12). The poignancy of the story derives from the very fact that it was the landlord's own son who was killed. Yet, if sending one's son is no major deal, Jesus' parable is clearly of no value.

What would it be? Paul is filled with appreciative amazement when he declares that God "spared not his own Son, but delivered him up for us all . . ." (Rom. 8:32 KJV). And he goes on to ask rhetorically, if God gave us this much, ". . . shall he not with him also freely give us all things?"

Yet it is John, more than any other single author, who most frequently drives home "what it would be" as he repeatedly proclaims the theme that "God so loved the world" this much—"that he gave us his one and only Son" to "save the world through him" (John 3:16–17). One passage from John's first epistle summarizes this heartbeat of the gospel well:

This is how God showed his love among us: He sent his one and only Son into the world that we might live through him. This is love: not that we loved God, but that he loved us and sent his Son as an atoning sacrifice for our sins. . . . And we have seen and testify that the Father has sent his Son to be the Savior of the world. If anyone acknowledges that Jesus is the Son of God, God lives in him and he in God. And so we know and rely on the love God has for us. [1 John 4:9–10, 14–16]

God sent his one and only Son to die and be the Savior of the world! *What would this be?* It would be, and in fact is, the greatest sacrifice God could ever make. I, like any decent parent, would rather have any sort of harm come to me than to see one of my children suffer pain. The excruciating physical pain I once suffered for several hours after having my spleen and intestines crushed in an accident was nothing compared to the complete emotional devastation I experienced when I had to see the pain and listen to the screams of my five-year-old daughter when she had to endure similar pain after having gashed her forehead open. And I, of course, am far from embodying perfect parental love.

Yet even our imperfect experiences of parental love, and hence of parental pain, provide us with a way of conceptualizing to a small degree the type of love and pain that lay behind the agony of the cross. God is so great, and so loving, that he can and did experience not only the firsthand pain of the cross as Son, but also the much more devastating nightmare of participating in this as something like a perfectly loving parent—as Father. That's "what it would be," and what in fact it *was*, for the Father to send his Son into the world to die on the cross.

Within Oneness theology, however, the "giving up" of the "Son" does not have, and cannot have, a centrally significant role. The "Son" is simply the human nature—some simply say "the body" (e.g., Norris, 12ff.)—that the Father assumed. It is his "tabernacle" or "garment" (see Reed, 279ff., 299ff.). The Father's attachment to "it," to the extent that there is any attachment, must be less than what he has for any human person, for a human person is at least a *full person* distinct from God himself. For Oneness theology, however, the Son is not a distinct person at all, but only a "nature." And how emotionally attached can one get to a nature?

Thus, the poignancy of the gospel proclamation that the sacrificed Jesus was the Father's "one and only Son" is completely lost. "One and only Son" has no personal connotation in Oneness theology! And thus there cannot in this thought be any appreciation for the Father's infinitely intense anguish over the hellish death of his beloved Son. Indeed, nothing personal is even touched on the cross.

For this reason, there is no sense of tragedy in Oneness theology when the Son is sacrificed for our salvation. There is no real sense that "this should not have been." Indeed, on Oneness terms the only purpose for which the Son was ever created in the first place was to be sacrificed! For trinitarian theology, in contrast, the central reason why the Son was *incarnated* was to die, but the loving relationship between the Father and Son is something that has gone on throughout eternity. That the Son had to take on this saving mission at all should never have been and hence represents a painful tragedy within the Godhead.

In the end, the chief difference between trinitarian and Oneness theology is that trinitarian theology is free to (and obliged to) conceive of the sacrifice of the cross in familial terms, and this gives the cross its sharpest, most poignant expression. Oneness theology, on the other hand, has no room for this and hence must see the cross only as a heroic event. For Oneness exponents, the suffering of Jesus on the cross is the suffering of a solitary individual only—worse, it is the suffering of the human nature only of that individual. By contrast, in trinitarian theology, the suffering of Jesus on the cross is the suffering of *God* (Acts 20:28; 1 Cor. 2:8) as an individual, but also—and even more so—something like the suffering of a parent over the suffering of his or her child.

The Son IS God Himself

This leads us to a final point as it concerns the language of "the Father's sending the Son." It is simply erroneous to say, as Oneness adherents frequently argue, that if God sent his divine Son to save the world, "he did not come himself." We have already shown that, as much as we differ from Oneness theology, trinitarians share the conviction with them that God cannot be "divided into thirds." We have also shown that there is no more "mystery" (and in fact much less difficulty) involved in the trinitarian affirmation of the complete divinity of Christ than there is in the Oneness affirmation. Both affirm a God who is "nonquantifiable" and hence is mysterious.

Thus, trinitarians would insist, along with most Oneness people, that what Jesus endured *the totality of the Godhead endured*. For the fullness of the Godhead was in Christ (Col. 2:9)! The Son is *himself* God (Heb. 1:8; 1 John 5:20).

But as I have intimated earlier, I would go further and argue that *only* trinitarians can *consistently* maintain that what Jesus endured on the cross God himself endured. For only one who admits that God exists within himself in personally distinct ways can affirm that God could truly humble himself in order to become a real full human being—he did not just "robe himself in human flesh"—while at the same time remaining the transcendent Father "in heaven." And thus only a trinitarian can maintain that God himself personally experienced God-forsakenness in his incarnate state while not ceasing to be personally God as Father and Spirit.

Oneness theologians recognize this and have attempted to get around the difficulty in two equally heretical ways. Some have maintained that Jesus was really forsaken by God, which means that he, at that point, ceased to be God incarnate. Others refuse to say that Jesus could ever cease to be God incarnate and thus maintain that he was not really God-forsaken. But what no Oneness theologian can consistently do is maintain *both* the reality of the Incarnation and the reality of the God-forsaken crucifixion.

For trinitarianism, however, God can fully and personally experience the hell of the cross as a full human person because the God who exists in three distinct personal ways does not exhaust himself by becoming incarnate. Thus God can and did experience the forsakenness of the cross not only in a firsthand personal manner as Son, but he endured it from the equally (if not more) painful perspective of Father as well. And, we see, it is only by affirming the reality of the second perspective that one can consistently maintain the reality of the first. God can personally be the crucified Jesus because God can personally at the same time be the transcendent Father.

Love as the Essence of the Trinity

God Is Love

Our discussion thus far has brought us to what has to constitute the most fundamental and important difference between Oneness theology and classical trinitarian theology. To state the matter succinctly, classical trinitarianism has always understood the love that bursts forth between the Father and the Son throughout the pages of Holy Scripture (not in four or five isolated verses) to constitute the very definition of God as love (1 John 4:8, 16). From eternity to eternity, God *is* love, passionate love, unconditional love, perfect love! For orthodox trinitarianism, God's innermost being is the totally interpenetrating loving union of the three "persons" of the Trinity. For orthodox Christianity, then, God's eternal union is, in some sense, a form of loving communion. God is not a God whose natural state of being, apart from or before creation, is solitude.

For classical trinitarianism, the perfect love of the Godhead is understood to be turned outward toward us as we behold the perfect love of Jesus leading him to lay aside completely his "divine prerogatives" to become a total human being and die the undeserved death of the cross (John 1:1, 14; 2 Cor. 8:9; Phil. 2:5–8). This love, according to the traditional teaching, is turned outward toward us further as we perceive the manifested and real loving interaction of the really distinct Father and the incarnate Son. How they love in time has always been taken by the church to be a true revelation of how they love in eternity.

Finally, God's eternal triune celebration of love within himself has historically been understood to be turned outward toward us to the point of enveloping us within it (John 17:20–24) as we come to know that the Father was willing to sacrifice his "one and only" Son, that the Son was willing to suffer the God-forsaken hell of the cross, and that the love of the Spirit dwells within us, transforming our lives from within.

This is the heart of the Good News: "For God so loved the world that he gave his one and only Son . . ." (John 3:16). For classical trinitarianism, far from being a "projected illusion," here is where we see God totally unveiled before us. The mutually self-sacrificing and perfectly loving relationship between the Father and the Son leads to the infinite pain of the cross—the infinite pain of the Father over sacrificing his Son, and the infinite pain of the Son over suffering God-forsakenness on the cross—so that we who are wholly unworthy of this love might be redeemed by it and drawn into it. Nothing could be truer of the eternal God than this: He burns with passionate love within himself throughout eternity, and this leads him to burn with passionate love toward us in time. God is toward us in time, just as he is toward himself in eternity. He is triune.

For Oneness theology, however, this dynamic suffering love occurring between the Father and Son can only be a somewhat artificially assumed "example," as we have seen. For Sabin, it is all a temporary appearance to accomplish something else. If I might bring in a personal element to this, the only thing with which I associated all of Scripture's "Father/Son" talk when I was with the United Pentecostal Church was a theological problem that had to be explained away. John 3:16, and all such talk about "the Father's giving up his Son," about "the Lamb of God," and so on, was something I needed to explain away (and ultimately failed to do). I could never simply let the text say what it plainly says, for I was too preoccupied with trying to prove it didn't say what I felt (and was taught) it couldn't say. Thus, none of this beautiful relational language ever moved me as it does now.

The bottom line is this: When one rejects what a text of Scripture plainly says for the sake of an assumed ideology (such as "God is absolutely one"), one loses the message and the passion of the text. More specifically, when one takes away the *interpersonal* dimension of the Father/Son relationship, which is so clearly displayed throughout the entire New Testament—when one exchanges this for an abstract concept of "two natures" for the sake of preserving some preconceived pseudo-concept of the "pure unity of God"—one has really taken away the very heart of the gospel. Nothing poignant remains.

Could a God of Solitude Be Essentially Loving?

The loving interpersonal relationality of the triune God is not simply a truth that must be believed on the authority of Scripture (though that, of course, is more than enough to warrant its belief). As a number of the church's best thinkers have seen throughout the ages, this doctrine can also be seen in hindsight to be a "truth of reason." If there is a God, these thinkers have observed, reason itself will confirm to us that this God *must* be internally relational.

There are two senses in which this is true. First, as I have already argued, the very notion of an undifferentiated, unrelated unity—of an "absolute Oneness"—is an unintelligible notion. "Pure unity" is equivalent to "nothingness," and is therefore neither picturable nor conceivable. It is, in short, meaningless.

Second, and more important, the notion that God is in his essence alone, that apart from and before creation God exists in *total solitude*, is completely incompatible with the Christian understanding that God is essentially love or even essentially personal. A God who existed throughout eternity in his own unrelated "onliness" (to utilize Sabin's phrase), a God who eternally existed in "relationship" only to the utter blackness of nothingness, would be a God who could not be *eternally personal*, could not be a God who was *eternally social*, and thus could not be a God who was *eternally loving*. This, rather, is a God whose essence is solitude.

To state the matter another way, the God of Oneness theology is not a God who could be *essentially* interpersonal, and thus *essentially* loving, for what belongs to God's essence belongs to God eternally. God does not, for example, choose to be omnipresent or omnipotent, for these are things that God eternally *is*. He could not be otherwise. But, for Oneness theology, God is not social, and therefore actively loving, in this sense. God, in Oneness thought, is essentially only alone. If he decides to be social and loving, this is a secondary and contingent matter for God (though of supreme importance for us!). If this "absolutely one" God is to have interpersonal relationality, and therefore if this God is to love, this is something he must choose to do by creating a reality distinct from himself.

The truth of this insight can be put yet a third way. If one agrees that God always does what is best (and what believer doubts this?), and yet if one agrees that it is better that interpersonal relationships and interpersonal love exist as opposed to their being absent (and who would doubt this?), one must accept one of two conclusions: Either God has always been in a loving relationship *with something other than himself,* or God has always been in a loving interpersonal relationship *within himself.*

If we accept the former, we deny that God is self-sufficient and posit the eternal existence of some sort of nondivine world. For example, in process theology God needs the world and the creation is not an act of grace. If we accept the latter, however, we *must* postulate something like an "I-Thou" relationship within the Godhead. For only if there is an "I" and a "Thou," a sense of genuine "personal otherness" within God, can there be the kind of interpersonal relationality and love that a God who eternally "does what is best" would have.

This is exactly what the doctrine of the Trinity, and it alone, maintains. Therefore, it alone can render coherent the understanding that God is essentially love and yet that throughout eternity God does not need anything other than himself to be perfectly happy and to be doing what is best. The fact that something other than God exists (i.e., we and our world) is therefore a matter of sheer grace, not necessity.

Our Sociality as the Image of God

It has been a long-established insight of Christian theology that our understanding of the nature of God affects our understanding of ourselves, our relationship to our world, and our relationship to each other. Theology, in other words, has psychological, ecological, and sociological consequences. In short, our lives ultimately mirror the God we worship.

This means that the issue over the nature of God—whether he is essentially lovingly related within himself or whether he is essentially "absolutely one"—has important consequences for our own self-understanding. Let us therefore inquire into what it means to be "made in the image of God" (Gen. 1:26–27) to see what distinct consequences these two contrasting views might have.

If God is essentially solitary, if relationships are not something that belong to God's essence, something similar must hold true for us who are made in God's image. Or, to put it another way, if interpersonal love is not the eternal essence of God, it cannot be the essence of those who are made in his image.

That is to say, one cannot in the Oneness view understand our relationship to the world or to other people as being essential to who we are. Our relationships, in this view, do not reach our core, for God's relationships do not affect his core, and we are made in his image. However much Oneness adherents may deny it, interpersonal sociality and love cannot be the supreme virtue in their theology, for the Creator who they worship, in whose image they are made, is essentially many things before he contingently decided to become interpersonal and loving. Indeed, God could have gotten by forever without any interpersonal relationships and love at all—and we are in his image.

This view, in my estimation, is tragic. On the one hand, it completely misses what is truest and best about human nature: namely, that we are created to be essentially related to other people, to love others. We are never complete in solitude. And, on the other hand, because this view exalts divine solitude, I believe it subtly prescribes an attitude that wrongly prioritizes behavior above love. For, in this view, who we are in relation to one another is not about our *essential being*, but only about our *contingent doing*—just as God's relationship to any other is not about his essential being, but only about his contingent doing.

All of this is directly related to my previous observation that the modalistic view of God undermines the genuineness of God's self-revelation. For, in this view, we never get behind the God who performs. All the revealed relationality of God in the New Testament thus has the air of "transient illusion" because it is not about God as he essentially is, but only about God as he has chosen to act.

This helps us to understand the fact (already discussed in chapter 6) that Oneness Pentecostalism tends toward works salvation. One is not saved, in this theology, by virtue of *being* in a gracious loving relationship with Christ alone. Rather, salvation is tied, in a most particular fashion, to what one *does*. Unless one speaks the exactly right words when baptized in exactly the right way, one's sins are not washed away. One must further show the one correct sign of having the Holy Spirit, speaking in tongues, or one is again lost. Furthermore, one must adhere to the "standards" supposedly set by God—women never cutting their hair, men having short hair, and so on—or one is again not saved. (See appendixes A, B, and C on these subjects.) One's saving acceptance by God hangs on all this activity. The God who performs, we should not be surprised to see, creates a people obsessed with performing.

It has been my experience, and the experience of many of the ex-UPCI believers I have conversed with, that this performance orientation tends to carry over into the social structure of many Oneness groups as well. This is what gives many Oneness churches a "cultic" quality.[8] The performance-oriented God who loves or damns because of behavior tends to create a people who accept or reject each other (and "outsiders") because of behavior. For again, we always tend to mirror the God we worship.

One is therefore likely to find an unusually high degree of behavioral conformity in Oneness churches. This is rendered inevitable, since acceptance into the saved community is usually contingent upon one's conforming to the behavior of the community—whether this is explicitly spoken by an authority figure or is simply communicated through peer pressure. Disconformity—individuality—thus often leads to the individuals being ostracized or even officially excommunicated from the community.

There is, then, simply no motivation to love and accept people unconditionally—whether inside or outside the church. In Oneness theology, such activities as loving and accepting are not about our being, but about our doing—for we are made in the image of "the God of solitude."

The Practical Significance of the Trinity

It may seem that we have gone off track from our discussion of the Trinity, but in fact we have never left it. And this, I think, simply shows how eminently practical this supposedly "abstract" and "theoretical" doctrine really is.

For trinitarians, God is essentially and eternally loving, for God is essentially and eternally social. And we who are created in his image are created to be mini-examples of this eternal sociality and this eternal lovingness. Therefore, our individual self-realization is not to be found in isolation from others, for the one triune God who created us is not a God whose essence is solitude. Rather, because we are made in the image of the triune God, our own self-actualization is achieved only when and as we engage with one another in loving interaction. This is true regardless of how "worthy" or "unworthy" the recipient of our love is. We love simply because it is our created and regenerated essence to do so. Hence we are created to love unconditionally.

What is more, because we know that God's eternal essence is pure love, we know that our being related to him is not something extraneous to who he eternally is. God is not "really" a God of solitude who is now just "appearing" to be related to us, as both ancient and modern modalism suggests. Rather, we know that God is naturally being the infinitely loving God who he eternally is precisely when he enters into the unconditional relationship with us that he desires. Hence we can understand how it is that we can be made whole, that we are "saved," only by God's grace. We don't need to—and we can't—*do* something to make God do something he wouldn't otherwise do. Our performance is not the issue.

To say this another way, a trinitarian who lives his or her theology will know and experience the unconditional love of God, for such a person will know and experience that God loves him or her in Christ with the same love God eternally has for his Son. In turn such a person will, through the Spirit, love God with the very same love the Son has for his Father. Because God is essentially social and loving, our loving relationship with him is not a sort of bridge to God we construct with our "good" behavior, as the Oneness theology requires. Rather, our relationship with him is something God himself accomplishes by opening up his loving sociality now to include us. Our acceptance before God is wholly based on God's performance—which manifests who God eternally is. It is not even related to *our* performance. Hence, in a word, as we are loved by God, and as we love God, *we participate in God's eternal triune love.* And nothing could be further from a solitary God who loves "on condition that. . . ."

This brings us back full circle to the issue surrounding the previously discussed problem of revelation posed by modalism. It is no mere coincidence that a view of God that undermines the authenticity of God's triune revelation ends up with a legalistic, behavioralistic Christianity. It is no coincidence that the "absolutely one" God who is hidden behind the three "illusory" roles he performs produces a people who need to hide behind their own performances. And it is no coincidence that a view of God that undermines the authenticity of his revelation also undermines the authenticity of his eternal love, for God's revelation is nothing other than his eternal love turned outward.

All these things so crucial to Christianity—God's revelation, love, and grace—are lost whenever one denies the eternal Trinity. For, when all is said and done, the doctrine of the Trinity simply means that God is a God of eternal love, a God of grace, and a God who is unconditionally and authentically open and revealed in the manifested activity of the Father, in the Son, through the Holy Spirit. If you deny the eternality of the three personal ways God is God, you end up undermining the very essence of Christianity.

Appendix A

Salvation, the Spirit, and Tongues

What made the Pentecostal movement distinctive from the start was its insistence that speaking in tongues is the "initial physical evidence" that always accompanies the baptism of the Holy Spirit referred to in the Book of Acts. No tongues, no Holy Spirit baptism.

For traditional Pentecostals, however, this didn't mean that one did not have the Holy Spirit and was not saved until one spoke in tongues. For faith, the Pentecostals rightly saw, was itself a work of the Spirit (1 Cor. 12:3), and faith in Jesus Christ was what saved a person. The "baptism in the Spirit" in Acts, therefore, was about "empowering for service" (Acts 1:8), not about salvation.

A more radical doctrine began to emerge, however, among the Oneness Pentecostals when they broke away from the trinitarians in 1916. Oneness preachers began to preach that unless one was baptized in the Holy Spirit with the evidence of speaking in tongues, one did not have the Holy Spirit at all. For these individuals there existed *no distinction* between the infilling of the Spirit spoken of in Acts (1:5, 8; 2:4; 4:31; etc.) and the possession of the Spirit referred to throughout the rest of the New Testament (Rom.

197

8:9–11; 1 Cor. 3:16; etc.). Hence, since Paul says that one without the Spirit of Christ "does not belong to Christ" (Rom. 8:9), it followed, for these misguided preachers, that anyone who had not spoken in tongues had *not yet been saved.* This person was yet a sinner who would die in his or her sins unless at some point tongues flowed from his or her mouth. This remains the teaching of the United Pentecostal Church and most other Oneness Pentecostal groups.

Though it is almost always minimized or completely overlooked in summaries of this movement, I believe that this doctrine of the necessity of tongues is, in terms of its direct effect upon people, the most psychologically harmful of all the teachings of the United Pentecostal Church and other "apostolic faith" groups. One simply *must* speak in tongues to be saved and to be a part of God's "holy community." This, obviously, puts tremendous psychological and sociological pressure on people to speak in tongues. Quite literally, more could not be at stake than what is at stake in whether or not one speaks in tongues. Each night you go to bed not yet having spoken in tongues, you go to bed without God's salvation.[1]

Unfortunately, some people have trouble, or find it impossible, to speak in tongues. (Is it even something one can and should "try" to do?) From a theological standpoint, this is not an ability God gives to everyone (1 Cor. 12:30), and psychologically it seems to require a certain degree of abandon that some people find difficult to accomplish.[2]

From the Oneness standpoint, however, the only reason why someone has not spoken in tongues is that he or she is not yet salvation-worthy. This person has not yet "completely yielded" to God (#6145, Pugh, 57), or does not yet have "sufficient faith" (Pugh, ch. 3, 34f.), or perhaps has not "really" repented of his or her sins (Pugh, 34–37). In any case, if individuals have not spoken in tongues, it is unquestionably their fault, not God's, for it is forever reiterated that God wants everyone to have the Holy Spirit and be saved (that is, to speak in tongues). Failure to speak in tongues, then, not only ostracizes a person from God's love and God's people; it is a direct indictment of his or her moral state.

How vividly, and sadly, I recall the numerous people in my UPCI experience who vigorously "sought" for the Holy Spirit for months and years on end. After nearly every service, these unfortunate souls would be up at the altar praying to God to save them, sometimes screaming, begging, and crying out to God to "give them the Holy Ghost" to save them. Why God was holding back on them they did not know. They, and everyone else, only knew it was *their* fault.

This doctrine, I firmly believe, gives the UPCI and similar Oneness groups the distinction of being the most legalistic "Christian" movement in church history. The heresy that we are saved by our works and that grace simply assists us in carrying out these works has popped its head up numerous times throughout the history of the church. But never before has it ever been suggested that one could actually do all the works, could completely believe in and love the Lord, could actually "keep all the rules," and even be baptized in the correct way—and yet *still* be unsaved! Never before has there been any form of Christianity, however heretical, that has suggested that one could want to be saved and do everything within one's power to be saved, and yet not be saved *and not even know why!* This is utterly, and tragically, and heretically, unique.

The Oneness Argument Stated

The UPCI understanding of the necessity of tongues as a sign of one's receiving the Holy Spirit is based entirely on four passages of Scripture, all of them from the Book of Acts. The first comes from the second chapter of Acts:

> When the day of Pentecost came, they [the disciples] were all together in one place. Suddenly a sound like the blowing of a violent wind came from heaven and filled the whole house where they were sitting. They saw what seemed to be tongues of fire that separated and came to rest on each of them. All of them were filled with the Holy Spirit and began to speak in other tongues as the Spirit enabled them. [Acts 2:1–4]

Oneness Pentecostals point out that tongues here was "the sign" that the disciples had received the Holy Spirit, which Jesus had previously promised (Luke 24:49; Acts 1:4–5). They ask, "Why think that the sign today should be any different?"

The second passage used to substantiate the "initial evidence" doctrine comes from Acts 8. Here we find that Philip had successfully preached the Good News to the Samaritans and to Simon the sorcerer, whom the people of Samaria had been following (vv. 5–11). In some sense the Samaritans and Simon himself had believed and obeyed Philip's preaching, for they had appropriately responded to his preaching by being baptized (v. 12). Still, something was missing. They had not received the Holy Spirit. Hence Philip called for Peter and John to come up from Jerusalem and pray that the Samaritans "might receive the Holy Spirit" (v. 15). John and Peter arrived in Samaria, and the narrative continues:

> Then Peter and John placed their hands on them, and they received the Holy Spirit. When Simon saw that the Spirit was given at the laying on of the apostles' hands, he offered them money and said, "Give me also this ability so that everyone on whom I lay my hands may receive the Holy Spirit." [Acts 8:17–19]

Tongues, of course, is not mentioned in this verse. But, the Oneness Pentecostals point out, Simon saw something. It must have been something visible and/or audible. And since tongues is mentioned as "the sign" in the other three accounts, is it not reasonable to assume that this is what Simon saw here?

The third passage used by the UPCI to establish this doctrine comes from Acts 10 in which Peter is shown preaching the first Gentile evangelistic sermon to the household of Cornelius. Beginning in verse 44 we read:

> While Peter was still speaking these words, the Holy Spirit came on all who heard the message. The circumcised believers who had come with Peter were astonished that the gift of the Holy Spirit had been poured out even on the Gentiles. For they heard them speaking in tongues and praising God. [10:44–46]

Again, the argument goes, the "evidence" that convinced Peter that the Gentiles had in fact been saved was that he heard them speaking in tongues. And so it should be today.

The fourth and final passage is in Acts 19. Here we find Paul confronting certain disciples concerning the adequacy of their Christian instruction. It turns out that they had not yet received Christian baptism, nor had they even heard of the Holy Spirit. To remedy this, Paul baptized them and began to pray with them and lay his hands on them. When he did this, the Scripture continues, "the Holy Spirit came on them, and they spoke in tongues and prophesied" (Acts 19:6).

Hence, the Oneness Pentecostals argue, tongues was always the sign for receiving the Holy Spirit in the Bible, and so it should be today. Without this sign, no one has the right to say that they have the Holy Spirit or that they belong to Christ (Rom. 8:9). (See Pugh, 29, 37; Reeves, Tongues, 33; Bernard, New Birth, ch. 9.)

The Spirit and Tongues in the Book of Acts

The Pattern in Acts

It is, I shall subsequently argue, precarious at best to base any doctrine on the historical record of Acts unless this doctrine is confirmed in some didactic portion of Scripture. But there are a number of problems with the Oneness position on tongues, even if we grant for the moment that Acts *can* be used in this fashion.

The first observation that needs to be made is that the "method" of "receiving the Holy Spirit" among Oneness churches does not, as a matter of fact, conform to the pattern found in the Book of Acts. There is, first of all, no instance of anyone seeking for the Holy Spirit, and certainly no instance of anyone seeking or looking for tongues as the initial evidence of the Holy Spirit. (The disciples in Acts 1 and 2 did wait in the upper room for the coming of the Holy Spirit at Pentecost, but these disciples were already saved, were not "seeking" or begging for the Spirit, and, so far as we can tell, were not expecting tongues.) In each instance in the Book of Acts the Holy Spirit simply "falls" on people, and the people are entirely passive, if not surprised, during the event (cf. Acts 4:31; 13:52). There is nothing in the Book of Acts, or anywhere else in the Bible, that comes close to the phenomenon of believing people begging God for the Holy Spirit or trying for days or years to purify or surrender themselves so that the Holy Spirit would come.

Relatedly, there is nothing in the Book of Acts suggesting that the reception of the Holy Spirit is at all contingent upon the subjective state of the believing individual, as though it were some kind of reward for someone who had (finally!) "completely" yielded himself. This is why in each of the four instances found in the Book of Acts the Holy Spirit falls on *all* the believers *at the same time*. Is one to believe that each of these believers just "happened" finally to purify and surrender themselves at the exact same moment? Of course not.

This is also why Jesus can unconditionally promise the disciples that the Holy Spirit will come upon all of them and empower them to witness (Luke

24:49; Acts 1:8). If this coming were dependent in any way upon the disciples' subjective state, it could not be unconditionally promised.

But these observations count decisively against the UPCI claim that they alone follow the "biblical pattern" for receiving the Holy Spirit. In Oneness churches the supposed reception of the Holy Spirit is directly contingent upon the moral and/or psychological state of the individual, and rarely, if ever, does the Holy Spirit "fall" upon entire groups. In my fifteen years of studying this movement, including four years from the inside, I have never seen this experience happen to more than one individual at a time. And the most I have ever seen experience this in one night is three. But, by the UPCI's own hermeneutics, this is without biblical precedent.

So, if one is going to use the Book of Acts as an absolute legalistic norm of how the salvation experience must always be, one should hold that the candidates for salvation cannot seek for the Holy Spirit, they cannot worry about tongues, and they cannot receive him by themselves, but only in groups. Oneness Pentecostals, however, want to seize upon tongues as the one normative element in Acts and bypass everything else.

The Spirit and Salvation in the Book of Acts

Relatedly, there is nothing in the Book of Acts to suggest that Luke the historian was attempting to teach his reader Theophilus (Luke 1:3; Acts 1:1) that the infilling of the Holy Spirit has anything to do with one's salvation. Rather, as just about everyone throughout church history except the Oneness Pentecostals has seen, Luke is referring to a special anointing from God that supernaturally empowers people to carry out God's will dynamically.

Hence Luke records the angel's promise to Elizabeth that her son John would "be great in the sight of the Lord" and would "be filled with the Holy Spirit even from birth" (Luke 1:15). Following the pattern of Old Testament heroes who were filled with the Holy Spirit in order to accomplish God's will (e.g., Exod. 31:3; Num. 11:25; Judg. 3:10; 6:34; 14:6; 1 Sam. 10:10; 16:13), Luke is here simply conveying that John the Baptist would be a dynamic man of God from a very early age. This obviously has nothing to do with John's personal salvation.

Later in this same chapter Elizabeth is said to have been "filled with the Holy Spirit" (Luke 1:41). Does this signify that she was finally saved? Of course not. Rather, her being filled with the Holy Spirit was for the purpose of the prophecy regarding Mary that she was to give (vv. 42–45). A few verses later, Zechariah is also "filled with the Holy Spirit" (v. 67) for the purpose of prophesying about the coming Messiah (vv. 68–79). Nothing could be farther from Luke's narrative intention here than the suggestion that the infilling of the Holy Spirit is somehow associated with Elizabeth's or Zechariah's personal salvation.

Finally, something very similar is later said in Luke's Gospel regarding Simeon (2:25) and Jesus himself (4:1). In each case the Holy Spirit is associated with God's dynamic anointing and presence in a person's life. One might also incidentally note that tongues played no role in any of these "infillings."

The only aspect of the Holy Spirit's work that changes in the church age, as recorded in Acts, is the scope of the Spirit's work. Whereas the Holy Spirit only occasionally "filled" certain individuals with a special calling in the time before Pentecost, now the Holy Spirit is to "fill" *all* believers. This is the essence of what Peter is saying to the Jews on the day of Pentecost immediately succeeding the disciples' experience in the upper room. When accused of having overindulged in wine, Peter responds by saying:

> "Fellow Jews and all of you who live in Jerusalem, let me explain this to you.
> . . . this is what was spoken by the prophet Joel:
>
> > 'In the last days, God says,
> > I will pour out my Spirit on all people.
> > Your sons and daughters will prophesy,
> >   your young men will see visions,
> >   your old men will dream dreams.
> > Even on my servants, both men and women,
> >   I will pour out my Spirit in those days,
> >   and they will prophesy.'"[Acts 2:14–18]

As an aside, one cannot help but notice that Peter does not record the prophecy as saying, "I will pour out my Spirit in those days and they will speak in tongues." The only place in Acts where something about the "evidence" of the Holy Spirit's coming is taught (not speculatively implied) associates it primarily with prophecy (cf. Num. 11:25f.; 1 Sam. 10:10f.; 19:20f.; Luke 1:41, 67; Acts 19:6). If one mistakenly felt compelled to come up with some biblical teaching about the "initial physical evidence" of the outpouring of the Holy Spirit, then, I would think, this would be it. But, as I shall shortly argue, the whole enterprise of seeking for a single "initial evidence" is wrongheaded.

In any case, what is important for us presently to note is that what is distinctive about the work of the Spirit in the church age, according to Peter, is that the Spirit will be poured out on all people. "The promise," Peter again proclaims, "is for you and your children and for all who are far off . . ." (Acts 2:39). Hence the supernatural phenomena (e.g., prophecy, visions, healings) that have always been associated with the Spirit will, after Pentecost, be available not just to one or two great men of God, but to the entire people of God! The point Peter is making is that the Spirit is for the church, and the church is for all people.

This is one more reason why it is significant that the Spirit's initial outpouring in Acts 2, 8, 10, and 19 (cf. also 4:31 and 13:52) occurs to groups and not individuals. And this is also why Luke has a different class of people represented in each of these outpourings. He is showing the universality of the gospel and the dynamic Spirit that accompanies the gospel. And all of this simply follows the pattern of Jesus' promise of what would happen after the Spirit was poured out (Acts 1:8).

Finally, a case can be made that it is Luke's understanding of the universality of the Spirit that leads him to find the presence of tongues to be significant enough to mention (along with prophecy and praise) in three of the four cases in which he records these groups as receiving the Holy Spirit. The manifestation of tongues among each of these unique classes of people may symbolize for Luke the universality of the Spirit, which begins to tear down the divisive walls represented by the different languages of humankind. The phenomenon of Pentecost, when everyone understands the praising disciples "in his own native language" (Acts 2:4–13), reverses the phenomenon of Babel, when for the first time groups of people were separated by a language barrier (Gen. 11:1–9).

In any case, it should by now be clear that Luke's intention in speaking about the "outpouring" or "baptism" of the Holy Spirit in his Gospel and in Acts has nothing to do with how individuals are supposed to be saved.

Everything else we read about the Spirit in Acts simply confirms this. Thus, when Jesus refers to the Spirit's future outpouring, he associates it with power to witness, not salvation (Acts 1:8). When the disciples receive the Spirit, there is nothing to suggest that they were all here saved for the first time. Rather, they were all here empowered and, as Jesus promised, turned into dynamic witnesses for him (Acts 2:4ff.; 3:12ff.; 4:8ff.; etc.).

Moreover, Acts 4 records that the Jerusalem community was again "filled with the Holy Spirit," and they therefore "spoke the word of God boldly"

(4:31). This "filling" empowered them to witness boldly; it did not save them. They were already saved (see Acts 2:41–47). So, too, Luke notes that Paul, Barnabas, and other disciples "were filled with joy and with the Holy Spirit" as a way of explaining the wonderful manner in which the Word of God was dynamically preached in the face of persecution among the Gentiles (Acts 13:49–52).

The connection Luke is making between the dynamic outpouring of the Spirit and spiritual dynamism in a believer's life is also made clear by the way he at crucial points describes individual believers as being "filled with the Holy Spirit." Peter, for example, is described as being "filled with the Holy Spirit" (Acts 4:8) just prior to his bold sermon before the Sanhedrin. Luke clearly is not in this verse simply saying that Peter was saved. He is describing Peter as being unusually energized by the Holy Spirit.

So, too, when the apostles are looking for deacons and ask the church to "choose seven men from among [them] who are known to be full of the Spirit" (Acts 6:3), they are not simply asking for seven saved people. This much would be true of the entire church. Salvation is not the issue surrounding the infilling of the Spirit; divine empowerment is.

Thus, when Stephen is two verses later described as "a man full of faith and of the Holy Spirit," Luke must be understood to be alluding to a distinctive aspect of this man. In other words, what is said of Stephen is something that cannot be said of all Christians all the time. He was a man "on fire" for God. With good reason, then, Luke later reminds his reader that Stephen was "full of the Holy Spirit" just prior to giving his final witness for Christ as a martyr (7:54–55). As Jesus promised, when one is saturated with ("baptized with," "filled with," etc.) the Holy Spirit, one does indeed become bold.

In just the same way, Jesus (10:38), Barnabas (11:24), and Paul (13:9) are all described as being "filled with the Holy Spirit," and in each of these instances this is said as a way of explaining how it is that they accomplished for God what they accomplished. In none of the instances does it have anything to do with salvation.

Of course, the work of the Holy Spirit is necessary for salvation, for faith is necessary for salvation, and we who are dead in our sins, who are by nature children of wrath, whose hearts are in and of themselves desperately wicked and at war with God, would never come to love and trust God for our salvation on our own (e.g., John 6:29, 44, 65; Acts 16:14; Rom. 3:9–20; 1 Cor.

12:3). Faith, then, is a gift. It is the result of the gracious internal working of the Spirit of God.

But this is not what Luke has in mind when he is phenomenologically describing members of the historical church as being "filled with the Spirit of God." Hence, whereas Paul, for example, primarily thinks about the personal transformation from desperate sinner to loving saint when he thinks of "the Spirit," Luke recollects the historical alteration from ordinary believer to extraordinary witness when he thinks of "the Spirit." This difference of perspective is due to the fact that Luke is writing theological history, whereas Paul is writing what we might call pastoral theology. The main point Luke is making to Theophilus, his reader, is that the early church exploded the way it did because the Holy Spirit was making extraordinary witnesses out of a lot of ordinary people like Peter, Stephen, Paul, and Barnabas. What occurred on occasion in the period of the Old Testament was widespread in the New Testament era, and it is still available to all today.

Mistaking Descriptive History for Prescriptive Doctrine

I argued above that even if the Book of Acts is understood to provide a normative pattern for how all individuals must receive the Holy Spirit, one still must reject the "apostolic faith" approach to this issue. For in Acts we never find anyone seeking for or even anticipating the outpouring of the Spirit. It comes spontaneously and without preparation. We never find such things as individuals or groups waiting for (let alone begging for) salvation, worrying about tongues (or even knowing about them ahead of time), or receiving the Holy Spirit in a group smaller than twelve. Therefore, the Oneness groups fail to follow even their own prescribed use of Acts as the normative pattern for how salvation should always occur.

What needs to be pointed out, however, is that even the attempt to use Acts in this fashion is really misguided. One of the most fundamental principles in interpreting the Bible is that we must interpret a writing in accordance with the purpose that the author had in composing the writing. We cannot, for example, derive literal information about (say) God's appearance or about a scientific cosmology from the Psalms (e.g., Ps. 18:7–15; 104:2–9), because these poems were not written with the intent of communicating this kind of information. In just the same fashion, we cannot derive a doctrinal or behavioral prescription directly from historical description. To say what happened is not the same as saying what should *always* happen.

Luke is writing as a historian, not a systematic theologian, in his Gospel-Acts volumes. He tells his reader Theophilus that he has "investigated everything from the beginning" so that he can now bring forth "an orderly account" of the life of Jesus and the early life of the church ("the things that have been fulfilled among us"). This history, he hopes, will help convince Theophilus that the gospel he has "been taught" is true (Luke 1:1–4). This explains Luke's above-mentioned concern to emphasize the supernatural work of the Holy Spirit in the early church.

The point to be taken here is that Luke presupposes that Theophilus has *already* been taught the gospel (Luke 1:4). His purpose, then, is not to reteach him this, but to now tell how all this came about. Therefore, if we look to Acts to be taught the gospel—how we should get saved—we are bound to go astray, for this work was never written for this purpose.

To turn specifically to the UPCI's interpretation of the references to tongues in Acts, we must first simply point out that Luke nowhere teaches that tongues-speaking is the initial evidence of the Holy Spirit. Only in one passage does he include any didactic material on the subject of what "signs" will follow the outpouring of the Spirit, but here it is prophecy, dreams, and visions that are mentioned, not tongues (Acts 2:17–18). Yet even here there is no intention of prescribing what exactly the outpouring of the Spirit must *always* look like. Peter is simply stating some of the more interesting phenomena that will generally accompany this outpouring "in the last days." He is not giving us anything like a legalistic formula.

Even less can the other passages in Acts be used to prescribe didactically what the outpouring of the Spirit must look like. In the second chapter of Acts a number of things are mentioned in connection with the outpouring of the Spirit—the sound of a violent blowing wind, tongues of fire appearing on each disciple's head, speaking in tongues, people understanding these tongues (2:1–4, 11)—yet there is no indication that any of these things is to be taken as normative for all church history. They are simply recorded because they happened. Indeed, Luke leaves them completely uninterpreted. They do have theological significance (which can be learned especially by studying the Old Testament), but they are not a normative prescription for the individual salvation experience.

The other occurrences of the Spirit's outpouring are recorded in similarly objective, uninterpreted fashion. In Acts 8:17 Luke simply tells us that the Samaritans all received the Holy Spirit when Peter and John placed their hands on them. Left open are the questions of why Peter and John had to come, why the Holy Spirit had not yet come, why the laying on of hands was significant, and how they all knew that the Spirit had come when he finally did come. What is certainly clear, however, is that Luke was not trying to teach Theophilus that the answer to any of these questions—whatever it might turn out to be—was normative and necessary for all time. What kind of pedagogy would that be? Rather, these questions are not addressed precisely because they were not germane to what Luke did want Theophilus to learn.

Acts 10:44–46 is no different. The Gentiles received the Holy Spirit in the middle of Peter's sermon, they spoke in tongues, they praised God, they were baptized, it was wonderful and miraculous. That was the end of Luke's interest. The fact that in this one case he states that the Jews knew the Gentiles had received the Holy Spirit because they started speaking in tongues and praising God (v. 46) tells us nothing more than one historical fact—namely, that when the Holy Spirit was first outpoured among the Gentiles, the Jews knew it to their own surprise because they heard them speak in tongues and praise God.

It is not taught, or even remotely suggested, that this is the way it had to happen then and has to happen now. One can no more take this passage as prescriptive for all time than one can deduce from Acts 4:32–37 that the contemporary church should sell all private property and share all things in common.

Finally, in Acts 19:6–7, Luke simply reports, without interpretation, that certain disciples "spoke in tongues and prophesied" when the Holy Spirit came on them through the laying on of hands. Was it Luke's intention here to teach that tongues is the necessary sign of the reception of the Holy Spirit? Or perhaps, since Peter mentions prophecy in his first sermon (Acts 2:17–18) and since this is a superior gift (1 Cor. 14:1–5), was Luke suggesting that the prophesying mentioned here is the necessary "initial physical evidence"? Or is he saying that one must lay hands on a person before they receive the Holy Spirit? Or that the Holy Spirit only comes to groups of twelve or more (since this, too, fits with the other three occurrences)?

The answer to all these questions is that we are asking the wrong questions! Luke is perfectly clear about saying what he wants to say. But he simply is not interested in saying the kind of thing these questions invite. Indeed, so uninterpreted is Luke's objective reporting that he leaves it up to us to infer why he even placed just these four accounts in his work rather than some other occurrences of the Spirit's initial outpouring. And, far from providing us with a normative pattern to follow, it seems that the best guess is that Luke included just these four occurrences of the Spirit's outpouring because they were *not* normative!

These four accounts are certainly not little glimpses into the everyday operation of the early church. In each of the Acts recordings we have the gospel surprisingly reaching out in unusual ways to people who had previously been excluded from the revelation of God. When this occurs, unusual things happen. Indeed, given the time span that Luke seeks to cover with his Acts volume, it is not surprising if he tends to lift out of the ordinarily mundane history of the early church those rare things that are most spectacular and unusual, for this is most likely what will convince his reader Theophilus that the church is indeed a work of God and that the gospel that it preaches is therefore true.

To set this work up as a norm for all church experience is thus to set up a very rich—and very unhealthy—diet for oneself indeed. Nothing but harm and heresy can come from such an endeavor. But this, in a nutshell, is precisely what we find occurring in Oneness Pentecostalism.

Four Final Objections

I will conclude my refutation of the standard Oneness Pentecostal view of tongues as the "initial evidence" for receiving the Holy Spirit by briefly articulating four final objections.

1. Not only is there no corroborating evidence in the Epistles that any New Testament church ever placed evidential and saving significance on tongues, there is actually some evidence *against* such a notion. In 1 Corinthians 12:30 Paul rhetorically asks his audience, "Do all speak in tongues?" The structure and context of the remark make it indisputably clear that the answer is assumed to be "of course not." Could Paul really have asked this if he (and the Corinthians) in fact believed that all saved Christians do at some point speak in tongues? I think it renders the question absurd.

Oneness Pentecostals are likely to respond to this argument by making a distinction between the "evidential" tongues referred to in Acts and the "gift of tongues" referred to in 1 Corinthians. And, their response goes, it is only the *latter* use of tongues that Paul assumes only some Christians have. All Christians, in other words, speak in tongues when they are initially filled with the Spirit, but only some continue to have this gift as it functions in the church and in private prayer.

This response, I think, fails to answer the objection. If Paul himself had at least hinted at some distinction between these two kinds of tongues, the response might carry some weight. But, as a matter of fact, no such hint is to be found. Paul speaks about tongues and its limited usage in this context without any qualification. Indeed, had Paul known of some sort of tongues distinction as the Oneness Pentecostals make, one would expect him to mention it here. Certainly if a pastor of a United Pentecostal Church today suggested flat out that not everyone speaks in tongues, he would have to make it clear immediately that he was referring only to the exercise of the "gift of tongues," not to the supposed "evidential" use of tongues.

What is more relevant, however, is that Paul does mention that tongues can indeed serve as a "sign" (1 Cor. 14:22–23), but not in any sense close to the way it functions as a "sign" in Oneness Pentecostal churches. For Paul here says that tongues "are a sign . . . for unbelievers." Although the precise meaning of this verse is a matter of some controversy, this need not detain us presently. I believe that one point from this is quite clear: If Paul and the Corinthians had known about a notion of tongues as a sign in any other sense than that being mentioned here, we would expect there to be some hint of it. The unqualified way he speaks of tongues as a "sign" in this context could only bring about confusion if in fact there existed another use of tongues as a "sign" that was really more important: namely, its function as evidence that one has initially received the Holy Spirit.

The Bible does say much, and in very plain language, about what the "evidence" of the reception of the Holy Spirit and of salvation is, but this talk never has to do with speaking in tongues. Indeed, a great percentage of one book of the Bible, 1 John, is about little other than this. Listen to a brief sampling of relevant verses from this epistle:

> . . . if anyone obeys his word, God's love is truly made complete in him. This is how we know we are in him. [2:5]

> This is how we know who the children of God are and who the children of the devil are: Anyone who does not do what is right is not a child of God; nor is anyone who does not love his brother. [3:10]

> This is how you can recognize the Spirit of God: Every spirit that acknowledges that Jesus Christ has come in the flesh is from God, but every spirit that does not acknowledge Jesus is not from God. . . . [4:2–3, cf. 1 Cor. 12:3]

> We are from God, and whoever knows God listens to us; but whoever is

not from God does not listen to us. This is how we recognize the
Spirit of truth and the spirit of falsehood. [4:6]

If anyone acknowledges that Jesus is the Son of God, God lives in him
and he in God. [4:15]

If the Oneness Pentecostals are correct in saying that the only way one can
know that one has the Spirit of God at all is by speaking in tongues, the
multitude of such biblical statements as these cannot be true, for in the Oneness view one can believe in, love, and obey God, and at least appear to have
the fruits of the Spirit, and yet not have the Holy Spirit—if one has not yet
spoken in tongues. In the biblical view, however, genuine faith in Jesus
Christ is all the evidence of salvation one ever needs.

2. The second concluding objection to be raised against the "initial evidence" doctrine concerns the contradiction it creates within Oneness theology itself. In a word, Oneness exponents have a great deal of trouble making
sense out of the multitude of Pentecostal and charismatic believers who have
spoken in tongues but have not been "correctly" baptized on the one hand,
and those Oneness Pentecostal people who have been "correctly" baptized but
have never spoken in tongues on the other. The former class of people suggests that there are some who are "acceptable" to God to the point where
God will come and dwell within them while their sins are not yet even forgiven. And the latter class of people suggests that there are some who have
had their sins forgiven, but who for some reason are not yet "acceptable" to
God!

Both conclusions, however, are absurd and render meaningless the Oneness understanding of both God's forgiveness and his indwelling Spirit, for
neither is by itself indicative of God's intention to save a person. What significance does God's indwelling Spirit have for us if it doesn't necessarily
mean that we are in a saving, loving relationship with the Father? And what
significance can God's forgiveness of sins (supposedly through Jesus' Name
baptism) have if God can yet have something against us (as he must if he
will not give us his Spirit)?

3. The third concluding argument concerning the Oneness "initial evidence" doctrine is that all the post-canonical evidence from the early Fathers
counts decisively against it. If tongues had anything close to saving significance in the apostolic period, one would expect this to be taught to the disciples of the apostles. Certainly everything else pertaining to salvation and
"entrusted to the saints" (Jude 3) was handed on successfully to the next

generation. At the very least, one would expect that if this saving belief was somehow "slipping between the cracks" in the second and third generations, someone would have noticed it or contended for it.

As it turns out, however, none of the writings of the second, third, or fourth centuries supplies a shred of evidence that the church ever held to anything like an "initial evidence" doctrine, let alone one invested with eternal saving significance. To the best of my knowledge, no patristic scholar, and not even any Oneness exponent, has attempted to defend such an impossibly unsubstantiated thesis.[3]

There are, of course, occasional references in these writings to such things as "the gifts of the Spirit," "prophecy," and "tongues," and there is good reason to believe that these gifts were practiced in many churches up through the third century. But these were always relatively incidental, peripheral aspects of the gospel and of church life. No charismata was ever associated with salvation or the reception of the Holy Spirit. This unfortunate notion is strictly a Oneness Pentecostal novelty.

4. The final argument against the Oneness Pentecostal view of tongues—and this could really be leveled against all aspects of the Oneness doctrine of salvation—is that it would require one to believe that for some nineteen centuries the church of Jesus Christ had lost its saving message, that the gates of hell had in fact prevailed against the church (cf. Matt. 16:18). If the Oneness Pentecostals are correct, even today—after the supposedly saving message of the Oneness of God, of Jesus' Name baptism, and of the Holy Spirit with the evidence of speaking in tongues has been "rediscovered"—it is still 99-percent true that the church of Jesus Christ is impotent and unsaving.

From that perspective, what a total flop Christ's body turned out to be! So far as I can conservatively guess, the Oneness doctrine of salvation, which has only been around for seventy-five years and is yet only held by approximately five million people today, rules out (of heaven) all but about 1/1000 of one percent of all people who have ever identified themselves as Christians!

The great saints of the church—Augustine, Thomas Aquinas, Francis of Assisi, Mother Teresa; and the great Protestant Reformers: John Calvin, Martin Luther, Jonathan Edwards, Charles Wesley; and the great revivalists who (we thought) won thousands or millions of souls for the Lord: John Witherspoon, Charles Finney, Billy Sunday, Billy Graham—all of these not only personally lost out with God, but in terms of salvation never accomplished anything for God! Or so most Oneness Pentecostals would have us believe. In all their love, piety, and scholarship, these saints supposedly missed the things necessary for salvation, things that only the Oneness Pentecostals have recently found. According to Oneness theology, they had the wrong understanding of Jesus, they baptized wrong, and they never spoke in tongues. And in terms of building the saving kingdom of God, their lives and the multitude of lives they touched were wasted in trinitarian futility.

For some of us, this horrifying implication is itself enough to prove the error of the Oneness doctrine of salvation that requires it.

The Holiness Standards and Works Salvation

he legalistic mind-set is very much a part of the Oneness Pentecostals' self-identity. It follows directly from their other doctrinal deviations, and it is frequently the doctrine that Oneness adherents first begin to question in their journeys away from this faith. I have seen from my own experience that the majority of people who end up leaving Oneness sects leave initially because of the strain of the group's legalism.

The Insufficiency of Grace

The intensity of the perfectionistic and legalistic mind-set of the United Pentecostal Church is evidenced in many of its published writings. Thus, we read the following in the UPCI's major published work on "the standards":

> If the sinner has to forsake sin in order to be saved, the Christian must live free from sin in order to stay saved . . . sin has to be dealt with in an individual's heart and life before he can have fellowship with God. Salvation is maintaining fellowship with Jesus Christ, and when that fellowship is broken there is no

215

salvation. Fellowship must be restored in order to have salvation. No sin will
enter heaven. If sin could enter heaven, it would cease to be heaven. Holiness is living a life of victory, free from sin and condemnation—a require-
ment for entering heaven. [Why?, 15]

It is very apparent from this text that the responsibility for being "free
from sin and condemnation," and thus compatible with heaven, is *ours*. And
it is also very clear that this must be done on a regular, uninterrupted basis,
for a lapse means a break in fellowship, and a break in fellowship means
"there is no salvation." Salvation here does not rest on God's character of
being unconditionally and graciously loving; it rests on the precarious
moment-by-moment work of our character. Being "covered by the blood" is
only true of the moment, and only so long as the "saint" keeps his or her
end of the deal—living "free from sin and condemnation" (but why, then, is
the blood even needed?).

One might be inclined to worry a bit over this teaching, because it seems
that if one is to be compatible with the all-holy God in heaven on one's
own effort, one would have to be perfect. And, as a matter of fact, this worry
is very well-founded. As the UPCI "Study in Christian Standards" states:
"Holiness must be perfected. . . . The responsibility for perfection lies within
the individual Christian. . . . He is the one who must perfect holiness in his
own life" (Why?, 152).

This, clearly, is quite a different understanding of salvation from that
upon which Protestantism was founded. Whereas the theology of John
Calvin and Martin Luther was founded upon Paul's beautiful and freeing
gospel that one is saved by grace alone, wholly apart from works (Rom.
4:1–8), the United Pentecostal Church explicitly argues against this position. It is maintained, in the most explicit fashion, that the grace of God
through the work of Christ is not alone sufficient for our salvation. Indeed,
one entire tract of the UPCI is devoted to just this point. It is entitled *"Grace
+ O = Salvation?"* and in it the UPCI explicitly argues *against* the view that
"there is nothing that can be added to grace to bring salvation to a soul.
Grace . . . wrought salvation with no strings attached. . . . Grace plus nothing equal [sic] salvation" (#6155).

In contrast to salvation by grace alone, the UPCI tract maintains that
"grace" merely "initiates salvation." But this initiation doesn't itself save
you. It is, rather, one's "obedience" that "activates salvation." As I was taught
as a young UPCI convert, one needs grace "at the beginning" of one's walk

because one is a baby in Christ. But in time one is expected "to learn how to walk on one's own." Obedience takes over what grace begins, and it is when it does so that salvation is "activated."

Hence, in contrast to the classically Protestant view, which holds that Grace + 0 *does* equal salvation, the UPCI and other Oneness groups maintain that it is "Grace + Faith + Obedience" that equals salvation (#6155). In the end, "everything that God can do for us depends upon a change in behavior" (Sabin, III, 3).

God the Behavioralist

God, in this view, is a supreme behavioralist. It seems that God is not in the business of loving and affirming people. Rather, God is in the business of loving and affirming—or hating and rejecting—behavior. If you do good, God approves of you. If you do bad, God rejects you. But this only means that in neither case is God dealing with *you*. It's your behavior that God is really interested in.

I recall as a young UPCI convert being told with the entire congregation by a pastor that anyone "caught" in a bowling alley when the Lord returned would be left behind. A terrifying thought for an impressionable young man who happened to like bowling. And I recall questioning, even this early on in my involvement with Oneness Pentecostalism, how it was that if God really loved *me*, he could be so uptight about my *behavior*. Sitting in that service, I quickly came to the logical but unfortunate conclusion that God didn't really love me—or anyone. What he really loved was the act of staying out of bowling alleys!

Thinking in this fashion inevitably exalts performing for God above honestly loving God, for it exalts God's estimation of our performance above God's estimation of our being. Indeed, what God thinks of us as beings is wholly contingent upon what God thinks of us as performers. In Oneness theology, the cross, so far as I've ever been able to see, does not factor into this issue at all. And I am convinced that this is why the adherents of this religion tend to become preoccupied, even obsessed, with their own ethical behavior. Virtually everything hangs on it.

The extent to which this religion is behavioralistic is evidenced in its theology of the Holy Spirit. The Bible clearly teaches, and traditional orthodox Christianity has always believed, that the Holy Spirit is the means by which one initially believes and then is subsequently and gradually sanctified.

Behavioral changes are thus not the *basis* of the Spirit's coming and of salvation. They are the *result* of the Spirit's coming and of salvation. This distinction is basic to the gospel of grace.

The United Pentecostal Church and other Oneness Pentecostal groups, however, believe just the opposite. The coming of the Holy Spirit, and of salvation, only occurs after, and as a result of, one's own self-purification. The "gift of the Holy Spirit" is therefore not a free gift. Since there are any number of preconditions that must be met, it is really only "a reward."

The extent to which this religion is behavioralistic is also evidenced in the legalistic way it tends to dictate how people live. Because the God of Oneness Pentecostalism sees and evaluates people in terms of their particular behavior, and because this God tends to be, as we have shown, a compulsive perfectionistic God (hanging eternity on a formula, for example), it should come as no surprise to find Oneness believers tending to be compulsive and perfectionistic in their definition of what "holy living" before this God means.

While congregations within the UPCI and general "apostolic movement" may vary a bit in their particular standards, depending largely on their geographical locations, they all tend to have certain rules in common. Any form of smoking or dancing, any use of alcoholic beverages, and/or any attendance at movie theaters is regarded as strictly immoral. Televisions are always frowned upon, if not expressly forbidden, especially for ministers (#126; Why?, 60ff.; Bernard, Holiness, 89ff.). Moreover, at least in all UPCI congregations, women are not supposed to be allowed to wear any kind of makeup or jewelry, to wear any sort of pants, or to ever cut their hair (see Appendix C), and men are to wear their hair short and, usually, always to wear long pants (Why?, *passim*; Gray, 115–202; Bernard, Holiness, 102–79, 261).

Beyond these standard rules, individual congregations may (and usually do) come up with a multitude of their own individual rules. In one church I attended, the women were made to wear their long hair always up in a bun (this was a common rule among UPCI churches). In some southern congregations, wearing long-sleeve shirts or blouses, as well as wearing bright colors, is "prohibited." Most congregations further prohibit attending, and sometimes playing in, any sports events. (See Bernard, Holiness, 26ff.). In one congregation I attended, no one could partake in any activity without the pastor's explicit permission. In a different congregation the pastor would not let anyone move away, regardless of his or her reason for doing so (e.g., finding new employment). In another congregation, to which I belonged for a period of time, the pastor had huge charts in the church recording how much one prayed—and paid—each week. Still other UPCI churches are served by pastors who tell married couples what kind of sexual behavior is and is not appropriate between them in the privacy of their own home.

If an individual voluntarily held to some of these convictions because of certain weaknesses in his or her own life (e.g., maybe sports is a tempting idol), or because that person felt it best to do so in order to witness to a certain group of unbelievers, that would be one thing. But that is not how the issue is generally viewed in the UPCI. Practices such as those listed above are part of what it means to live in holiness, without which "no one will see the Lord" (Heb. 12:14; cf. Why?, 15). Staying out of bowling alleys was for me not a matter of individual conviction, but of salvation!

The New Testament and Grace

Because the God of Oneness theology hides behind the "masks" he wears in history, he is a performing God (see ch. 8). And because he is a performing God, he creates a performing people. What he thinks of a person is directly tied up with what he thinks of that person's behavior. Therefore, Oneness Pentecostals are quite legitimately forever worried about what God thinks of their performance. Their obedience becomes a means of their salvation, and it is at this point that their preoccupation with meticulous rules goes from being merely unhealthy to being absolutely heretical.

In contrast to this view, the God revealed in Jesus Christ is, in a word, a God who loves and saves on the basis of how *he* performs, not on the basis of how *we* perform. Indeed, God's evaluation of us as based on his performance in Jesus Christ runs directly against all of our "performance," for even our righteous deeds are as "filthy rags" in comparison to the perfection that God's holiness requires (Isa. 64:6; cf. Rom. 3:9–20). Thus, if "perfection" was in fact our responsibility, as the UPCI theology suggests, we would all be hopelessly lost.

But the true God revealed in Jesus Christ saves us, not *because* of what we do, but *in spite of* all we do. Everything the believer is and ever shall be is once and for all accomplished by what God does in and through the saving work of his Son Jesus Christ. Thus, in the most striking terms possible, Paul writes: "Now when a man works, his wages are not credited to him as a gift, but as an obligation. However, to the man who does not work but trusts God who justifies the wicked, his faith is credited as righteousness" (Rom. 4:4–5).

If salvation depended at all on our behavior, on our supposedly "righteous" working, God would be a debtor paying off those who habitually "work." On that basis, salvation could not be an unconditional gift. But, as a matter of fact, God will not be indebted to anyone. The text therefore proclaims that God justifies—he credits righteousness to—those of us who know we are so ungodly that we do not think of working to impress God and make him a debtor (cf. Luke 18: 9–14). We have nothing of our own to give but can only trust God for his ability to save the ungodly.

Just this is meant by Paul's declaration that there is "no condemnation for those who are in Christ Jesus" (Rom. 8:1). This is true of us in spite of the fact that we would deserve condemnation if our behavior *was* at issue (cf. Rom. 7:7–25). But being "in Christ" means nothing unless it means that our behavior is no longer the issue. This is also why, later in this chapter, Paul exclaims, "Who will bring any charge against those whom God has chosen? It is God who justifies. Who is it that condemns? Christ Jesus, who died—more than that, who was raised to life—is at the right hand of God and is also interceding for us" (Rom. 8:33–34).

It is because the Son of God now lives and is interceding for us, and because Christ Jesus is the highest authority in heaven and earth, that no one can bring any charge of unworthiness against those who are in Christ Jesus, God's elect. This has nothing to do with how worthy or unworthy we think we are and therefore act. Rather, it has everything to do with who Jesus is. By his one sacrifice, our high priest "has made perfect forever those who are being made holy" (Heb. 10:14). This perfection is given to us, not created by us, for it is the righteousness of God himself (2 Cor. 5:21), and it comes exclusively from God himself (Rom. 1:17; 3:21). All we are or ever shall be before God, then, is because of what he did, in spite of what we do.

Frankly, to make salvation conditional upon the particular do's and don'ts that we perform in our life is to deny Christ's glory and to disparage God's grace. This is precisely what the Christians at Galatia did by thinking that the little act of circumcision somehow, in some degree, supplemented the work of Christ in making them righteous and was therefore a prerequisite to salvation (see Gal. 5:1–12). In no other place in his writings does Paul come close to expressing the degree of anger and horror he expresses toward the "foolish Galatians" (see 3:1–5; cf. 1:6–9).

Paul was outraged at the Galatians because he knew that if one thinks it is possible to add *anything* to the righteousness of God that comes from God because of Jesus Christ, he or she does not at all understand the righteousness of God. Such persons simply do not understand or accept Jesus Christ. Paul writes, "If you let yourselves be circumcised, Christ will be of no value to you at all" (Gal. 5:2). Indeed, to try "to be justified by the law" is to be "alienated from Christ" and "fallen away from grace" (v. 4). If good behavior could impress God, Christ died for nothing (3:21). Therefore, we cannot be justified if our thinking about our relationship with God is tied to, and contingent upon, human effort, upon the keeping of any set of rules (3:11; 5:4; cf. Rom. 3:28). The idea of a self-produced legal way into heaven is nothing but a "curse" (Gal. 3:10, 13).

In the end, Paul's basic message is that either grace-plus-nothing amounts to salvation, or one isn't talking about salvation at all!

If this is true of Christians who simply thought that circumcision could make them "more okay" with God than if they only trusted in Jesus, how much more true it is of believers who somehow think that a well-defined long list of ethical prerequisites is necessary if one is to be "okay" with God at all!

Whether or not one is circumcised, whether one wears a dress or pants, whether one wears one's hair long or short, and whether one eats meat and drinks wine (Rom. 14; 1 Cor. 10:23–33) are matters that may or may not be important to particular individuals within particular cultures at particular times. But in no case must we ever think that they have anything to do with what God essentially thinks about us. The ground motivation to live and grow in the sanctified life to which Christ calls us is love for God, based on what he has already done, and a love for others that flows from God's unconditional love received into one's life.

If a person is in fact saved, what God thinks about that person is based entirely on what Jesus Christ has done for him or her. If a person is not saved, what God thinks about that person is based entirely on what he or she does—nothing such people do can get them right with God as they are.

With Christ, it's an all-or-nothing deal.

Appendix C

Hair

One distinctive belief of the United Pentecostal Church and a number of other Oneness Pentecostal groups is their teaching that a woman must never cut her hair. While this is not a central doctrine of these groups, it is an important one, which is why I have included this appendix. For one thing, this teaching obviously has tremendous consequences for women who belong to these groups. A woman who converts into the United Pentecostal Church is expected never to cut her hair again. At least for some women, this is cruelly oppressive.

If one can help a UPCI woman see the error of this teaching, one may help her to experience more of the freedom before God that Christ has won for her. Relatedly, one may thereby help her see the error of the entire legalistic UPCI system. Since the UPCI sets itself up as "*the* truth," finding a crack in this so-called truth, especially on something that impacts one's lifestyle as much as this teaching does, may help free the person from the authority of the group altogether.

The UPCI teaching on this subject is based entirely on 1 Corinthians 11:2–16. According to the UPCI, verses 14 and 15—which speak about long hair as "a covering"—reveal that Paul has been speaking about hair all along. This is, the UPCI contends, also why Paul says in verses 5 and 6 that if a woman is to have her head uncovered, she may as well have her hair cut short ("shorn," KJV) or be completely bald ("shaved"). Indeed, it is argued that the word *shorn* in verse 6 simply means "to have one's hair cut," and the word for "long hair" in verse 15 means "to let grow" and hence implies that hair should never be cut (Why?, 47; Gray, 178–79; Bernard, Holiness, 136ff.).[1] Supposedly, that is also why Paul says that "nature itself" teaches us that a woman should have long hair—nature (not scissors), in other words, should determine "the proper length for each woman" (Bernard, ibid.).[2] Hence it is concluded that "what the Lord is saying is that a woman might as well shave all the hair off her head as to trim it. God counts a woman trimming her hair to be sinning as if she cut it all off and shaved her head" (Gray, 179; cf. Jordan, 105).

I believe there are at least three considerations that count strongly against this exegesis.

First, the very fact that no one in church history until the Oneness Pentecostals ever interpreted this passage in this fashion strongly suggests that their interpretation is askew. Neither the early church, nor the church throughout the ages, has ever held to the very eccentric notion that a woman should never cut her hair.

Second, the fact that Paul is throughout this chapter speaking about propriety during a worship service suggests that he is not speaking about a permanent condition. It is during the activity of "praying or prophesying" that a woman is to have her head "covered" and a man to have his head "uncovered." But if Paul is interested here in hair length in general, why would he restrict his comments to these activities? This would be like telling people that you don't want them to be more than six feet tall when they serve communion! Hair length, like height, is not the sort of thing one can alter back and forth between activities. No, Paul is in this passage clearly speaking about something that can be put on and taken off, depending on the activity.

Third, if Paul is talking about hair in verses 4 through 6, why doesn't he simply say so? He uses the word *katakalupto*, which ordinarily refers to some sort of clothing covering.[3] If Paul is in fact referring to hair here, then, he is speaking in a most unusual and cryptic fashion.

Indeed, the suggestion that Paul is referring to hair when he speaks of "a covering" is refuted by the UPCI's own interpretation of this passage. As we have seen, this group maintains that Paul in verse 6 is saying that if a woman will not cover her head, she might as well have her hair also shorn (cut) or shaven (bald). But if "covering" already refers to uncut hair, how could Paul say that if she does not cover her head she may as well go further and cut her hair or shave it off? On the UPCI interpretation, Paul would in effect be saying "if a woman is unwilling to have uncut hair, she may as well also cut it." But this, of course, is ludicrously redundant.

What is Paul really driving at throughout this passage? The central problem Paul is addressing is that the Corinthian women have interpreted his message of grace as a license to throw off all customary gender distinctions in religious worship. Paul is therefore concerned with preserving this distinction and the church traditions that embody them (vv. 2, 16). To this end he reminds the Corinthians that there was, even in the original creation, a difference between men and women. Christ is the head of man, and man is the head of woman (vv. 3, 8, 12).[4] This difference, therefore, should be manifested in assembly worship. A man should not have his head covered, and a woman should. This is the church custom, and the Corinthian women are being scandalous in throwing this custom aside (see v. 16).

Also to this end Paul appeals to the Corinthians' own first-century common sense. Men and women look different! "Judge for yourselves: Is it proper . . . ?" (v. 13). It is simply "natural"—in Corinth in the first century, at least—for women to have longer hair than men (vv. 14–15). Paul is not prescribing an eternal truth here; he is simply referring to a commonly acknowledged cultural fact.

It should also be noted that Paul's statement that a woman's hair is "given to her as a covering" does not at all imply that he has been (cryptically) referring to her hair with his use of "covering" in verses 4 through 6. Indeed, he uses an altogether different word here for "covering" [*peribolaion*].[5] Rather, he is appealing to the woman's customary hair length, which hangs down on her—in contrast to the man's shorter hair—to support his contention that the woman, but not the man, ought to wear a covering when she prays or prophesies. Social decency, in other words, entails ecclesiastical decency.

For Paul, then, a woman's refusal to wear a covering while performing religious functions is akin to her cutting her hair short or even going completely bald (vv. 5–6). This is shameful, according to Jewish tradition as well as to the Greco-Roman society. The bottom line is that one's behavior in church should not shock the sensibilities of other Christians or the sense of decency of the culture in which the church finds itself.

This leads us to my final point. Whatever interpretation of this passage one arrives at, this does not in and of itself tell us how the passage is to be applied today. There is a great deal of relativity concerning propriety in personal appearance even within the Bible itself, and this should caution us against assuming that the letter (and not just the spirit) of Paul's advice here is intended to be binding law throughout all time. If, for example, it is some sort of universal principle that long hair on a man is "shameful," it is hard to understand why it was in certain circumstances God's will for a man to have long hair as a sign of holiness (e.g., Lev. 21:5; Num. 6:1–5; Judg. 13:5).

That there is some cultural relativity involved in Scripture, including the New Testament, is recognized even by the UPCI. This group apparently recognizes that the injunction against women having "braided hair" (1 Tim. 2:9; 1 Peter 3:3) had a first-century application that it does not have today, for UPCI women are known, both in and outside the church, for their fancy braided hairstyles. Similarly, the UPCI recognized, long before many other Protestant groups, that Paul's mandate to Timothy that a woman cannot teach or have any authority over a man (1 Tim. 2:12) was culturally relative, for the "apostolic faith" movement has been ordaining women from the start.

But why, then, does the UPCI give its eccentric interpretation of 1 Corinthians 11 the status of law, the fulfillment of which is one more prerequisite for women to please God? To the contrary, whether Paul is speaking in this passage about women wearing veils, or about a particular hairstyle, or even about women having long hair, there is no good reason to assume that this is anything more than a cultural issue. Though the scriptural principle that Christians should retain the propriety of gender distinctions in church and society is a permanent one, how this is done will vary from culture to culture. In our culture, it simply is no longer the case that women with short hair are thought of shamefully, like lesbians and/or prostitutes in the first century (see note #1). It follows that the application of this principle will differ from that of the first-century Corinthians.

Appendix D

Statistics on Oneness Pentecostal Groups

The size of the Oneness movement is difficult to ascertain with any exactitude. Anything beyond an informed approximation is impossible, since the Oneness movement is not centralized outside of relatively small fellowships, since many Oneness groups do not keep membership roles, and, finally, since there are hundreds of Oneness churches that remain completely independent of any larger fellowship. My own research suggests that there are in the United States about one million Oneness Pentecostals as a most conservative estimate, or approximately 25 percent of the total number of Pentecostals in this country. James Dunn has a similar estimate.[1]

David Barrett provides an authoritative estimate of 4.2 million worldwide, but this report is now nine years old, and if the rate of growth of Oneness Pentecostals has remained constant during this time, the actual number would now be over 5 million,[2] a number Russell Spittler arrives at in his research.[3]

If these figures are accurate, Oneness Pentecostals rank as the third-largest antitrinitarian professing Christian group, behind the Mormons (who number over 7 million worldwide) and Jehovah's Witnesses (who number about

4 million dedicated members and about 9 million followers worldwide). It should be noted that all three groups are growing at an alarming rate. The number of Mormons has more than doubled since 1970, while the number of Jehovah's Witnesses has tripled! Meanwhile, the number of Oneness Pentecostals in the world has also almost doubled since 1970.

(Mormonism is classed here as an antitrinitarian movement since Mormons explicitly reject the orthodox doctrine of the Trinity as represented by the creeds and confessions of orthodox Christianity. Although they do use the word *Trinity*, their doctrine is not trinitarian, since they hold that the Father, Son, and Holy Ghost are three separate Gods.)

Some of the larger Oneness or Apostolic Pentecostal groups (with their approximate reported number of members in the U.S.A.) are the following:

United Pentecostal Church International (400,000)

Pentecostal Assemblies of the World (200,000)

Bible Way Church of Our Lord Jesus Christ (100,000)

United Church of Jesus Christ (100,000)

Church of Our Lord Jesus Christ of the Apostolic Faith (45,000)

Pentecostal Churches of Apostolic Faith (25,000)

Beyond this there are some thirty other Oneness denominations listed in standard reference works on religious bodies in the United States.[4]

Notes

Chapter 1: *Understanding Oneness Pentecostalism*

1. I shall throughout this work place the word "person" in quotation marks when I am referring to the Father, Son, or Holy Spirit. I do this to avoid the modern trinitarian tendency to overliteralize and overindividualize the threefoldness of the Trinity. This tendency has frequently encumbered the doctrinal discussion on the Godhead between trinitarians and Oneness believers. The quotation marks are intended to remind us that we are speaking analogically about God. This is further discussed in the next chapter.

2. Because the deity of Christ is not the issue in our present discussion, I have omitted any discussion of the various grammatical issues surrounding these passages. For such discussions, consult Raymond Brown, *Jesus, God and Man* (Milwaukee: Bruce Publishing Co., 1967); Oscar Cullmann, *The Christology of the New Testament,* tr. Shirley Guthrie, Charles Hall (Philadelphia: Westminster Press, rev. ed. 1963), ch. 11, Wainwright, ch. 4; and Dunn, 192ff., 239ff.

3. See Francis Brown, S. R. Driver, and C. A. Briggs, eds., *Hebrew and English Lexicon of the Old Testament,* (Clarendon Press: Oxford, rep. 1978), 43; G. Johannes Botterweck and Helmer Ringgren, eds., *Theological Dictionary of the Old Testament,* vol. 1, trans. John Willis (Grand Rapids, Mich.: William B. Eerdmans, 1974), 272ff.; and William Albright, *From the Stone Age to Christianity,* 2d ed. (Baltimore: Johns Hopkins Press, 1957), 213.

Chapter 2: *The Trinity: Truth or Error?*

1. See Dunn, chs. V–VII; Wainwright, ch. 2 and pp. 132–34; and Larry Hurtado, *One God and One Lord* (Philadelphia: Fortress Press, 1988), ch. 2, for detailed discussions of this matter. There has been an ongoing debate as to whether the references to personified attributes of God in the intertestamental period were merely literary conventions (the view held by Dunn and Hurtado) or whether they were understood as constituting actual "hypostatic" (substantial) distinctions in God, a view endorsed by Wainwright and H. Ringgren in *Word and Wisdom: Studies in the Hypostatization of Divine Qualities and Functions in the Ancient Near East* (Hakan Oholsson: Lund, 1947).

For our purposes, little hinges on this debate. But if Wainwright and Ringgren are correct, it is somewhat easier to understand how the first-century Jewish Christians were already culturally prepared to understand the Father, Son, and Holy Spirit as being personally distinct from each other, while at the same time constituting one God. Either theory, however, readily explains the New Testament authors' literary convention of referring to the Son and Spirit alongside of God, while not thereby suggesting that the Son and Spirit are not themselves God.

2. There is also a possible theological explanation for why the Father is alone called God when referred to alongside the Son and Spirit. In traditional trinitarian theology the Father is perceived of as being "the beginning and source" of the Trinity, not in a temporal sense, but in an ontological sense. See, for example, John Calvin, *The Institutes of the Christian Religion,* vol. 1, trans. F. L. Battles, ed. J. T. McNeil (Philadelphia: Westminster Press, n.d.), 144–45.

3. See, for example, Carl Jung's, "The Psychological Approach to the Doctrine of the Trinity," found in *Psychology and Religion, West and East,* trans. R.F.C. Hull (Princeton, N.J.: Princeton University Press, 2d ed., 1968), 109–200.

4. In my work *Trinity and Process* (forthcoming from Peter Lang Publishers), I maintain that the very structure of rationality itself requires a view of ultimate reality as triune.

Chapter 4:
Did the Son of God Exist Before His Birth?

1. As noted in chapter 1, there is a minority of Oneness writers who do not limit Christ's distinctness from the Father to his human birth, but who rather come closer to trinitarianism in maintaining that from "the beginning" (of the world, or from eternity) God had a "Word," an "Image," or a "Form" that later became human as Jesus Christ. I am not addressing this small group in the refutations of this chapter except insofar as I shall be demonstrating that Christ preexisted not just as *an aspect* of God, as an *"it,"* but as *the Son* of God himself, as a "who."

2. I have followed the NIV and other modern translations in omitting from this passage the additional phrase "who is in heaven" found in some ancient manuscripts. For a brief discussion, see Bruce Metzger, *A Textual Commentary on the Greek New Testament* (London and New York: United Bible Societies, 1971), 203–4.

3. I am indebted to Robert Bowman, who first utilized this insightful argument against Robert Sabin in a debate held on January 8–9, 1990, at the Apostolic Bible Church, St. Paul, Minn. See Sabin, Debate.

4. For a discussion, see Dunn, 71, 113ff.; 187ff.; G. Lampe, *God as Spirit* (Oxford: Clarendon Press, 1977), 120–25; G. Caird, "The Development of the Doctrine of Christ in the New Testament," in *Christ for Us Today,* ed. N. Pittenger (London: SCM, 1968). No less an authority than Wolfson, however, regards even most of the Rabbinic talk about preexistent entities as implying some sort of actual preexistence. See *The Philosophy of the Church Fathers,* vol. 1 (Cambridge: Harvard University Press, 1956), 155.

5. This passage need not, and probably should not, be taken to imply that Melchizedek was himself some sort of eternal divine figure. The author is simply employing a common Rabbinic exegetical principle, which holds that one may draw lessons from what Scripture does not say as well as from what it does say. See H. L. Strack and P. Billerbeck, *Kommentar zum Neuen Testament aus Talmud und Midrasch* (Munchen, 1926–28), vol. III, 694. Hence, the fact that Scripture does not mention anything about Melchizedek's lineage is taken as an allegorical lesson about Christ's eternality.

6. See Walter Bauer, *A Greek-English Lexicon of the New Testament and Other Early Christian Literature,* 2d ed., rev. and aug. by F. W. Gingrich and F. W. Danken from the 5th German ed. (Chicago: University of Chicago Press), 527; and George R. Beasley-Murray, "John," *Word Biblical Commentary,* vol. 36 (Waco, Tex.: Word Books, 1987), 14.

Chapter 5: *Is Jesus the Holy Spirit?*

1. See Alasdair Heron, *The Holy Spirit* (Philadelphia: Westminster Press, 1983), chs. 1–2; George Montague, S.M., *The Holy Spirit: Growth of a Biblical Tradition* (New York: Paulist Press, 1976), part I.

2. While John 14:23 is the clearest instance of a divinely spoken first-person plural referring to the Trinity, there are four other instances where God speaks this way in the Old Testament (Gen. 1:26; 3:22; 11:7; Isa. 6:8). While some attempt to explain these verses as God either speaking to angels or using a supposed "plural of majesty," both of these explanations are problematic. The texts seem to imply some sort of internal relationality within God, especially when read in the light of the New Testament. In any case, neither alternative explanation is relevant to John 14:23.

Chapter 6: *Baptism, Salvation, and The Name*

1. For an excellent succinct discussion of this, see G. R. Beasley Murray, *Baptism in the New Testament* (Grand Rapids, Mich.: William B. Eerdmans, rep. 1977), 90ff.

2. Ibid.

3. It is sad, yet in a sense almost comical, to learn that there are a number of Oneness groups that have split over, and continue to debate, what is the one true proper baptismal formula. Is it "in the name of Jesus" or "into Jesus' name" or "in the name of the Lord Jesus" or "into the name of the Lord Jesus Christ" etc.? For the most part, each group believes that its formula alone truly washes away sin! One must simply be amazed at the dysfunctional view of the Deity presupposed in this entire debate.

Chapter 7: *Was the Early Church Oneness?*

1. As the famous church historian J.N.D. Kelly argues, the early church did not sharply distinguish between the authority of Scripture and the authority of the apostolic tradition. Hence, to alter the apostles' "rule of faith" in any way was to tamper with the Word of God itself! The earliest Fathers, therefore, deemed it their sole function to pass on, without alteration, what the apostles had taught as well as what the biblical authors wrote. See his *Early Christian Doctrines*, rev. ed. (San Francisco: Harper & Row, 1978), ch. 2. Also informative on the role of the apostolic tradition in the early church is Kelly's *Early Christian Creeds*, 3d ed. (New York: Longman, 1972).

2. Citations in this chapter are from the second edition of *The Apostolic Fathers*, trans. J. B. Lightfoot and J. R. Harner, ed. and rev. Michael Holmes (Grand Rapids, Mich.: Baker Book, 1989), except for the writings of the Apologists and Irenaeus, references to which are taken from *The Apostolic Fathers*, vols. 1–2, Alexander Roberts and James Donaldson, eds. (Grand Rapids, Mich.: William B. Eerdmans, rep. 1979).

3. It should, in fairness, be mentioned that Bernard is coming out with a far more comprehensive work on the issue of the early church and the Oneness doctrine tentatively entitled *Oneness and Trinity, A.D. 100–300*. I have consulted the rough draft of this manuscript, but Bernard asked me not to quote from it as it is yet unfinished. Suffice it to say that this work is certainly the most thorough work to be published from a Oneness perspective and an attempt is made to address the trinitarian-sounding passages in these authors. In my estimation, however, the attempt is no more successful than previous attempts, largely because it is based on the same sort of "cross-referencing" hermenuetics that, we have seen, characterize the Oneness treatment of the Bible.

4. Kelly, for example, describes the Apologists as "loyal churchmen" who "made it their business to proclaim the church's faith, the pattern of which was of course triadic" (*Early Christian Doctrines*, 101).

Chapter 8: *The Inescapable Trinity*

1. While no Oneness group officially endorses this position, some individual Oneness churches believe that sincere trinitarians may not go to hell, though they certainly won't go to heaven either. These churches hold to an intermediate state theory, a place (called "the New Earth") between heaven and hell. While this belief is utterly without biblical foundation, it helps soften the offensiveness of the Oneness claim to exclusivity.

2. For an excellent discussion concerning the ancient concepts originally used in developing the doctrine of the Trinity such as *hypostasis, prosopon, persona,* and *ousia,* see Prestige, God, ch. 8 to end. For a sampling of some prominent trinitarian theologians speaking on the issue of whether or not the word "person" should be retained in contemporary trinitarian confessions, see Karl Barth, *Church Dogmatics,* vol. 1, pt. 1: *The Doctrine of the Word of God,* G. W. Bromiley and T. F. Torrance, eds., 2d ed. (Edinburgh: T&T Clarke, 1975), 351–60; Gustaf Aulen, *The Faith of the Christian Church,* trans. Eric Wahlstrom (Philadelphia: Fortress Press, 1976), 225ff.; and Karl Rahner, *The Trinity,* trans. Joseph Donceel (New York: Seabury Press, 1974), 103–15.

3. See Otto Weber's discussion in *Foundations of Dogmatics,* vol. 1., trans. Darrell Guder (Grand Rapids, Mich.: William B. Eerdmans, 1981), 377.

4. This is similar to the way most models in physics, for example, provide ways for us to conceive of aspects of physical reality without providing anything like a literal picture of the reality. For a nice discussion comparing the roles of models in science and theology, see Alister McGrath, *Understanding the Trinity* (Grand Rapids, Mich.: Zondervan, 1988), ch 4.

5. "God is one in the same sense that a person is one" is the answer Bernard gave to me in a public dialogue on the Oneness doctrine during the 1982 Harvard Symposium on Oneness Pentecostalism.

6. I argue this point extensively throughout my work, *Trinity and Process: The A Priori Construction of a Process-Trinitarian Metaphysic From a Critical Evaluation of Harshorne's Di-Polar Theism* (New York: Peter Lang Publishers, 1992).

7. Stated in common theological terminology, "the economic and immanent Trinity are one." Only with grave theological consequences can one divorce God's eternal being from God's temporal revelation. This has been a resounding theme in contemporary theological discussions since Barth. See Barth, *Church Dogmatics,* 316ff., 364ff., 422ff.; Weber, *Foundations,* 388; and Rahner, *The Trinity,* 99–100.

8. According to the cult expert Ronald Enroth, a cult, sociologically defined, is a group that embodies any number of the following characteristics—They tend to be (1) authoritarian, (2) oppositional, (3) exclusivistic, (4) legalistic, (5) persecution conscious, (7) sanction-oriented, (8) esoteric, and (9) anti-sacerdotal. (See Guide, ch. 1.) Without here entering into a full discussion over whether or not the UPCI should be classified as a cult, I would at least say that I have met few persons who have left the UPCI who did not admit that this group meets, without qualification, a minimum of five of these criteria, with many saying that it actually meets all nine.

Appendix A: *Salvation, the Spirit, and Tongues*

1. A number of ex-Oneness believers have reported to me that they frequently had nightmares of "missing the rapture" and/or of going to hell before they "were able" to speak in tongues (or before they gave up thinking it was something necessary).

2. The Oneness author J. T. Pugh implicitly acknowledges the psychological dimension of glossolalia in the context of Oneness Pentecostalism throughout his widely read book, *How to Receive the Holy Ghost*. For example, he states that a person "seeking for the Holy Ghost" must "condition himself in much the same manner" as a "person being instructed in the process of diving into water" in that he must "[yield] himself over to an element and influence he is not well acquainted with" (57). He further suggests that the seeker try repeating a word or phrase over and over again as a part of the seeker's effort to loose himself from "the fleshly process of thought" (58). This will help him "suspend himself in the state of willingness and yielding" (58–59). Indeed, Pugh suggests that the seeker should "deliberately . . . move away from our own language" and "go backward to the babblings of a baby" (60). These babblings may not initially be Spirit inspired, but if the believer "continues in the state of spiritual suspension and yielding" to the place where he comes to "a psychic zero," he will be filled with the Spirit (59–60). This method, Pugh promises, "cannot fail" (60).

That there is nothing remotely analogous to this in Scripture is sad enough. But what is tragic is that literally millions of Oneness Pentecostals think that one's eternal salvation rests on such shallow manipulative ploys.

3. Bernard appears to attempt this in chapter 11 of his work *The New Birth*, since he claims to be tracing "the existence of the Holy Spirit baptism with tongues in church history . . ." (282). What he in fact does, however, is simply show that the post-apostolic church still believed in the gift of tongues. But this doesn't address the issue of whether or not the early church thought of tongues as anything like the "necessary initial physical evidence" for receiving the Holy Spirit, which was, further, itself necessary for salvation.

Appendix C: *Hair*

1. The word translated "shorn" in the KJV is *keiro*. It is used of Paul when he took a religious vow in Acts 18:18, where it clearly implies more than a simple haircut. It is also the word used for shearing sheep (cf. Acts 8:32). As used of women in the context of 1 Corinthians 11, it clearly implies hair cut uncustomarily short. The cultural assumption Paul is appealing to here is the assumption that it is shameful for a woman to have a "mannish" hairstyle. It was, among other things, an indication of lesbianism and/or (possibly) prostitution. For an excellent discussion on this point, see Gordon Fee, "The First Epistle of the Corinthians," *New International Commentary on the New Testament* (Grand Rapids, Mich.: William B. Eerdmans, 1987), 510–12. This work is informative concerning the whole of 1 Corinthians 11 and was written by a Pentecostal (trinitarian).

There is, finally, simply no evidence for the Oneness contention that the verb for "wearing long hair" in verse 15 (*komao*) means wearing uncut hair (Why?, 47; Gray, 178). See Walter Bauer's *A Greek-English Lexicon of the New Testament*, 442.

2. Paul's appeal to "nature" need not be taken as a natural law, as though it were somehow in the nature of things that women should have long (uncut!) hair and men short hair. Biblical customs and cultural customs have always varied a great deal on this. Rather, "for Paul it is a question of propriety and of 'custom' (vv. 13, 16) which carries with it 'disgrace' or 'glory' (vv. 14–15). Hence, this is an appeal to the 'way things are'—to the 'natural feeling' that they shared together as part of their contemporary culture" (Fee, op. cit., 527). Ironically,

the same UPCI that holds this to be a "natural law" also understands the mandate for women to have long hair to be one of the "special marks which separates them [God's true people] from the rest of the world" (Bernard, Holiness, 134). But if uncut hair was a law of nature, how would this set them apart?

Nor is there any basis whatsoever for David Bernard's incredible exegesis that Paul's appeal to "nature" here implies that the women would let nature determine the length of their hair (Bernard, op. cit. 136; see also Gray, 178). Among a host of impossible difficulties, one is left wondering how Paul could argue on this same basis that men are to have short hair.

3. The word is a combination of *kata* (down) and *katalupto* (to cover). It contrasts with the phrase *kata kephalas exon* (lit. "hanging down from the head"), which a man is not to have when praying or prophesying. The noun *kalumma* means a "covering" or "veil." Hence *katalupto* is most easily understood to refer to some sort of clothing that hangs down from the head. See Fee, 507; Bauer, 411. It is not impossible, however, that Paul could be referring to an issue over a woman's hairstyle in church. But even if correct, this thesis counts as much against the UPCI view as does the more traditional, and more likely, interpretation of "covering" as a veil.

4. For our purposes it does not matter whether "head" here means "authority figure" or "source." Even if "authority figure" is correct, this does not imply any essential inequality, but only functional submission. On "head" as "source," see Fee, 502–04.

5. On the UPCI interpretation, one would have expected Paul to use *kalumma* instead of *peribolaion.*

Appendix D:
Statistics on Oneness Pentecostal Groups

1. Tim Dowley, ed., *Eerdmans Handbook to the History of Christianity* (Grand Rapids, Mich.: William B. Eerdmans, 1977), 619.

2. David Barrett, ed., *World Christian Encyclopedia* (New York: Oxford University Press, 1982), 837.

3. Rubin Keeley, ed., *An Eerdmans Handbook: Christianity in Today's World* (Grand Rapids, Mich.: William B. Eerdmans, 1985), 77–81.

4. See Constant Jacquet, Jr., ed., *Yearbook of American and Canadian Churches, 1989* (Nashville: Abingdon Press, 1989); J. Gordon Melton, *The Encyclopedia of American Religions*, 3d ed. (Detroit: Gale Research Co., 1989); and J. Gordon Melton, ed. *The Encyclopedia of American Religions: Religious Creeds*, 1st ed. (Detroit: Gale Research Co., 1985). My membership information is based on these sources as well as from personal phone conversations with recognized leaders of the various Oneness fellowships.

Made in the USA
Middletown, DE
30 April 2021

Oneness Pentecostals
and the Trinity